ELECTRIC BICYCLES

Buyers' Guide   -   Technology   -   History

The Complete Guide

ROTATION

EXCELLENT BOOKS PLAN

EXCELLENT BOOKS
94 Bradford Road, Wakefield WF1 2AE
Tel: (01924) 315147
www.excellentbooks.co.uk
Printed 2010

With thanks to: Bert Cebular of NYCeWheels, New York. Wai Won Ching, eZee.
Lloyd Clarkson, Raleigh. Tony Flecchia. Alyson France. Neil Guthrie. Peter Henshaw. Elizabeth Holman.
Cor de Jong, Gazelle, Netherlands. Phil Key, OnBike. Justin Lemire-Elmore, Grin Technologies, Vancouver.
Andrew Pattle, Iceni CAM. Larry Pizzi and Mitch Robb, IZIP USA. Diana Powell.
Steve Punchard, Electric Mountain Bikes. Annick Roetynck of ETRA. Theo Schmidt.
Mark Searles, Cytronex. Eric Sundin of Electric Bikes Northwest, Seattle.

ISBN 978-1-901464-24-5

Printed in the UK by JF Print, Sparkford, Somerset.

Contents

Choosing an electric bike can be confusing, but get the right one for you and it will bring endless pleasure.

Foreword

When a book says its going to be a 'Complete Guide' that's exactly what I want, so thank goodness David and Richard have produced the authoritative, comprehensive book on electric bikes that they promised.

I've been trying to live a 21st century lifestyle, but with a reduced impact on the planet, since moving to my smallholding in Cornwall six years ago. Many of us see bicycles as an urban transport solution, but transport is also a major issue in the country, as rural communities seldom have the transport infrastructure they need to allow them to move around without resorting to cars. We have an eclectic bunch of bikes here, from high performance mountain bikes, through multi-geared workhorses (complete with trailers) all the way to a much loved, ancient tandem that allows those who fear too much exertion to take the back seat. They all have one thing in common, other than being slightly tatty; when used in our beautiful, somewhat hilly, part of Cornwall, they guarantee to raise your heart rate and ensure you end up sweaty and knackered. Enter the electric bicycle!

Understanding the pros and cons of electric bikes is essential before investing hard earned cash on the perfect two wheeled chariot. The first big question must be 'is an electric bicycle right for me?' This book provides you with all the necessary information (including lots of details on costs, technical choices, environmental assessments and even lifestyle factors) to turn you into an intelligent customer, and, therefore, empower you so you can decide for yourself if you should buy your very own electric bike. To the uninitiated electric bikes may seem straightforward, however, dig a little deeper and it can be a minefield. There are many areas you need to investigate and understand. Batteries are hugely important; who wants to end up with insufficient range? What about the legal issues, or safety, or the possibility of converting your own bike - the list is long!

After a little research, the financial, health and environmental advantages of an electric bike are apparent, but you may need just a little more information to take the plunge. This book is both digestible and comprehensive, so is a must for anyone who is at all serious about changing their transportation for the future.

Dick Strawbridge 2010

About the Authors

I shall never forget the day I discovered electric bikes. We'd known about the bikes since the late 1990s, and had tested a few for *A to B* magazine, but despite living without a car in a fairly rustic corner of Somerset, we'd never been tempted to buy one ourselves. The turning point came one day in the spring of 2002 a few months after our first son Alexander had been enrolled at play-school.

The group we preferred was three miles from home on quiet back roads, the six-mile round trip with a child trailer being hardish, but quite practical. Then one day I asked my wife Jane if she could go another couple of miles to pick up a new seal for the washing machine.

That day, of course, there was a howling gale, and the ten mile round trip turned into an exhausting nightmare. Living without a car in a remote rural area had been fine for a young couple, but the extra complications of child-carrying had added a new ingredient. It was 'green' enough, but - to borrow a much over-used phrase - it was not sustainable.

A few days later we bought a Heinzmann power kit and fitted it to a Fold-it folding bike. By modern standards the bike was slow, and the range was quite limited, but it changed trailer towing from a chore to a pleasure. The Heinzmann restored our mobility: we could take long rides into the country for picnics, choose the nursery school (and then the primary school) we wanted, rather than being forced to use the closest, and we could visit grandparents more often (17 miles away over a very challenging route). As *A to B* magazine grew, the Heinzmann enabled us to continue carrying mail bags to the Post Office by bike, something that was becoming increasingly difficult. In short, it arrived just in time to save our 'life beyond cars' experiment.

The Heinzmann wasn't in front line service for very long, because in the summer of 2002 we bought a Giant Lafree Comfort, a much loved machine that is still in service today, more than eight years later, hauling a new trailer and a new child. In those eight years, we've raced electric bikes, pulled massive loads, taken an electric bike on holiday and test-ridden just about every electric bike in production. Alexander, now 11, has taken up percussion, adding another whole layer of tricky transport head-scratchers. Or perhaps not. We've carried timpanis (admittedly one at a time), a glockenspiel, a complete drum kit (in two loads) and a 'travel' drum kit *and* glockenspiel in one go. All using a large cycle trailer towed by an electric bike. A dozen or so times a year, we hire a car for journeys beyond electric bike range and away from public transport routes, but for day-to-day transport the electric bike has enabled our growing family to remain car-free.

In the early days the bicycle establishment was openly hostile to the electric bike concept, but today, all but the real diehards have been won round. Electric bicycles may not be quite as green as conventional bikes (even this is disputed, as we will discuss later on), but they are several orders of magnitude greener than a car.

After a decade or so, electric bikes have a proven track record for keeping bums on saddles, and even replacing second cars. And that's all that really matters.
So join with us in an exploration of the fascinating world of the electric bike. You might not think you have a need for one, and you might be right, but the chances are you just haven't realised what the application is yet!

David Henshaw Editor, *A to B* **magazine**
November 2010

Winning the 2006 Tour de Presteigne on the original and now classic eZee Torq.

One thing leads to another, or so the saying goes, and it certainly applies to the way I became a user then an avid fan of and writer about electric bikes.

I got into cycling by a rather serendipitous route in my late 20s. I just happened to be taking a mini career-break when I saw a sign for a local cycle route and was intrigued that such things existed (this was 1994 when traffic-free cycling trails were a rarefied novelty and not something to be found in nearly every corner of the country, as they are today). I decided it might be a fun and interesting thing to do to write a little guidebook to the route, which, it turned out, visited some of the most beautiful and interesting corners of the Yorkshire Dales. It would be a welcome diversion too, before I had to go back and face the cold reality of a nine to five working existence.

Fast forward to 16 years later and I have somehow managed to produce over twenty cycling books and maps and countless articles in the interim and the career break has become a career change. This unforeseen outpouring of work would very probably have proved impossible had I not started to use electric bikes after reading about them in David's superb magazine, *A to B*.

In a remarkably short space of time I progressed from having never heard of electric bikes to regularly trying out a wide variety of machines. When my old Ford Fiesta finally packed in, the advantages offered by my electric steeds meant getting a replacement car made little sense - from whichever angle I thought about it.

I can't imagine doing without a folding electric bike (specifically a Nano-Brompton). I also get great fun and immense satisfaction from riding and reviewing a large variety of electric bikes. In particular, electric bikes have allowed me to take on European cycle tours of many hundreds of miles that would have seemed forbiddingly prohibitive without them; they've taken me into the scirrocco wind of Southern France and up the Alps - not things I would have relished on a conventional bike, but relish them I did on an electric.

It seems a particularly exciting and suitable time to have written a book on electric bikes; in the UK widespread ignorance of their existence has changed, over the years, into what currently seems to be a veritable thirst for knowledge. It's quite rare nowadays that people want to know *what* it is I'm riding but they do often approach me with a list of seemingly pre-prepared specific questions: how far does it go on a battery charge, how much did it cost, is it heavy...and so on and so on. Hopefully, this book will answer all the questions of the who-knows-how-many curious there are out there, looking for reliable and realistic information. Just as importantly I hope readers are inspired to hop on an electric bike and discover for themselves the unalloyed joy and immense practicality they can bring to their lives.

Richard Peace Publisher, Excellent Books
November 2010

Phil Key of Onbike on an E-motion
pedelec enjoys cresting a hill at the Presteigne electric bike rally. Photo by Pete MacKenzie

What, Why, Who?

What are electric bikes?

The electric bike - essentially a conventional bicycle with an electric motor added to make pedalling easier - is a machine with truly revolutionary potential. It very neatly fills the troublesome gap between journeys short enough to be made on foot or by conventional bike and much longer trips where a car or train might be necessary. The best electric bikes are supremely practical, bringing all the advantages and joys of cycling, without many of the difficulties. They are, quite simply, one of the most efficient, useful, cost-effective and *fun* modes of transport in the world today. Mass take-up has occurred on a significant scale in two main areas, underpinned by two entirely different types of electric bike. In China relatively heavy lead-acid battery powered bikes have become everyday transport for millions of people (over 20 million electric bikes were sold in China in 2009 alone) and they have transformed the transport scene there over the last decade. They have also, in part, been responsible for a rapid decrease in the use of conventional bikes. Meanwhile, in north-west continental Europe electric bicycles are now, at the end of the first decade of the 21st century, enormously popular. They account for around one in every ten bikes sold in the western world's foremost cycling nation, the Netherlands.

Electric cycling in Northern Europe has been a huge success in recent years. The riders are just as likely to be female as male and the bikes are generally designed for both comfort and speed.

Speedy and easy commuting is just one use amongst many for electric bikes. Modern Chinese made bikes, like the eZee (above), have large batteries and are capable of covering a lot of ground quickly.

The British designed GoCycle (pictured in an entertaining, but slightly optimistic advertisement below), is intended specifically for urban use - it has a smaller battery giving a shorter range than most but is still very speedy and is light by electric bike standards. It also takes apart for easier storage and transportation when not in use.

Electric bikes come in all shapes and sizes. The typical Chinese machine is a throttle-controlled behemoth (often having more in common with a moped than a bicycle). In the Netherlands a typical machine blends traditional Dutch sit-up-and-beg town bike styling with state of the art electronics. In Japan, home of the original 'pedal and go' or 'Pedelec' type machines, the target markets tend to be mothers, or older riders. In contrast to the heavy, long-range machines sold in China, and lighter equally long-range European bikes, Japanese electric bikes are mostly very light, often small-wheeled folding machines, with high-tech batteries. In less than twenty years, the technology has evolved to suit the local conditions, and it continues to evolve rapidly.

Why use one?

There are some compelling practical, economic and environmental arguments for riding an electric bike - in addition to the fact that they offer pure enjoyment!

1 They're faster

A good electric bike allows the averagely fit cyclist to travel at least as fast as - and often faster than - a much fitter cyclist on a conventional bike, and with far less effort (though don't expect to outpace all non-assisted cyclists!). This is of enormous importance, because it means a cycling speed of four or five times walking pace is now attainable for a huge segment of society - anyone who can ride a bike can ride an electric equivalent. And in 'stop/start' town conditions, up hills and against headwinds - conditions where you need to put substantially more energy into pedalling a conventional bike - the extra power of an electric bike means quicker, easier progress and less sweat.

In congested towns and cities the electric bike magnifies the advantages of the conventional cycle. Like the non-assisted bike it's a largely 'congestion proof' mode of transport but with added ease of use and higher, more consistent average speed. Trials seem to back up this claim - for example Shrewsbury commuters tested an electric bike against the bus, car (in conjunction with park & ride), an ordinary car, an electric car and an ordinary bike over a 2.5 mile course in the morning rush hour. The electric bike won in a time of 11 minutes, a full 12 minutes ahead of the car, with an average speed of 12.5 mph.

Energy use compared

The table shows energy measured in kilowatt hours (kWh) used per 100km per passenger for different travel modes.

Whilst these are very approximate averages - there are variations of energy use depending on the exact type of vehicle and the number of passengers it is assumed to be carrying - they give a good idea of the order of magnitude of energy used by different transport modes. They are mainly based on figures researched by David MacKay for his book *Sustainable Energy - Without the Hot Air.*

Modern Intercontinental Jet
(average number of seats filled)
50 kWh per 100 passenger km

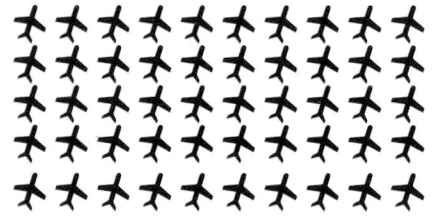

Average UK Car (urban use
2 people occupancy)
40 kWh per 100 passenger km

Average Electric Car
(manufacturers' figures, upper-end averages)
25 kWh per 100 passenger km

Coach (half full)
16 kWh per passenger km

Vectrix Electric Scooter or Small Electric Motorbike
10 kWh per 100 passenger km

Average Train (half full)
10 kWh per 100 passenger km

Electric bike
1 kWh per 100 passenger km

2 They're cheaper

As far as the law is concerned an electric bike is effectively an ordinary bicycle, so there is no need for the expensive red tape that powered vehicles tend to attract, such as road tax and compulsory insurance. In many ways the electric bike is a very privileged vehicle.

Here are typical comparative running costs for different travel modes:

Conventional (non-electric) Bike	3 - 7 pence per mile A to B magazine*
Electric Bike	8 - 12 p/m A to B magazine, 2007-2009 test bikes*
Small Car	32-145 p/m AA 2010 figures, 10,000 - 20,000 annual mileage
Small Car - local use only	64-256 p/m AA 2010 figures, 5,000 annual mileage
Bus (Oyster Card)	18 p/m**
Bus (cash)	40 p/m**
Train - peak fares	40-60 p/m***
Trains - off-peak fares	20 p/m***

* Based on depreciation over 10 years and annual mileage of 2,000 miles (conventional bike) and 2,500 miles (electric bike)
** From www.whatgreencar.com
*** Provided by rail expert Barry Doe - www.barrydoe.plus.com

3 They're hugely energy efficient

A few comparisons reveal a lot. Electric bikes typically use energy at an average rate of 100 to 150 watts, against 15,000 or so for a car. In terms of fuel consumption, an electric bike achieves about 800-2,000mpg (280 - 700 km/litre). Put another way, if your average electric bike ran on petrol it would consume 40 times less than your average car. So a trip to the fuel pump for 25 litres of fuel costing £30 at 2010 prices, would translate into 0.63 litres at a cost of 76p in electric bike terms! Electric bikes have other running costs, such as battery depreciation, but no other commercially available vehicle can match figures of this kind.

4 Ride safer

It sounds unlikely, doesn't it? But there is some logic to this, especially in particular cycling situations.

Think of a steep and busy road, with cars climbing at 30mph. If you previously slogged up the hill at 6mph, but can tackle the same gradient at 12mph with an electric bike, you will see 33% fewer cars, and they will pass you at 18mph rather than 24mph.

The same general principle applies to road junctions - the faster your acceleration, the more easily you will be able to move between other vehicles. And with no need to rush the hills, you won't be tempted to ride downhill at breakneck speed...

5 Still get some exercise

Most of today's electric bikes have a handlebar mounted switch that allows you to simply turn off the power whilst on the move. The more advanced models have variable power levels, so that a typical low power setting will leave the cyclist contributing around two-thirds of the power needed. As cyclists typically burn anything from 200 calories (sedate shopping trip) to 950 calories per hour (full-on racing over hills) that can still mean plenty of exercise. So a one hour ride on an electric bike - with power set at a low level to stop you getting exhausted on hills - could easily burn 300-500 calories. That's equivalent to all but the most strenuous of sporting activities.

Recent developments in battery technology have revolutionised their capability: weight for weight, today's lithium-ion batteries provide eight times as much power as the lead-acid batteries used in the first electric bikes. This means lighter machines that take little more effort to ride with the power off than a conventional bicycle. UK company Modern Times produces the Cytronex range for exactly this kind of riding - its Cannondale Super Six, weighing in at only 12.9kg, would be quite light even in conventional bicycle terms.

Although there has been little scientific study on the matter, two exploratory studies have demonstrated that electric-assist cycling is likely to be sufficiently intensive to yield fitness and health benefits.

If you love getting some exercise on sporty bikes some electric bikes allow you to do just that.
The Cytronex Capo rides pretty much like a normal bike until you need power, which it delivers at the touch of a button. It's also remarkably simple - a single gear allows you to cruise up and down hills at a pretty constant 16mph.

Who uses them and why?

Electric bikes have suffered from an image problem, without a doubt. But there is a range of bikes available today to suit just about anyone's transport needs - local trips, commuting, leisure riding, shopping trips or child carrying. Even if you don't think you have a need for an electric bike, you probably do! It's worth highlighting how specific groups of users might benefit:

Older people

Many want to continue cycling, or even take it up for the first time, with advancing years but feel physically unable. There is now a good range of light 'comfort bikes' especially suitable for older riders. If pedalling is a problem, a throttle-controlled E-bike rather than a 'pedal and go' pedelec may be more suitable.

Some older riders may prefer throttle-controlled bikes - especially if they have difficulty pedalling.

Pre-moped and younger riders

Whilst several reports suggest that the over 40s are the main group to use electric bikes, there is a move in the industry, especially in Germany and Switzerland, to attract younger age groups into the fold. Ave (with the JD Eagle), Riese & Muller and Swiss Flyer have all introduced models styled for and aimed at the youth market.

Cyclists towing trailers and carrying passengers

Most bicycle trailers are rated to carry 25-40kg, but pulling this sort of weight by human power alone, especially on hills, is another matter. An electric bike with plenty of low speed torque (that's the pulling power of the motor) is particularly useful for towing heavier loads. There are a few bikes that are designed to carry passengers - both small and large - for example Surly, Yuba and Madsen - and these can all be motorised (some specialist dealers can supply a passenger carrying bike with assistance off-the-peg).

Most cargo bikes can be adapted with electric hub motors. Here a bike made by Surly has had an Alien (Suzhou-Bafang) motor added.

Commuters

Electric bikes can effectively extend the range and speed of commuting for those wanting to bike into work, making a long commute quicker, easier, faster and more reliable, whatever the wind and weather. Bikes such as the Cytronex and some of the Kalkhoff range deliberately set out to appeal to young professionals who want to get about quickly and reliably.

Electric bikes bought through employers signed up to the UK government's Cycle to Work scheme will be eligible for tax relief on the purchase, meaning savings of between 30 and 50% (though many employers impose a £1,000 cap on bikes bought under the scheme to avoid extra red tape imposed by consumer credit laws).

Non-sweaty riding

Surveys into why people don't cycle to work have revealed looking sweaty and dishevelled as a major turn-off. Women in particular have quoted this as a major reason they don't travel by bike.

Hill conquerors

Hills were once a huge barrier to all but the fittest cyclists, but with an electric bike steep hills cease to be a problem.

Other cyclists in need of a little assistance

Those with medical conditions leading to loss of power or movement in the legs and people carrying children to school are just two groups who can benefit from the extra power of an electric bike. For those with balance problems electric tricycles are available. And of course, just like conventional bikes, electric machines play a role in preventing chronic diseases related to sedentary living as well as having a rehabilitative role for those who have had serious illness.

Organisations have found electric bikes the best vehicle for their special needs - the following examples show its great versatility:
- **Law enforcement agencies** - US and Swiss police forces, and the Royal Parks police in London.

Currie was one of the first companies to supply police forces with electric bikes.

- **Postal services.** In April 2010 Deutsche Post purchased around 7,000 electric bikes for use in hilly areas, and as a partial answer to the problem of an ageing workforce, allowing them to keep valuable, experienced but more elderly workers for longer. Electric bikes are also used for deliveries by the French and Dutch postal services, amongst many others, and were briefly trialled in the UK. In 2009

the Belgian post office declared it was aiming to reduce its CO2 emissions by a staggering 35% by 2010. To do so it started pedelec trials to test the possibility of replacing its current fleet of mopeds.

Private couriers have seen the logistic and economic benefit of electric bikes too. FedEx uses a fleet of 12 power-assisted tricycles, capable of carrying a large volume of parcels, to help with its Paris deliveries.

A German post office electric bike.

- Electric bikes ridden by **trained medical staff a**nd carrying life-saving equipment only debuted in 2008 but have since become a common sight at many places where full vehicle access is difficult, such as large concerts, congested city centres and traffic-restricted areas.

eZee hub motor bikes have been adapted for medical use in central Holland.

- Electric bikes hold some potential for **low impact tourism**, especially in relieving motor traffic, in popular outdoor destinations which may be poorly supported by public transport. Swiss Flyer in Switzerland is associated with several schemes that allow the public to rent their bikes and provide a network of places that will exchange empty batteries for full ones. To give just one example, the traffic-free village of Wengen in Switzerland offers e-bikes for hire – perfect for climbing to the foot of the Eiger! Indeed, in Germany there are many hundreds of electric bikes to rent in several popular tourist areas. "Paris Charms & Secrets" is a tourist tour based around electric bikes and one of the first to combine tourism and electric bikes in a city environment.

Peter Henshaw tried out the Swiss Flyer hire scheme in Wengen in 2010. Swiss Flyer have teamed up with national cycling organisation Veloland to create a national hire and battery exchange network.

Evidence on use

Just why people ride electric bikes has been indicated by some recent surveys*:

• There is certainly some evidence that electric bikes **appeal to women in particular**. One industry analyst commented particularly on this point '....worldwide... the usual buyer is a woman and she is buying transportation. In China 80% of buyers are women and in the US it's now over half.' Trek's own electric bike expert noted that one of the most popular reasons given for buying an electric bike was to allow a wife to ride with her husband. And a study from the Basel canton of Switzerland noted that pedelec buyers showed, overall, an even distribution between the sexes (not something found very often with the purchase of conventional bikes) and in the 20-39 age group women were actually in a majority.

• Electric bikes are very popular amongst **older riders** (the 40-60 age group or the over-60s depending which survey you give most weight to).

• **Commuters** are also an important group of users - increasingly so, meaning that the current trend is for the average age of buyers of electric bikes (specifically pedelecs) to decrease.

• Two of the surveys stressed how the electric bike had been **used to replace car journeys** - in one, nearly a quarter of users replaced a car with an electric bike and a further 16% replaced a moped or motorbike with an electric bike.

Whatever an individual's reasons given for choosing an electric bike - and everyone will have a range of motivations - one thing seems clear; people believe the bikes will make life easier for them, and undoubtedly they often do. As the results from a Dutch survey of 2008 reveal, electric bikes are generally a way of overcoming a difficulty or achieving an end in the most effective manner possible:

Reason for using a pedelec	Pedelec Users	Interested in using pedelecs
Conventional cycling too difficult (or may become so)	66%	65%
Cycling into headwind easier	52%	36%
Long distance cycling with less effort	46%	33%
Easier hill-climbing	29%	19%
Not very sporty but wanting more exercise	17%	-
Reduce travel time without extra effort	11%	13%
Alternative to less environmentally-friendly transport	10%	20%
To get to work without sweating	8%	7%
Other	4%	1%

* The surveys were: a 2001 UK survey by Neil Guthrie, research student at Leeds University, a 2008 study by Dutch cycling policy organisation Fiets Beraad, a study from Brussels University, a long-standing survey by the Swiss Canton of Basel and a 2009 online survey by Halfords.

All the evidence suggests women in particular are drawn to electric bikes such as the very practical Panasonic crank-motored Monark Eco (above) and the sporty, nippy JD Eagle (right).

Step-thru frames are particularly popular, for example on the Gazelle Chamonix (left). Some women might prefer the greater speed and sportiness of bikes such as the Velocity (above). This is one of the few companies that produces bikes that fall into the 'Swiss fast class' (see page 218).

13

Are electric bikes really green?

Green is a word so over-used and under-explained that it seems to have lost any real meaning. In transport terms it's perhaps more helpful to think in terms of carbon emissions. Climate scientists now generally agree that the amount of carbon in the atmosphere is increasing very much faster than natural systems are able to remove it. The net result is that the planet is slowly starting to cook itself. So, a good measure of how 'green' electric bikes are would be the amount of carbon they put into the atmosphere. The manufacture and distribution of the high-tech batteries used in modern electric bikes do bring their own environmental problems, and these are discussed in later chapters, but there is little doubt that electric bikes are an extremely low carbon form of transport, comparatively speaking - as the figures in the table below indicate.

Carbon emissions compared

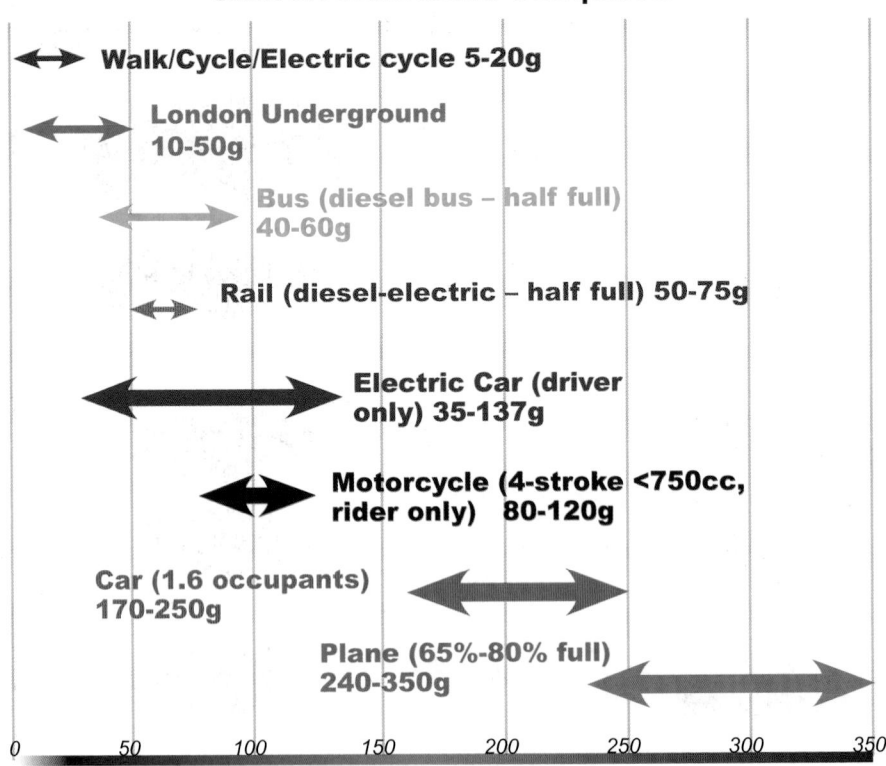

CO2 emissions in grammes per passenger km for different transport modes
(source: www.travelfootprint.org except electric bikes - based on a 2008 study by Cherry,
Weinert & Xinmao).

There seems to be an anomaly here. How can a machine that is - in part - electrically powered result in similar emissions to a conventional bike, or even walking? When riding a non-electric bicycle you are still, of course, expending energy, but in this case the energy has to come from food (and after using energy cycling, you will eat a quantifiable amount of extra food). Growing, transporting, processing and cooking that food has a surprisingly high energy cost.

So, the amount of carbon that can be attributed to a conventional cycle ride rather depends on your diet. Similarly, with electric-assist cycling much will depend on the source of the electricity. Some examples illustrate the point.

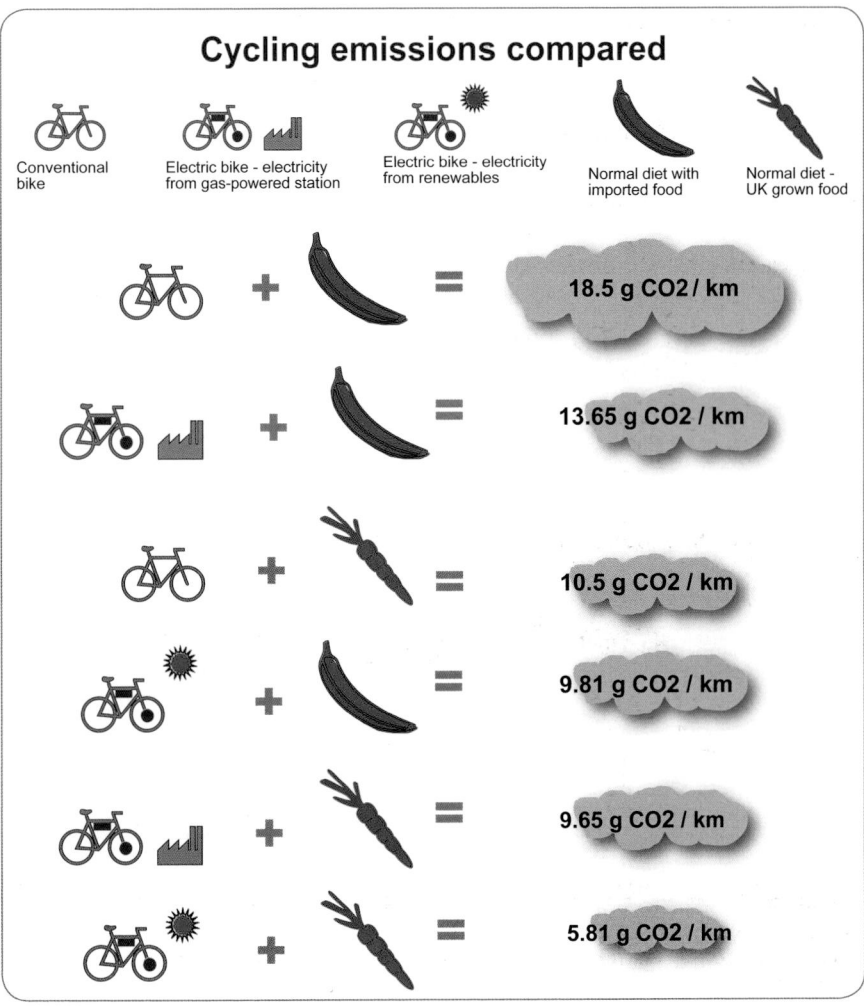

Cycling emissions compared

Conventional bike

Electric bike - electricity from gas-powered station

Electric bike - electricity from renewables

Normal diet with imported food

Normal diet - UK grown food

18.5 g CO2 / km

13.65 g CO2 / km

10.5 g CO2 / km

9.81 g CO2 / km

9.65 g CO2 / km

5.81 g CO2 / km

15

No doubt many people are simply waiting for the electric car to be perfected before changing their habits. With media reports touting electric cars as 'green' and 'emissions free' why bother swapping to a bike when you can continue to sit in the weatherproof comfort of your own personal space without emitting carbon?

It's a nice thought, but not the quick fix it at first seems, because cars, compared to electric bikes, are heavy, inefficient and require huge amounts of energy to move about. If motor vehicles all went electric tomorrow they would simply get their power from a more remote source of carbon emissions, the coal or gas-fuelled power station, rather than from petrol in the tank. In the UK alone, providing enough renewable energy to power all-electric road transport would mean covering an area the size of Wales with wind turbines. Or you could always build 100 new nuclear powered stations.

That is not to say electric cars aren't preferable to petrol powered ones, especially if powered by renewable electricity - but the actual prospect of this happening begins to look incredible in view of the very small percentage of electricity generated from renewables and the huge amount of extra renewable electricity that would be required for a widespread switch to electric cars. Batteries too, consume a great deal of energy in their manufacture. This applies to electric bikes as well, of course, but a typical electric car battery is 100 times bigger than a typical electric bike battery, so the problem is proportionately much more serious.

These German El Moto electric motorbikes demonstrate quite clearly why this transport mode will never be as green as electric bicycles; heavy, bulky and with no pedals to share the motor's workload!

Electric motorbikes are affected by the same issues, as a typical high-performance motorcycle can consume as much or more fuel than a car. To quote from the British Motorcyclists' Federation website: 'Why are bikes so poor at conserving fuel stocks? Easy. They're designed for performance. Massive choke sizes for carb or injector bodies to pass massive volumes of air at high engine speeds are not conducive to good fuel consumption'. The very facts that they travel at four or five times the speed of an electric bicycle and their drag coefficient is generally quite poor, also means they have to fight against a huge amount of wind resistance. In their current form - petrol driven, electric or otherwise - these facts will remain true for as long as the laws of physics do! And unlike cars, which are at least able to carry a large battery, motorcycles are strictly limited in terms of battery size and weight. These factors all combine to make electric motorcycles a uniquely difficult technological challenge.

Potential downsides

Despite the huge advantages of electric bikes compared to other modes of transport, there are drawbacks. Probably the biggest of these for today's typical electric bike is that the lithium-ion battery technology used has a relatively short life (holding 80% of full charge after two years seems to be the currently accepted but unofficial industry 'best practice'). When put together with the replacement cost of a battery (usually several hundred pounds) this factor alone adds significantly to the running costs of modern electric bikes. A few stalwarts have stuck with traditional battery chemistry - Currie and Powabyke with lead-acid and Sparta and GoCycle with NiMH - but the vast majority of electric bikes now sold in the western world are Li-ion equipped. We look at this problem in more depth, and the possible ways ahead, in the chapter *The Battery*.

In the UK, electric bikes inhabit a legal grey area, and this confusion has discouraged the cycle trade from promoting and selling the whole concept. Add in a general reluctance among the public, and the specialist skills needed to service and repair electrical products, and it's easy to see why the electric bike has not been welcomed with open arms by the cycle trade, certainly in Britain.

Similar problems seem to have cropped up in the US too - there are different laws on electric bikes in different states and public reaction has, historically, been cool. But in the pre-eminent European cycling countries, such as the Netherlands and Germany, servicing, repair and back-up for electric bikes is taken much more seriously. However, more on this in later chapters...

あたる坂道 *Sel!*

電動ハイブリッド自転車
ニッケル水素電池採
電動伸縮ハイブリッ

BE-EBD41

本体標準価格　178,000円(バッ
専用充電器標準価格 10,000円(リフレ

合計**188,000**円(税別)
本体と専用充電器、セットでお買い

Panasonic's Dracle, seen here on the right, may not seem like a good idea with the hindsight history affords, but it was given an enthusiastic launch in Japan in 1999. The Dracle used electricity not only to help you ride but to telescope itself into a smaller folded package! Panasonic seems to have had the last laugh though, as today its crank-drive system is used on a massive range of high quality electric bikes.

Electric Bike History, Classics & Flops

The history of the electric bike - up until the 1980s at least - was one of false starts. Certainly the idea of electric bikes predates the 20th century, as witnessed by early patents and reported discussion of the concept. But internal combustion engines fitted to bicycles consistently proved more of a commercial proposition, not least because a tank of fuel would take you much further, more quickly than a heavy battery-powered electric bike.

However, two developments starting in the 1980s set electric bikes on an upward trajectory from which they haven't looked back. Firstly, staggering Chinese economic growth created a seemingly insatiable demand for affordable personal mobility and the electric bike (albeit with heavy lead-acid batteries) gave commuters something close to the speed of a small moped whilst avoiding the growing legal clampdowns on petrol power, forced on many city authorities struggling with traffic congestion and pollution. Secondly, from the early 1980s onwards, in many western countries and Japan, lighter battery technologies, the miniaturisation of electronics, the development of torque sensors (allowing electric bikes to be use in the same way as conventional bikes) and legal recognition of this new breed of transport saw sales begin to take off.

Recent history has revealed an almost insatiable demand for very keenly priced electric bikes in China.

Electric bike timeline

1859 Frenchman Gaston Planté develops the first practical lead-acid battery that could be recharged - the model for the lead-acid battery still in use today.

1868 Sylvester Howard Roper develops a steam-powered bicycle and exhibits it at fairs and circuses around the eastern USA.

1885 In Germany, Maybach and Daimler invent the first petrol-powered bike, named the Reitwagen (riding carriage).

1890s Various patents are filed in the USA for electric bike designs, but it is unclear which of these were actually produced. Despite this it seems highly likely that quite a number of electric bikes were made and sold - after all, 1899 and 1900 were the highpoint for electric cars in America where they outsold all other types, including petrol and steam powered ones.

1893 Thedore Cummins produces a bicycle powered by compressed air.

1895 Ogden Bolton Junior is granted a patent for 'a 6-pole brush-and-commutator direct current (DC) hub motor mounted in the rear wheel'. There were no gears and the motor could draw up to 100 amps from a 10-volt battery. This implies a rather heavy brutish device, but the principle of a battery-powered hub motor remains the basis of the vast majority of today's electric bikes.
Even in these early days of the electric bike there was an ideological debate springing up about whether electric power (or assistance) was a suitable addition to a bicycle. For example, a reporter at Pope's Hartford plant in the US in 1896 found 'many advocates of the power bicycle' who anticipated that the article would come into demand'. The same reporter also found that many industry leaders 'did not believe that the great army of bicycle riders throughout the country will take kindly to the idea of sitting idly in the saddle and merely balancing the machine whilst the motor does the work... the chief element in the popularity of bicycling is the enjoyment the rider gets from the wholesome exercise. If a person were too indolent or feeble to pedal himself along he would probably discard the bicycle altogether in favour of an automobile.' Prophetic words!

1897 In another foreshadowing of the resurgence of electric bikes in the late 20th century, Hosea Libby comes up with a design for 'a double electric motor' that is housed around - and drives through - the crank.

1898 An electric machine was produced by Humber - a modified, stretched tandem bicycle with batteries between the two riders. It was used as a pacer in the Bol d'Or 24 hour paced track race of 1899 in Paris. It was almost immediately superseded by the petrol-engined motorcycle for this purpose.

Humber was best known for making all manner of petrol-engined vehicles. The size of the batteries required on this model gives more than a clue as to why electric bikes would have to wait almost a century before they started to come of age.

1899 John Schnepf introduces the idea of a friction drive for electric bikes in his US patent application.

1914 - 1925 Electric propulsion for bicycles is overshadowed by the success of the UK-designed, American-made Wall Auto Wheel. Many thousands were made and were fitted to other vehicles too, such as railroad repair vehicles.

1918 Howard Hughes, later aviator and multi-millionaire, designed a motor power attachment for his bicycle.

1920 German company Heinzmann produces the first commercially available electric bicycle motor. It is fitted to a twin-seater bicycle. The company goes on to develop a whole series of high quality and reliable electric motors for bicycles (amongst many other applications), later supplying motors for German postal service bikes.

1927 Despite the preponderance of petrol power, electric scooters appear to gain some measure of popularity, though the technology doesn't seem to have made any widespread migration to bicycles. The French Electrocyclette - a 1927 electric scooter from AEM - appears on the scene. The reported specification is: length 1.8m, weight 75kg, battery 150Ah, 0.5 horsepower motor, top speed 25km/h, range 30km. The battery was said to be easily removable. One review of the time sums it up as 'quiet and economic, small, quite quick..replacing the tiring effort of cycling'.

The French Electrocyclette was lauded for its performance figures

1930s The LeJay Manufacturing Company of Minneapolis starts producing a booklet (pages shown right and on opposite page, bottom) describing unusual electrical projects, most using car generators. One of the projects details plans for the GoBike. It claims 50-75 miles from a single charge of a battery and 'no more pedalling'! The idea was to recycle an old Ford Model T generator mounted in a box, sidecar style, and driving through its own wheel.

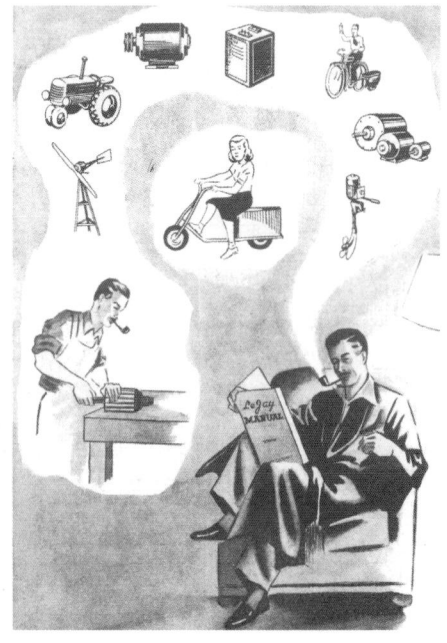

1932 EMI / Philips produces an electric bike powered by a 12-volt battery. During the 1930s the same basic design is adopted by several European bike companies but Gazelle - the most successful in sales terms - only produces 117.

The Philips electric bike (© Philips)

DIY plans from the LeJay Manufacturing Company looked pretty complex - maybe the idea was to seduce buyers with the promise of home-build, knowing that in reality many would buy a ready-made version, produced in LeJay's own factory.

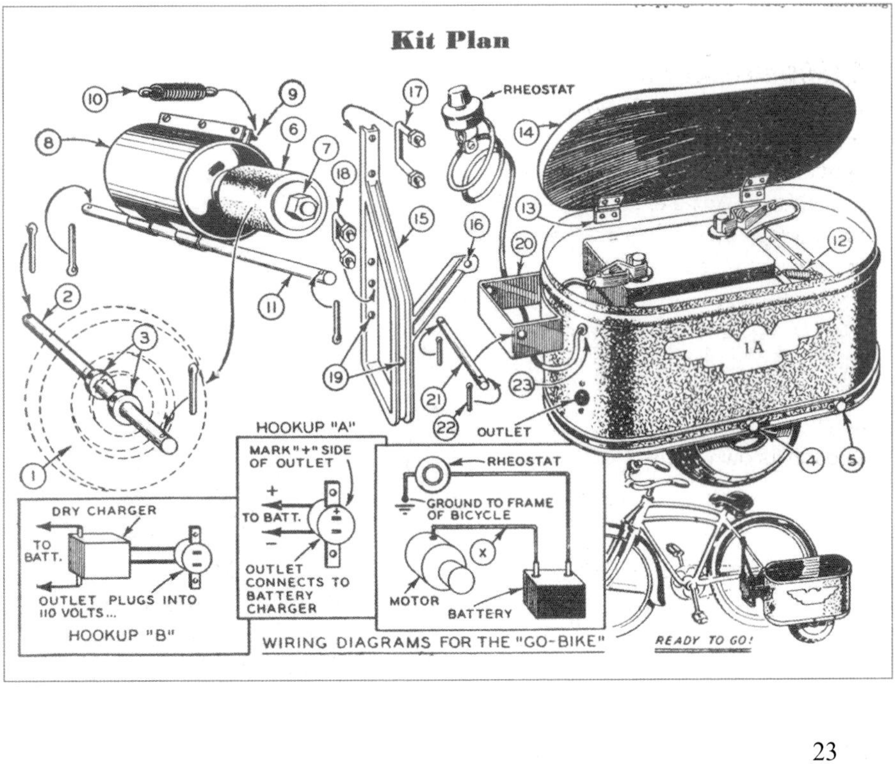

Kit Plan

HOOKUP "A"

MARK "+" SIDE OF OUTLET

TO BATT.

OUTLET CONNECTS TO BATTERY CHARGER

DRY CHARGER

TO BATT.

OUTLET PLUGS INTO 110 VOLTS...

HOOKUP "B"

RHEOSTAT

GROUND TO FRAME OF BICYCLE

MOTOR BATTERY

WIRING DIAGRAMS FOR THE "GO-BIKE"

READY TO GO!

RHEOSTAT

OUTLET

1A

1946 In the UK Ben Bowden tries to get his 'Bicycle of the Future' manufactured. After working with Donald Healey to produce streamlined bodywork for high performance cars, Bowden attempts to get manufacturers to take up his idea for an electric bike with a frame made from pressed steel or alloy sheets (a method later used in the mass manufacture of mopeds). A model prototype is exhibited at the September 1946 'Britain Can Make It' exhibition at the Victoria & Albert Museum. It received many advance orders, including one for six from King Farouk of Egypt! The 1946 patent reveals many ideas ahead of their time in the world of bike design, including the option of a shaft drive, batteries housed within the frame and internal cable runs and wiring. Perhaps the most advanced of Bowden's ideas was to incorporate a hub motor into the rear wheel (the motor also functioning as a dynamo to feed charge back to the batteries). The patent envisages the motor as being capable of powering the bike up a one-in-ten hill at 5mph, a far cry from the performance of today's electric bikes... Reportedly a working prototype of the electric bike was made, though its fate is unknown.

The idea appears to have been roundly rejected by UK manufacturing industry and a scheme to have the bike manufactured in a South Wales factory using unemployed miners fails. Bowden moves to South Africa in 1949 where a government-backed scheme for his bicycle came within a hair's breadth of starting up. Capital was raised and tooling was on its way from the UK when a change of fiscal policy meant a ban on imports and the collapse of the venture, including the confiscation of the working prototype. His design is later manufactured in 1960s USA as the 'Bowden Spacelander' - but without the motorised component.

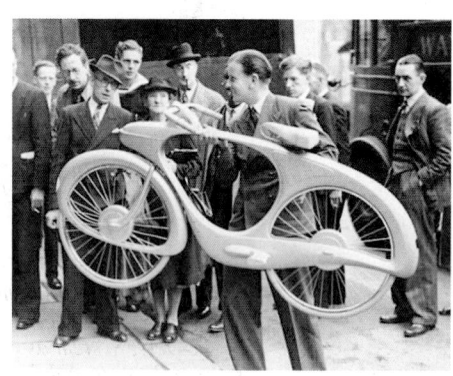

Bowden with his 'Bicycle of the Future' at the 1946 'Britain Can Make It' exhibition.

1954 Pearson, Fuller and Chapin pioneer solar generation of electrical power.

1959 Francis T Bacon designs alkaline fuel cells capable of producing 5kW of electricity. The technology is subsequently taken up by NASA and used on Gemini and Apollo spacecraft, but remains too expensive for everyday applications.

1966 Moulton Consultants Ltd patent a chainwheel drive system for a power-assisted bicycle. It noted, 'the risk of overloading the gearbox will be less with smaller as opposed to conventionally-sized wheels..When motorised power is transmitted to a wheel of small diameter through a hub gear box it has been found it...operates satisfactorily for long periods because it functions at higher revolutions but at lower torque for a given gear ratio and road speed than if fitted to a larger wheel.'

The Moulton was one of the most popular and innovative bikes of the 1960s. It was quick, comfortable and caught the mood of the swinging 60's. Unfortunately it seems the patent was never put into effect commercially.

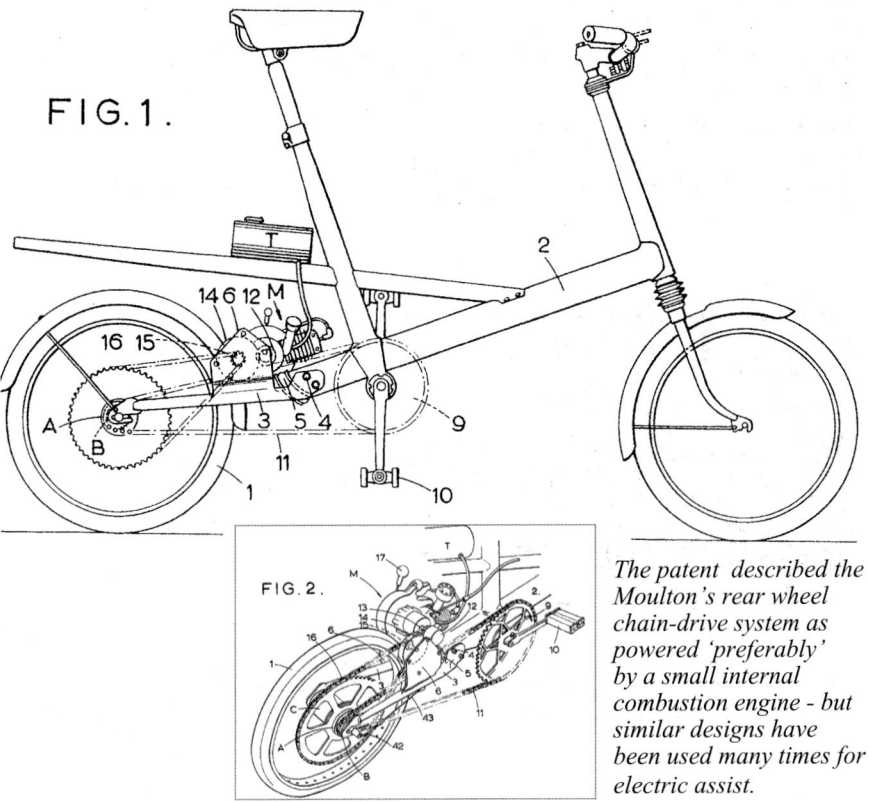

FIG.1.

The patent described the Moulton's rear wheel chain-drive system as powered 'preferably' by a small internal combustion engine - but similar designs have been used many times for electric assist.

1970s China's communist government starts to promote electric bikes.
Partly inspired by the youthful moped craze of previous decades, a mini-rash of electric moped style bikes are launched in the early 70s, remarkably similar in basic design to the 1927 Electrocyclette! Large lead-acid batteries are encased by a low slung, box mainframe where the feet can rest (pedal power is an option on many models too).

Models include the Solo Electra, the Flandria-Electro and the Zundapp Electro-Mofa. Ranging from 48 to 67kg in weight, they all belong in a class of vehicle subject to a legal speed cap of 25km/h. The French magazine *Moto-Revue* spells out the more advantageous German laws for such vehicles, but goes on to outline some interesting possible uses: '..on the other side of the Rhine (i.e. Germany) the Electra falls into the 'Mofa' class (cyclemotors limited to 25km/h) where it is perfectly competitive. In France, because of the 40km/h cyclemotor limit, the Solo will be seriously handicapped with its 25km/h limit. On the other hand, its silence and cleanliness give it a privileged place for use inside (factories, stations, exhibition halls, warehouses) or in areas normally forbidden to motor traffic.'

The 70s: although presented as fashionable and the way to a clean, green future, pedalable electric mini-mopeds never really caught on.

1973 The first oil crisis, when Arab oil producers declare an embargo on oil exports as a protest against US support for Israel in the Yom Kippur war, prompts research into electric bikes in both Japan and the USA.

Palmer Industries of Endicott, New York state, begins making the Electa Ride - a 12-volt friction drive add-on kit for tricycles. It later produced a similar kit for bicycles. Electric bikes find little public acceptance however, not least because they are still classified as motor vehicles in many countries, with all the attendant inconvenience and expense.

1975 First known Series Hybrid (SH) Bicycle is designed by Augustus Kinzel. In this design, the pedals turn a small generator, transforming pedal motion into electricity which can be fed straight into the motor. SH electric bicycles remain extremely rare, the vast majority being Parallel Hybrids (PH) where both pedal and motor power are delivered, in varying proportions, directly to the cycle's wheel.

1979 The second oil crisis, sparked by the chaos of the Iranian revolution, prompts another surge of interest in electric vehicles, including bicycles.

1980 Austrian company Schachner produce a prototype electric bike. UK auto parts manufacturer Lucas Industries Ltd patents an electric motor for driving through the bicycle's bottom bracket. A prototype BAB (Battery-Assisted Bicycle) is actually built. A press report from the time describes the BAB as being fitted with a 16Ah battery and having a range of four miles with constant power assistance and 13 miles with intermittent use. It uses a Lucas SIBA PM300T motor and specially designed gearbox.

The Lucas BAB prototype had a rather Heath Robinson appearance.

1983 The Electrically-Assisted Pedal Cycles legislation prompts several UK companies to try their hands at electric bikes throughout the 1980s. One example is the Pandora P3 (shown below), a toothed belt-driven machine made in Birmingham.

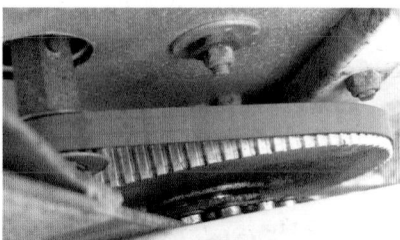

A. Freeman from Rugby, UK self publishes 'Solar Energy for Motive Power' detailing his Solarcycle, a 21 watt solar panel charged by a 25 volt 12Ah lead-acid battery giving a claimed range of 15mph. It has no pedals. Freeman claims the solar panel alone will power the vehicle at 8mph and predicts that 'future solar cell technology' will increase this to 15mph!

1985 Sir Clive Sinclair launches the now infamous Sinclair C5. Essentially a fully-faired electric three-wheeled recumbent, it fails to capture the public imagination, even though UK law was specially modified for its introduction (see 1983). By October 1985 Sinclair Vehicles was in receivership and subsequent reports suggest sales of the C5 totalled between 12,000 and 17,000. Since its demise the C5 has become something of a cult item, changing hands for large sums of money. In 1996 a heavily modified C5 reached a top speed of 150 mph (241 km/h) and did 0 to 60 mph in 5 seconds, taking the land speed record for an electric vehicle!
The first Tour de Sol solar-powered race takes place in Switzerland at Lake Constance. It includes a category for hybrid pedal and electric power.

1986 Twike I pedal-powered, faired recumbent trike is first developed by a group of Swiss students for the WorldEXPO in Vancouver, Canada. Twike I is entirely human-powered, but Twike II is soon developed as an electro-human hybrid. It is powered by an AC motor and 336 volt NiCd batteries.

Dennis Doerffel chooses to lift the front of this Twike.
A wise choice as the batteries and motor are in the rear...

1987 The Swiss government begin tests on the first solar/hydrogen vehicle, based on a design by Theo Schmidt, a pioneer of many types of hybrid-powered vehicles . US company AeroVironment Inc develops a solar powered electric race car designed for the World Solar Challenge in Australia, where it wins first prize. Hughes Aircraft are responsible for installing 8800 solar cells on it. AeroVironment Inc. goes on to develop the Charger electric bike, launched in 1998.

1989 In Germany the groundbreaking Hercules Electra and Saxonette are introduced. The Electra and Saxonette were unusual in being developed around the same Dutch town bike style frames but with the respective models being offered with an auxiliary electric motor (driving the rear wheel via a separate chain) or an internal combustion engine located around the rear axle. The Electra was offered in two designs - the Comfort, below and the much more eye-pleasing Classic, opposite. Unlike European electric bikes of today, the Electra was fitted with a twistgrip throttle. Electra's publicity material claimed, rather disingenuously, that it was 'the first electric bike on the market'. Perhaps a claim to being the first mass-market electric bike would have been more justifiable. They can still be found secondhand in Germany today, selling for a few hundred Euros.

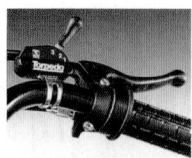  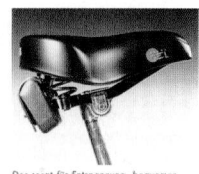 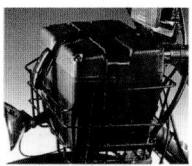

Sachs Torpedo 3-Gangschaltung: sportliche Übersetzung, sichere Bedienung, zuverlässige Rücktrittbremse.

Wenn's drauf ankommt: Die Alu-Trommelbremse packt kräftig zu. In jeder Situation, bei jedem Wetter.

Der sorgt für Entspannung: bequemer Comus Gelsattel mit stabiler Doppelfeder.

Das Energiepaket: die wiederaufladbare Batterie von Sanyo. Reicht für ca. 20 km ohne Tretunterstützung.

Unlike bikes sold in the UK or US, the German Hercules Electra made a selling point of 'dependable....weather-proof' hub brakes and a comfortable double sprung seat. The claimed battery range was 20km without pedalling.

Unusually, for a bike that was supposed to be a groundbreaking 'new' form of transport, the lines of the Electra Classic (above) seemed to draw inspiration from previous eras and offered reassuringly solid construction.

Both the Comfort and Classic models were also offered with a small internal combustion engine (left) instead of the electric assist motor. This offered a cylinder capacity of 30cc and would take 1.5l of two-stroke petrol mix. Hercules claimed well over 100km range on a single tank, against a claimed range of only 20km for its lead-acid battery-powered electric cousin! The stated weight of both models was 30kg.

1990s The development of sophisticated torque sensors and electronic power controls revolutionises the world of electric bikes. Both Giant and Yamaha enter the electric bike market with pedelec models that will provide a template for the next two decades of development.

NiCd batteries begin to be replaced by cleaner and more reliable NiMH technology.

31

1990 Yamaha produces prototype 'Vehicle A' which it claims to be 'the world's first electro-hybrid bicycle' - that's to say one that produces motor assistance in proportion to pedalling force (nowadays known as pedelecs). The following year another prototype, 'Vehicle Z', appears to confirm the concept's commercial potential.

Yamaha's prototype 'Vehicle A'. Claimed to be the world's first true human-electric hybrid.

1991 The first rechargeable lithium-ion batteries come on the market - another quantum leap towards a truly lightweight electric bike. Dogged by safety and reliability issues at first, they would not appear as standard offerings on electric bikes until well into the next decade.

1992 Dutch company Antec claims to have launched the first pedelec on the European market.
Sinclair Research Ltd of the UK produces the Zike, brainchild of Clive Sinclair - a 10.9kg (24lb) mini electric bike with NiCd battery and a claimed range of an hour with the motor doing all the work, or 90 minutes with rider input. Modestly promoted as "the greatest invention since the bicycle," the Zike is a small-wheeled design, with a £499.99 price tag and a claimed top speed of about 10mph (16 km/h). Unusually, it has regenerative braking, recharging the battery when ridden downhill. In sales terms, it proves even less successful than the Sinclair C5 (see 1995), selling only 2,000 units, and production - intended to be 10,000 a month - ends after only six months.

The first batch of 30 Velocity bikes roll out in Switzerland. The brainchild of Michael Kutter of Basel, the Velocity mixed pedal and motor torque using an 'Evo-Drive', a planetary differential gear unit in the rear wheel. Michael had been experimenting with prototypes for several years.

The clever technology that blends human and electric power in the early Velocity models (a 1992 model is seen here) still forms the basis of its bikes today.

AeroVironment of the US begins developing electric bicycles. It has previously been involved with the Bionic Bat electric and human powered airplane and the Sunraycer solar vehicle (see 1987).

1993 Yamaha introduces its PAS (Power Assist System) electric bike but, rather cautiously, sales are restricted to Tokyo, Kobe and Shizuoka. It weighs 31kg, has a range of around 20km and takes ten hours to recharge.
The Japanese government confirms to Yamaha that pedelecs such as its PAS system would be defined in legal terms as conventional bikes.
In the UK the Royal Mail starts trials of electric-assist bicycles for delivering mail.

1994 Undeterred by earlier failures, Sir Clive Sinclair launches the ZETA add-on kit for bikes. It is criticised as being extremely underpowered, and despite being developed into Mark 2 and 3 versions, with supposedly more powerful motors, it is still a commercial failure.

The Yamaha PAS is launched nationwide in Japan and encourages a steady stream of competition throughout the 1990s - Honda in 1995, Sanyo, Suzuki and Panasonic in 1996 and Bridgestone, Miyata and Mitsubishi in 1997.

1995 The Twike III power-assisted tricycle is launched and in the following year 190 vehicles are sold, mainly in Switzerland and Germany.

Currie's EV Warrior launched in the US. A product of a collaboration between Malcolm Currie (former head of Hughes Aircraft) and entrepreneur Malcolm Bricklin (US importer of the budget Yugo car, and inventor of a gullwing sports car that bore his name), the 12 volt lead-acid powered EV Warrior sells through car dealerships for $900 to $1500. It has all the typical street legal motorcycle features, such as full head and tail lights, brake lights, turn signals (LEDs embedded in the side view mirrors), rear view mirrors and a loud horn. It even has room in the rear to mount a motorcycle licence plate, with light.

Like the later Ebike from Lee Iacocca's EV Global, the EV Warrior from Malcolm Currie and Malcolm Bricklin was sold, not very successfully, through car dealerships.

1996 US designed and manufactured ZAP friction drive launched.

Backed by the US government, the Los Alamos National Laboratory develops a new breed of smaller and lighter fuel cells.

Former Chrysler chairman Lee Iacocca forms EV Global Motors. which goes on to produce the Ebike range of electric bicycles. Giant of Taiwan is to build the bike and Iacocca, who had raised US$10 million from investors, mainly in Switzerland and Sweden, promised production within a year. Ambitious sales targets aim at 50,000 bikes for the first year, with a prediction of an eventual million bikes per year, even though no one else had so far managed to sell more than a few thousand electric bikes in the United States.

Customers didn't receive their first electric bikes until March 1999, with prices starting at US$995. Initially sold through car dealerships, the bikes were later distributed widely through bike dealers, but by 2001 Forbes Magazine was reporting that EV Global had only sold 12,000 Ebikes. However, the company had emerged as the leading seller of electric bikes in the United States, outselling such competitors as Giant and Currie.

Lee Iacocca's EV Global Ebike. EV Global went on to offer step-thru, folding and trike variants, but the company stopped producing electric bikes altogether in 2004.

1997 Raleigh Select electric bike (shown below) launched, using a Sanyo power system. Like the Yamaha PAS, the Select has a proportional power control system that automatically monitors and matches the rider's energy input, switching into electric assistance only when required. It sells for about £1,000, but general opinion is that it is too expensive for the UK public, for whom electric bikes were still a very new concept.

minimal effort meets low maintenance

The Electric Bicycle Company, the concern behind the EV Warrior, goes bankrupt with much of the blame falling on the shoulders of Malcolm Bricklin. Creditors include Sanyo North America ($5.45 million) and co-founder Malcolm Currie ($1.5 million). In the same year however, Currie, together with Richard Mayer, goes on to file a patent for a 'precision direct drive mechanism for a power-assist apparatus for a bicycle'. This goes on to become the Currie Electro Drive, one of the best-selling systems in the US and still being made today.

US folding mountain bike manufacturer Montague receives a two-year grant from the Defense Advanced Research Projects Agency (DARPA), who recognise the importance of folding bikes, to work with the United States Marines in developing the Tactical Electric No Signature (TENS) mountain bike. For this project Montague develops a new faster folding design and increases the load capacity of the bike. It was expected to be dropped from military aircraft with paratroopers and special forces.

1998 BionX introduces the EPS (Energy & Propulsion System) as either an add-on kit or ready fitted. Unusually it has a direct drive motor and regenerative braking (see chapter 4 for more detail on types of motor).

California state legislation decrees that 2% of all vehicles sold must be electric. The Velocity Dolphin - one of the first commercially available 'superbikes' - goes into serious production. It weighs about 30kg and according to tests of the time delivers impressive results - it is claimed to have a range of 60km (37 miles) at 32km/h (20mph) with a non-standard double range battery. Like the original Velocity, it uses the 'Evo-Drive' system which went on to be used in many other models such as Swizzbee.

Americans Alec Brooks and Alan Abbott launch the Charger electric bike (shown below), claiming power-assist up to four times the level of the pedal force. It's stated vital statistics were; top speed 20mph, range up to 40 miles and a total weight of around 30kg. The Charger venture was subsequently taken over by creditors such as Shimano, though the original stock was still for sale on the web in 2010, retailing for $775 - just less than half the original retail price.

1999 Powabyke launched in the UK. This Chinese design uses a DC motor and 36-volt lead-acid battery. Heavy and a bit crude, but cheap and effectively marketed, the company sells 1,000 of them in the first four months.

Giant - the largest bicycle maker in Taiwan and therefore one of the largest in the world - launches its first electric bike, the Lafree Sport. With a 10.6kg 432Wh lead-acid battery it weighed a hefty 27.4kg and was not a commercial success.

The ETC Traveller launched. An electric folding bike with an unusual saddle-shaped friction drive unit over the rear wheel. It is not a success and is soon withdrawn.

The very compact and efficient Electric Wheel hub motor is announced. The brainchild of O.J. Birkestrand of the Rabbit Tool Company, Illinois, it never goes into production, but the rights are later sold to Sanyo.

Panasonic's extraordinary Dracle is announced - an electric bike that uses the battery not only to power the bike but to telescope the body into a smaller package for easier transport.

Late 1990's The Chinese cities of Shanghai, Guangzhou, Shijiazhuang, and Suzhou begin drafting laws to restrict the use of petrol-powered motorcycles and ease restrictions on E-bikes.

2000 Panasonic claims it has produced the world's lightest electric bike at 19.9kg. Honda responds with the Step Combo, a folding electric bike weighing 18.7kg, using Honda's own NiMH-powered crank-drive. The Giant Lafree is redesigned in the Netherlands to make it lighter and more stylish and appeal to the European market. The new bike is fitted with a new Panasonic NiMH crank-drive.

In 2000 Honda's Step Combo was at the forefront of electric bike design. Unfortunately, it has since stopped producing electric bikes altogether.

38

Currie Technologies expands its range of electric machines in the US in an attempt to appeal to the mass market. Included in the range are a folding bike, tricycle, cruiser bike and a foot scooter.

Clive Sinclair's Zeta kit is relaunched in 'upgraded' form as the Zeta 3 ZA10. Eagerly anticipated - not least because of the reasonable price tag of £130 – it suffers from the same fatal design flaws as earlier incarnations - lack of power, poor range and excessive noise.

2001 eZee bikes of Shanghai starts manufacturing electric bikes.

Panasonic launches the Porta Ranger electric folding bike on the Japanese market. It uses the same Panasonic crank-drive fitted to the Giant Lafree, but with a smaller battery.

US electric vehicle maker ZAP displays a hydrogen fuel cell powered electric-assist bicycle at a shareholders meeting, declaring it will be the first commercially available fuel cell powered electric bike when launched in 2002.

2002 Panasonic introduce the world's first commercially available lithium-ion electric bike. The bike is powered by a re-engineered version of the Panasonic crank-drive, fitted with a tiny 1.7kg Li-ion battery. Although designed for the domestic Japanese market, the new drive unit has caused a great deal of interest elsewhere, with a number of European bike manufacturers signing up to use it. First in the queue is Biketec of Switzerland in late 2003.

The Segway electric travel vehicle (a high-tech self-balancing scooter) is launched. Much anticipated (its financial backers claimed it is going to be 'more important than the internet' before they reveal what it actually is), it turns out to be extremely pricey - some $4950 - which limits sales to corporate users and the very wealthy. Heavy at 36kg (80lbs), and illegal to ride on most public highways and pavements, the Segway never comes close to fulfilling the 10,000 a week sales prophesy (some say well under 1,000 in the leanest years), but the company stays in business.

The Sachs/SRAM Sparc hub motor pedelec kit is finally launched after appearing on 'demo' bikes since before 2,000. The long gestation (caused in part by Sachs being absorbed into US giant SRAM) has left the device looking old-fashioned even before the launch. The combined 5-speed hub and motor drive is clever, but assistance is weak, and the lead-acid battery is too heavy and too small The battery is later upgraded to NiMH, but the Sparc is never a big seller.

Outclassed and outsold by the new Panasonic Li-ion drive, Yamaha ceases production of own-brand PAS electric bike, made in St Quentin, Southern France, but continues to sell drive units to other manufacturers until existing contracts have been worked through.

The European Union introduces construction rules for powered two-wheeled vehicles.

2003 China's annual electric bike sales top 4 million.
Panasonic claim the world's lightest folding electric bike (again) at 16.9kg.

2004 US company EV Global stops producing electric bikes, only five years after the first one was sold amidst much hype.

2005 The Giant Revive Spirit is launched - an electrically assisted semi-recumbent, powered by the Panasonic Li-ion crank-drive. Although attractive and comfortable, it turns out to be a massive flop.
Kalkhoff, part of the Derby Cycle group that also includes Raleigh, launches its first electric bike, built – once again – around the Panasonic crank-drive. Kalkhoff quickly gains a name for producing high quality, reliable and well-equipped electric bikes.
SRAM releases an upgraded version of Sparc with NiMH battery and improved electronics. It's still underpowered, but goes a lot further.

SRAM's Sparc system was used in the off-the-peg Carrera Sparc system, sold in the UK through Halford's. Despite being a brave attempt to integrate five internal gears and an electric motor in the rear wheel, it was underpowered and not a great success commercially.

Panasonic Will electric folding bike launched.
The first working model of the very small, seat tube-housed Gruber Assist motor system appears in Austria.

Powacycle launches its range of low-cost but reasonable quality electric bikes in the UK. Head of the Akhter Group (of which Powacycles is a part), Humayun Mughal, speaks of making electric bike technology 'acceptable and reliable' for the mass market. Launched with simple spec and NiMH batteries, the bicycles prove solid and reliable performers and are later upgraded to Li-ion.
Annual electric bike sales in China top 10 million.

2006 The classic Giant Lafree is withdrawn after disappointing sales of 20,000 over a five year period - very small beer for a massive company like Giant. Its replacement is the Suede, an ill-conceived hub motor bike that is axed the following year.
The e-Solex is launched in France - an electric version of a hugely popular moped originally launched in 1947. Powered by a 49cc petrol engine fitted above the front wheel, the original moped went on to become a French icon with 8 million being sold over 41 years and, at the peak, 11 different models. The company ceased production in 1988 but corporate business deals lead to a 2004 rebirth and, finally in 2006 the e-Solex. On this new variant, styled by Pininfarina, the petrol engine was exchanged for a 400 watt electric motor in the rear wheel hub, with a 540Wh Li-ion battery, which took eight hours to charge. The official specification was: weight 44 kg, maximum speed 35 km/h and a range of around 40km. Although priced to undercut most petrol-powered mopeds at €1150, the e-Solex doesn't seem to have been a big sales success.

2007 Nano-Brompton hub motor system launched in the UK but, despite (or perhaps because of) excellent reviews, the small company behind the project fails to keep up with demand and fulfil orders. Production proves to be spasmodic. The machine is fitted with a Tongxin front hub motor and a Li-ion battery in the removable front carrier bag.
Giant launches the Twist series of hub motor electric bikes.
US company Schwinn gets it all wrong, launching an electric bike range fitted with a Protanium battery and a poorly designed and unreliable control system that takes a while to sort out.

2008 Panasonic and Sanyo introduce a new electric bike system offering regenerative braking. The Panasonic Vivi RX-10S and Sanyo Eneloop, initially selling in Japan only, are fitted with a geared front hub motor without a freewheel, so the motor is spinning whenever the bike is moving. This enables it to function as a generator when riding downhill or braking. Although BionX had used regenerative braking on its gearless motor system for some years, it is surprising and intriguing to see the big Japanese electric bike manufacturers go down this road.

Powacycle launches the Infineum sub-brand to market an unusual machine featuring a front hub motor and rack-mounted stackable Li-ion batteries. Although each battery has a capacity of only 234Wh, several can be stacked for longer journeys. Technical problems mean the Infineum Extreme is not ready for sale until the summer of 2009.

Kalkhoff introduce the Agattu 'F' bike, a Panasonic front hub pedelec system similar to the Eneloop, but without regenerative braking. Unlike the crank-drive, the 'F' can be used with a back-pedal 'coaster' rear hub brake, popular in Europe.

Jealous of Panasonic's success, Yamaha introduce a new PAS (Power Assist System), and Hungarian company Gepida - one of the first Eastern European countries to produce a serious electric bike – is the first big user. Yamaha faces an uphill struggle against a deeply entrenched Panasonic.

Schwinn tries again, launching the Tailwind, equipped with a Toshiba Li-ion battery claimed to take a full charge in 30 minutes and have a life cycle of 2,000 to 3,000 charges (plus a unique two year/20,000 mile warranty). The downside is a battery capacity of only 120Wh, less than half that of rivals. Despite the interesting specification, the Tailwind seems not to have been a success.

The Yamaha crank-drive system is still in use on some Gepida bikes today.

Cytronex brand launched in the UK by Modern Times Ltd. The Cytronex range are built around standard machines, fitted with the Tongxin motor used on the Nano-Brompton and a NiMH battery disguised as a water bottle. Although range is limited, the bikes quickly gain a reputation for quality and attention to detail.

42

2009 Another NiMH-powered bicycle, the GoCycle, is finally launched in the UK. This demountable electric bike is custom designed, from its quick-release wheels to its magnesium frame, but technical problems have delayed the launch. Recalls and other issues continue for some months after the launch too, but the bike develops an enthusiastic following.

The French e-Solex is relaunched as e-Solex 2.0 as a response to the mixed reception received by the 2006 version. It now proclaims a lighter battery, a longer range, optional indicators and a number of other minor changes. It costs €1595.

The e-Solex 2.0 - could it resurrect the fortunes of a classic French petrol-engined brand that once sold in millions?

Lightweight Powabyke X-Byke launched. The new, small capacity lithium-ion battery weighs only 1.8kg, but offers a limited 15 mile range. By the end of the year, Powabyke is in receivership, but soon back on its feet.

Modern Times, manufacturer of the Cytronex, claims the tag of 'world's lightest production electric bicycle' with a 12.9kg carbon-framed racing bike and Tongxin motor-assist, based on the Cytronex Cannondale Super Six.

Currie Electro Drive kit relaunched.

The Tongxin motor fitted to the Nano-Brompton kit is now available in a narrower version to suit the Brompton front forks.

The BionX IGH3 integrates the BionX rear hub motor with SRAM's 3-speed hub gear.

The Gazelle Chamonix Innergy collects the prestigious Dutch Bike of the Year award - the first time an electric bike has achieved this accolade.

Sanyo reveals its solar-powered charging station.

The Chinese government announces a new law to clamp down on the perceived problems caused by electric bikes, but appears to U-turn in the face of popular criticism and industry protest.

2010 Yike Bike, designed by New Zealander Grant Ryan, is launched onto the European market - at a price. The folding, 10kg pedal-less electric 'bike' is dubbed a mini electric Penny Farthing and retails at £2,995. Unfortunately, as it doesn't have pedals, it cannot be ridden on the road under current electric bicycle regulations.

Grant Ryan, designer of the Yike Bike, sits proudly on his creation.

The next generation of Sanyo Eneloop bikes is launched.

Currie's IZIP Express is launched, aimed primarily at the US market. Its stated stats are weight 30.2kg and range of 37 miles at an average speed of 17.5mph. It's a collaboration between Currie, Dolphin and Sturmey Archer (hybrid drive transmission based on the Velocity 'Evo-Drive'), Trinamic of Germany (control systems) and Taiwan's Fairly Bike (manufacturing).

Irish company GoEco starts fitting electric motor drives to traditional style Irish bikes known as 'High Nellies'.

Yamaha announces that it wants to raise $812 million to dedicate to the development of alternative engine technology across its range of transport vehicles - including electric bikes.

Sir Clive Sinclair unveils plans for the successor to the C5 - the X-1 is a fully-faired two-wheeled electric assist recumbent. Plans are for a 2011 launch.

Raleigh re-enters the electric bike market using 'badge engineered' versions of the Kalkhoff range, the first being the Raleigh Dover, based on the excellent Kalkhoff Agattu. Raleigh had previously experimented with various Powabyke machines in an arrangement that didn't last.

2010 saw Raleigh produce its first own-branded electric bikes since 1997

2011 A veritable wave of European companies is set to launch electric bikes or electric bike systems onto the market:

Shimano showcases the STePS pedelec system - a collection of components to be sold initially to bike manufacturers as original equipment. It features a front hub motor and a rather small rear rack-mounted battery with claimed life of eight years. It also boasts regenerative braking. Shimano has clearly listened to consumer demands, but the jury is still out on the actual performance of the system as none are released yet into the public domain.

Bosch launches a crank-drive motor system with multi-power settings and a claimed range of 35 to 80km. Initially released on Cannondale and Scott bikes, amongst others, Bosch also says a retrofit option is 'a possibility'. The system claims ultra-efficient and precise sensing and control technology.

Suntour show a number of 'concept bikes' with a rather similar system to the Shimano STePS. The system is called HESC - Human Electro Synergy components.

Cube Bike's two EPO models feature a swathe of expensive components, including wireless technology - one of the very first electric bikes to do so.

For UK consumers the launch of the Raleigh Velo-City and Velo-Trail models holds great promise. They offer European hub motor pedelec quality at under a thousand pounds and appear to be bestsellers in waiting.

Cube's EPO electric bike promised a whole new level of technology. The bike was a talking point at Eurobike in late 2010.

Cannondale was a development partner on Bosch's crank-drive system, although it will be available on a wide variety of other makes of bikes from 2011.

Classics & Flops

Sinclair C5 1985 only * Zike 1992 only * Zeta 1994-2001

Sir Clive Sinclair is a British inventor with a long and somewhat mixed track record as an inventive genius. After doing very well in the early days of computers, he decided that the future lay in electric vehicles. This was something of a leap of faith in the early 1980s, because there wasn't a great deal of evidence for such a prognosis at the time. Batteries were composed of heavy and unwieldy lead-acid cells that hadn't advanced for decades, and there was very little development going on. On the other hand, petrol had dramatically increased in price (and came close to being rationed for a time), new battery chemistries looked promising, and after lobbying from Sinclair Vehicles, the government had legalised low-powered electric bikes and trikes. The time seemed right.

Introduced in 1985 at a reasonable £399 (£940 at 2010 prices), the Sinclair C5 was Sir Clive's answer to what many believed to be an impending energy crisis. It was effectively a faired recumbent tricycle, power-assisted with a small DC motor (produced by vacuum cleaner company Hoover) and a car battery. Although the

Sinclair teamed up with Hoover, better known as vacuum cleaner makers, for motor manufacture and after-sales servicing.

Lotus-designed polypropylene bodyshell looked suitably futuristic, the C5 was built around nice straightforward technology, and it was tailored to suit the new electric vehicle legislation, so although powered, it could be driven by anyone aged 14 or older without a licence, insurance or other motor vehicle legislative requirements. Had the ongoing political turbulence in the Middle East resulted in a long-term oil shortage, the C5 would undoubtedly have been a huge success, but the gamble failed. C5s did sell in modest numbers initially, but the usefulness of the little

C5 *driver*

THE OFFICIAL MAGAZINE
FOR THE SINCLAIR C5 VEHICLE

JANUARY 1985

45p

machines was seriously curtailed by the cars it was intended to replace. Although quite an upright recumbent, and highly visible on the road, the C5 was labelled as dangerous in traffic, and with the immediate crisis over, the roads became busier and sales dwindled. In truth, there were very few accidents. Figures from the Department for Transport revealed that in the first six months after the launch, with as many as 8,000 C5s tootling about, there were only two reported accidents, neither involving other vehicles. But the perception stuck.

A more serious issue was the C5's single 38-inch pedal gear, giving a top pedal speed of less than 10mph, so once the machine was running faster, up to its 15mph maximum, the pedals were useless, leaving the motor to do all the work. Range was claimed to be 20 miles (40 miles with an optional second battery), but it tended to be much less in practice.

Sinclair Vehicles had confidently predicted sales of 2,000 a week, but the reality was a peak of barely one fifth of that level and as unsold stock began to pile up, production was soon cut to a nominal 100 a week. Within a year, Sinclair Vehicles was in receivership, and the remaining stock of 7,000 C5s (more than half the production run of 12,000) was sold off to a quick-witted entrepreneur. They were soon changing hands for more than the original launch price of £399.

In more pragmatic markets, such as the Netherlands, where the trikes could roam free on the country's superb cycle path network, sales had been quite strong, and the C5 remained popular there long after production had ceased. Today, the C5 has rightly attained classic status in many countries and good examples change hands for £750 or even more.

Undeterred by the C5's monumental failure, Sir Clive went on to launch an electric bicycle called the Zike in February 1992. This was a diminutive machine with small wheels and a rather frail looking alloy frame containing the battery pack. There were several weaknesses. As with the C5, the Zike had a single gear, so pedal assistance was not a very practical option, but the bicycle had a much smaller NiMH battery, so range was necessarily rather limited. The little motor was a noisy high-speed device driving the rear wheel via a toothed belt. At £500 (£820 at 2010 prices), the Zike was rather expensive for what it was, and sales - estimated at 10,000 a month - had barely reached a total of 2,000 before production at the Scottish factory was wound up after only six months.

Interestingly, the Zike looked like a folder, and a folding version was under development when the plug was pulled. As a folding bike, the downsides of small wheels and limited range would have been much less of a handicap, but this does not seem to have been considered in the development stage.

The Sinclair Zike was marketed as an accessory for young executives, but today it's more likely to be found in the hands of car-boot salesmen. An unfortunate flop.

After ten unsuccessful years, most entrepreneurs would have crawled away to lick their wounds, but Sir Clive was made of sterner stuff, and in 1994 he came back with his cheapest and least satisfactory electric machine yet, the Zeta. Rather than an electric vehicle, the Zeta was a £145 power-assist module that could be fitted to a normal bike. In essence it was a shoebox-sized device that fitted above the rear wheel (the front wheel on later models), containing a small lead-acid battery and a motor linked by a toothed drive belt to a large idler pulley. When the unit was dropped against the tyre under spring pressure, the smooth reverse side of the belt contacted the tyre, transmitting the drive. There was no power regulation – just a simple on/off switch on the handlebars.

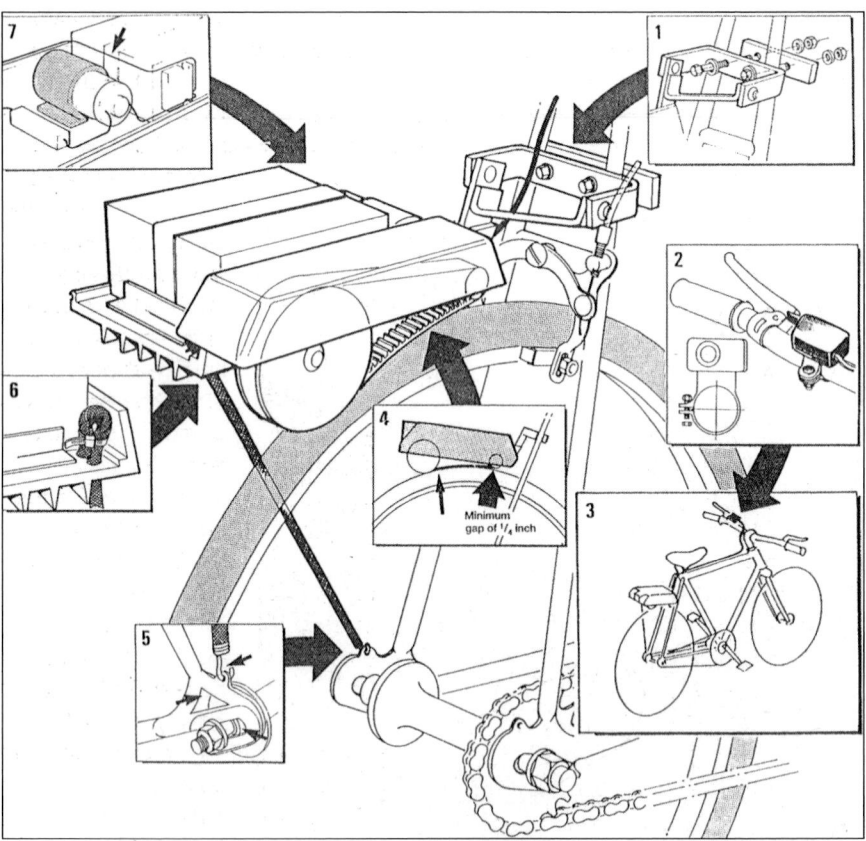

Fitting and operation of the Zeta looked straightforward but the assistance was of virtually no use.

This all sounded good in theory, but the practical limitations went on and on. The device had to be fitted very carefully to work correctly, and when it did, the power was limited, the belt didn't work well with knobbly tyres, and it was noisy and unreliable. Once underway, the Zeta put a lot of extra weight high up on the rear wheel or steering, which did nothing for the handling, and as it couldn't easily be retracted from the tyre (again, this was sorted later) there was no mechanism to freewheel, or pedal with the motor turned off. Despite all these problems, the Zeta sold well enough to at least stay in production for a while. As late as 2,000, it was being relaunched in Mark 3 form with a more powerful motor and slicker looks. Range was optimistically claimed to be 10 to 15 miles at 'up to' 12mph, but few users seemed to have made the thing work for long enough to find out in everyday conditions. Some critics argued that the bicycle was actually slower with the Zeta than without! A tongue-in-cheek comment no doubt, but it was an understandable impression when comparing the noise and vibration of the motor with the delicious silence with it was turned off and retracted (or better still, removed).

The irony for Sinclair was that his original prophecy had by this time been proved correct: electric cars and motorcycles were in their infancy, but electric bikes were starting to make quite an impact, and they were mostly very much better than the Zeta. A machine like the Powabyke cost more than three times as much, but it could go for dozens of miles at 15mph while the motive force of the Zeta was barely detectable.

The final version, the Zeta 3, seems to have sold fitfully for a few years, but its day had already long passed.

A decade later, in 2010, Sir Clive Sinclair announced that he was looking for backers to help

Even with the power transferred from rear to front wheel, the Zeta 3 was still a woeful under-performer

produce a larger electric vehicle called the X-1. Unveiled in late 2010 it turned out to be an attractive, and practical single seater semi-recumbent, and in many ways a worthy successor to the C5. At the time of writing details remain sketchy, but the X-1 is expected to have a relatively small Li-ion battery and a low powered motor. Delivery is promised for July 2011, and the price – astonishingly - is estimated to be £595.

Powabyke Classic 1999-

In 1999, when electric bikes were still regarded as innovative technology, the Powabyke Classic arrived on the scene. Sold in China as the Shanghai Elite, the Powabyke branding was added by a company in Bath, United Kingdom: it was heavy (36.5kg) and crude (DC motor, lead-acid battery), but it was more reliable than most, and in an era when a range of 15 miles was considered acceptable, the Powabyke's 20-30 miles was quite an achievement. In 2000, the Classic became the Euro (later the Eurobike), so-called because it could be switched between a crude pedelec mode for Europe, or twistgrip E-bike mode for the UK. At the same time, the price rose from £500/£550 to £700, but sales don't seem to have suffered. Powabyke was the first electric bike manufacturer to put a lot of work into developing a dealer network, sellers in those early days including all sorts of businesses, from moped outlets to trailer shops, as the cycle trade was generally unwilling to invest in electrics. This diverse but strong dealer network helped the Powabyke brand to take off, opening up the UK market in a way that hadn't been achieved before.

The Powabyke was propelled by three 12-volt lead-acid batteries in an unusually wide battery case that nestled between double top tubes in the main frame. This resulted in a rather ungainly riding style, with knees forced apart more than is generally considered comfortable, or indeed ladylike! The power was regulated by a simple transistor controller in a rather tacky plastic housing on the handlebars, and the motor was fitted in the front or rear wheel.

At its peak, Powabyke produced quite a range of models, from the upright single-speed step-thru Shopper, to the 24-speed Commuter. Its market was predominantly the elderly and infirm, but a few Commuters were bought by younger people looking for day-to-day transport.

The Euro 6-speed was probably the best all-rounder, and certainly the best seller. Gearing was a bit low, but it was cheap (£645 in 2005) and it did most things reasonably well. On later models the gearing was improved, but by this time the price was creeping up, and it wasn't quite the bargain it had been a few years before.

Something all Powabykes had in common was enormous weight - 36 or 37kg was typical, but some models were very close to the 40kg legal weight limit for electric bikes, and when sold with panniers, the Commuter actually exceeded it slightly. A third of the weight was accounted for by the 13kg battery, which was too heavy for some customers to lift unaided. This massive battery was the Powabyke's weakest element, and the weight led to many battery casings and mountings breaking on rough roads.

Batteries apart, Powabykes were fairly reliable machines. The motors could be noisy, and in theory they needed occasional gear lubrication and brush replacement, although the bikes usually fell to bits before these service items became due. As the years passed, the brand came under increasing pressure from newer, more innovative machines, such as the Giant Lafree, which weighed barely half as much, and from copycat machines like the Sakura, marketed by former Powabyke director Dan Hornsby.

By 2006, the Powabyke range was looking increasingly archaic, but sales were holding up well, and Powabyke scored a decisive blow in its search for new markets by securing an unlikely deal to sell its bikes through the big and prestigious Raleigh dealer network. One positive side-effect of the deal was a completely new Powabyke. The X-byke, launched in early 2009, was built around a conventional Raleigh bicycle. Some components – such as the old control unit and the anachronistic motor – were big and heavy, but others like the water-bottle battery, were amongst the smallest and lightest available. Overall, the bike weighed a reasonable 23.6kg, but the range of only 13.4 miles put it at a disadvantage against competitors (or traditional Powabyke models) that went more than twice as far.

It looked heavy and it was heavy, but reliability and price made the Classic a classic.

Replacing most of the previous bikes, the X-byke was a brave attempt to leap-frog several steps ahead of the opposition, but the concept was flawed and in late 2009, Powabyke went into administration. Fortunately, the company soon found investors, and the X-bykes and 'Classic' Eurobike range - including the 6-speed – were soon back on sale. In late 2010, the X-byke was upgraded with a modern BLDC motor and a larger 296Wh battery, but the classic 6-speed was kept in the catalogue and Powabyke insists there are no plans to withdraw it.

Interestingly, with the price of lithium-ion batteries rising fast, and continuing worries over reliability, many consumers are looking again at the simple, lead-acid Powabyke, which has outlasted all of its 20th Century competitors and continues to sell well today at a bargain £600. A great survivor.

Aprilia Enjoy 2001-?

For some reason, the Italians never quite seem to have managed to get their electric bike act together. That is not to say that they will never do so, but the fact remains that the Italian past seems to be littered with also-rans and lost opportunities. One of the most interesting was the Aprilia Enjoy, previewed as a hydrogen fuel cell-powered prototype in early 2001, and launched with NiMH battery power later the same year. The Enjoy had a sharply-styled alloy frame, attractive 'moped-style' crank motor and a very large 312Wh battery. With this spec, the Enjoy should have offered considerable performance and sold by the thousand, but the bike was an absolute disaster. Why? The only conclusion one can draw is that the thrust of the development had gone into styling rather than testing, because in practice the machine simply didn't work.

The Aprilia Enjoy looked way ahead of its time, but the technology employed was ill-conceived and the project seems to have sunk without trace.

The Enjoy suffered from an interwoven tangle of technical faults and issues: the gearing was much too high (46 to 111 inches), the motor (presumably US spec) was too powerful, the control systems were crude and inefficient, and the motorcycle style frame was too heavy and difficult to put human power into effectively. The result was unprecedented energy consumption of 32Wh/mile, and a range of only 16 miles. A less suitable test-bed for a fuel cell is hard to imagine, and the hydrogen version, which Aprilia had confidently predicted would be on sale within five years, was quietly shelved. It was, in any event, a slightly dubious prospect. The hydrogen, compressed to 4,000psi, was to be carried in a carbon fibre flask inside the top tube, with a fuel cell stack mounted in front of the handlebars. Range was put at 47 miles, and overall weight at 24kg, 6kg lighter than the battery version.

The Aprilia Enjoy must have cost millions of lire to develop, but it was dogged by technical problems with the control systems, motor and battery, and didn't stay in production for very long. Even today, this stylish and fascinating machine has an enthusiastic specialist following, and many of the bikes remain in (occasional) use, often rebuilt with modern controllers and batteries.

Giant Lafree 2001-2006

Although it was the biggest bicycle manufacturer in the world, Giant came rather late to electric assist. Its first venture, the Sport, was launched in the late 1990s, and wisely sub-branded 'Lafree' rather than Giant. It was a heavy, ugly, brutish lead-acid machine. This beast seems to have sold relatively well in America, but bombed in Europe, and other markets where bicycles and cycling were taken a bit more seriously. Unusually for a multinational, Giant then did the right thing, handing the electric bike project over to its European Design Centre based in the Netherlands. The Dutch engineers were given a free rein, with the proviso that the bike must utilise a crank-motor, similar to that of the new Yamaha electric bikes.

The engineering team, led by Robbert Broekhof, settled on the Panasonic crank-drive (basically it was either that or the Yamaha PAS) and designed a light, airy and elegant bicycle around the Japanese electronics.

This synthesis of European design, Japanese electronic genius and Taiwanese manufacturing knowhow proved a potent formula, and when it appeared in 2001, the new Lafree was far and away the best electric bike available. The basic version weighed just 22kg (lighter than some unassisted Dutch roadsters) and the quiet, effective motor gave it a range of over 20 miles from a relatively small NiMH battery. At this point Giant made its first big mistake. Uncertain whether electric bikes would gain widespread acceptance, the decision was made to stick with the Lafree brand, rather than badge the bike as a Giant. This lack of confidence, and unwillingness to back the bike with its well-respected brand name, was to cause a lot of confusion and cost many sales. To the public, and most bike dealers, it was the Giant Lafree, but Giant insisted it was the Lafree Twist. Later, the company gave in to pressure from US dealers and renamed it the Giant Lite, but that caused even more confusion, and in any event, it was much too late.

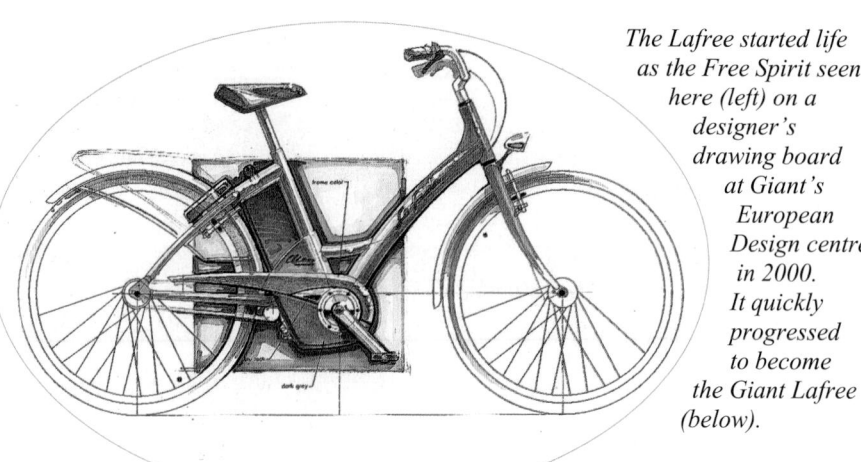

The Lafree started life as the Free Spirit seen here (left) on a designer's drawing board at Giant's European Design centre in 2000. It quickly progressed to become the Giant Lafree (below).

The Lite M (right) was designed to appeal especially to the US market. It was sold without mudguards and rack to enhance its sales potential.

Despite the over-cautious marketing, and some technical issues with chargers and control systems, the Lafree proved to be a wonderful bike, and news of its arrival spread almost by word of mouth. With all the elegance of a traditional Dutch roadster, and the convenience of power-assist, the Lafree was the first electric bike to gain real acceptance amongst serious cyclists and women in particular. And in an era when electric bikes were designed for, and marketed at, the elderly, it succeeded in attracting younger riders too.

Ironically, despite a reasonable price, a long list of favourable attributes and glowing reviews, the Lafree really had arrived too soon, and although it paved the way for a generation of similar machines, and set in motion an electric bike boom in Europe that continues to this day, it sold in pitifully small numbers.

By 2006, when Giant ruefully pulled the plug on the project, only 20,000 had been sold: 5,000 in the USA and 3,000 in the UK, with the balance – crucially – in the fast growing markets of Holland and Germany. Within a few years these markets had tripled in size, thanks in part to Giant's trail-blazing Lafree.

Today, the Lafree is the only early electric bike with an appreciable resale value, good used examples selling for £500 or more. This healthy interest is largely down to the bike being withdrawn before the arrival of the lighter, but more troublesome and expensive Li-ion battery. As the NiMH batteries have a proven life of five years or more, running costs can be appreciably lower than a modern machine, and in that respect at least, the Lafree has yet to be beaten.

Post-Lafree, Giant went on to score a series of expensive own goals. Looking for cheaper technology, the company settled on a more conventional system based around a front hub motor, but nothing quite seemed to work out. The short-lived Suede had gear and battery problems, and the replacement Twist just didn't seem to measure up to the Lafree on any criteria except range in twin-battery form. Ironically, the Lafree concept - a conventional looking roadster or hybrid with a neat and unobtrusive crank-drive - went on to become a runaway success, and today most quality bikes follow this general pattern.

Giant Revive 2005-?

As we've seen, Giant didn't always get it right. In the early years of the 21st Century, the company seems to have been either awash with creative talent, or thrashing around with no clear direction, or very possibly both! Amongst many interesting developments at this time was the Revive, a comfortable but heavy semi-recumbent non-electric bicycle.

Although enjoying a healthy enthusiast following, recumbents have never really broken through into the mainstream for a number of reasons: the sheer innovation puts off many riders and bike shops, and there are practical problems too – visibility in traffic being a common (although not necessarily justified) criticism, and the bikes and trikes are usually longer and very often heavier than the norm. The weight is an inevitable consequence of getting away from the classic diamond or step-thru bicycle design: other patterns may give better wind resistance or rolling resistance, or be ideal for specialist functions, but they almost always need more frame material and thus weigh more, unless exotic materials are used in their construction. So recumbents can be lighter than 'wedgies', but only if they are very expensive.

At the time, Giant had a hunch that a recumbent might work, and as the British engineering genius Mike Burrows was working for them at the time, they asked him to do the initial design work. As is so often the case, the production bike ended up heavier, more complex and – for various reasons - a fairly upright semi-recumbent. The Revive put the rider higher than a normal recumbent, but the riding position was still very much feet-first, with a comfortable seat rather than a saddle. It looked, and was, very pleasant to ride, but it was a heavy and expensive bicycle, and the geometry didn't lend itself well to hard pedalling on steep hills. The public certainly don't seem to have been convinced by the comfort angle and the bike was not a good seller.

The Revive looked power-assisted, but it wasn't, and it desperately needed to be. Giant responded with the Revive Spirit, released in the summer of 2005. Like the Lafree (still in production, but with only a year to live), the Spirit was fitted with a Panasonic crank-drive – not the venerable NiMH version, but a brand new Li-ion battery variant. This should have been good news, but designed for the Japanese market, the early Li-ion batteries were rather small, with options of 86Wh or 144Wh, neither of which was capable of driving this heavy machine very far or very fast. Aimed fair and square at the US market, the Spirit had a healthy top speed of 18mph, but had been crudely detuned for Europe by taking a tap from the speedometer sensor, and using these impulses to cut the motor at 15mph. This caused power to cut out rather abruptly at the legal maximum, and then 'hunt' in and out of engagement. Even in this unsatisfactory restricted form, range from the larger battery was only about 16 miles.

The Revive Spirit looked a million dollars and was comfortable and fun to ride, but you needed to be very keen on the concept to buy one. It's instructive to compare it point for point with the Lafree, which itself had proved something of a sales flop for Giant, and was close to being withdrawn. At £1500 the Spirit was 30% more expensive, the (smaller) battery was 40% more expensive, and at 33.2kg the bike was 30% heavier than the heaviest Lafree. It's no surprise that the Spirit had 29% less range. Is it any wonder this ponderous machine went down like a lead balloon? Firm sales figures for disastrous flops are generally hard to come by, but estimates for the Spirit may break all records. According to the handful of US electric bike dealers willing to try the machine, total dealer sales in the States may have amounted to less than bikes. It was, said one, 'Too expensive, too weird, and under-powered.' Sales in the UK would certainly have been even lower than the US, and there's no evidence that the Revive sold in any appreciable numbers elsewhere. After the bike was quietly withdrawn, Giant began selling the unwanted machines at a substantial discount, a process that was to continue for some time. Nevertheless, in a process strangely reminiscent of the Sinclair C5, the remarkable Revive Spirit is already (and quite rightly) becoming a sought after classic.

Bikes ahead of their time often looked great but failed to perform in practice or sell in the shops. The Giant Revive Spirit was no exception.

Could it have been better? And would it have fared any better if it had? Increased battery capacity would have given the flexibility to fit a more powerful crank-drive, whilst adding very little to the weight. The Revive battery weighed 2.1kg and delivered 144Wh, whereas five years later, the Derby Cycles battery (now an option on the same Panasonic crank-drive) weighs 3.3kg and has a capacity of 486Wh. A battery of this capacity would have given range of 40 miles, or a significant performance boost, but of course in 2005, neither the battery nor more powerful crank-drive were available. With today's improved technology, and much wider acceptance of electric bikes, it probably would be a success (although whether it would sell in sufficient numbers to satisfy Giant is another matter). Like the C5 and the Lafree, the Revive simply came on the scene too early.

eZee Torq 2005 on

The Shanghai eZee Kinetic Technology company, formed by Singaporean entrepreneur Waiwon Ching, was amongst the first of the modern breed of Chinese manufacturers, producing its first bike back in 2003. This was the Forza (almost immediately renamed the Sprint to avoid political connotations in Italy!), a successful, if slightly frumpy machine. The Sprint weighed less than 30kg, which was good for the time, and had a range of more than 30 miles (or 20 miles without pedalling) which was ground-breaking stuff.

By 2005, eZee was well established, the Sprint having been joined by the cheaper Rider, and the folding Quando. These were satisfactory, but even frumpier machines, so when the revolutionary Torq arrived in the summer of 2005 it took the electric bike world entirely by surprise.

The magic of the machine was an over-sized and slightly stretched MTB-style frame, fitted with big free-running 28-inch wheels, 9-speed Shimano Acera gears, the compact new 8FUN motor and a large, and at the time truly revolutionary lithium-ion battery. Any one of these ingredients would have resulted in a noteworthy new electric bike, but putting the package together produced a devastatingly effective machine. The prototype Torq had a huge 133-inch top gear, and the tiny motor was geared to give a top speed of about 23mph, thanks to the large wheels and high voltage output from the Li-ion battery. With high pedal and motor gearing, the bike could be ridden long distances at impressive (and totally illegal) speeds, and although range was only 23 miles, the bike's near silent wafting power made a tremendous impression on those who were considering buying an electric bike, and crucially, many people who weren't too. Like the Lafree, the eZee Torq was one of the first bikes to really break out of the 'geriatric' electric bike mould, appealing to much younger, and indeed, fitter people than any previous machine.

Gear range and quality were slightly downgraded for production, the brakes were terrible (but no-one seems to have minded much) and the price inevitably rose, but the Torq was in a class of it's own, and sales seem to have been quite strong.

The eZee Torq became as legendary as the model

What no-one knew is that the bike was living on borrowed time. The early lithium-ion battery had not seen sufficient testing, and within a few months there was a rash of premature failures that turned into an epidemic. Led along by over-ambitious claims from the battery manufacturers - that Li-ion would provide at least 1,000 charges and rapidly fall in price - eZee had launched the technology on an unsuspecting public much too early.

Over the next two or three years, the company thrashed around in a desperate attempt to find a lithium battery that could deal with the demands made by this fast and furious bicycle, but although battery life did rapidly improve from the initial three months or so, the problem was never fully cracked. The early Phylion batteries were re-engineered several times before eZee adopted Sanyo cells in early 2008, the Japanese cells later being replaced with a cheaper alternative (allegedly from Samsung), and then yet another brand.

Meanwhile, the 24kg Torq had gained in weight, and suffered the ignominy of being legally restricted for a while (a decision rapidly reversed following vigorous customer protests!). In 2008, the Torq was replaced by the Torq 2, fitted with a custom-made, 'high torque' motor, in place of the delightfully high geared 8FUN. Unfortunately, it seemed to have less torque than its remarkable predecessor and it was certainly noisier.

Despite all the battery issues, two changes of UK distributor, and weaker performance, the Torq 2 continues to sell today. The modern machine is much better equipped than its predecessor, and the latest Alfine variant has Shimano Alfine gearing and hydraulic brakes, an electronic analyst and larger 518Wh battery, but at £1,900 it costs as much as a decent European electric bike. It's a measure of the strength of the Torq brand and mythology that it continues to sell in reasonable numbers. Second-hand bikes can be found for as little as £300 to £400, but a second hand bike will almost certainly need a new battery, and that will cost another £500.

Nano-Brompton 2006 on

With a few honourable exceptions, folding electric bikes have tended to be rather laughable machines. A folding bike needs certain key attributes to succeed: it has to be light enough for anyone to lift and carry a reasonable distance, compact enough to fit easily into a car boot or a busy commuter train, and ridable enough to stand in for a big-wheeled bike on short or medium length journeys.

Designing a conventional folding bike able to satisfy these three conflicting requirements is hard enough, but with the weight and bulk of power-assist, it's very nearly impossible. Most Chinese manufacturers have made a rather half-hearted attempt to fulfil the folding brief, but as a general rule these machines are little more than cheap fold-in-half frames fitted with full-size electric bike equipment. The result can be guaranteed to fail in at least one of the three folder requirements, with many failing in all three.

The better machines tend to be based on known and respected conventional folding bikes, with battery, controller and motor carefully chosen to add minimum weight and maximum performance. Of this select group, the best by a considerable margin is the Nano-Brompton, produced by Wiltshire boffin Tony Castles.

Back in 2006, Tony settled on the Brompton as the basis for his bike. It wasn't the lightest folding bike on the market, but it was one of the smallest, and it had a reputation for a quality ride, and a quick and effortless fold. However good the bike, it would have been ruined with a big heavy electric motor, but it just so happened that Hangzhou University in China had designed a delightful little sensorless BLDC hub motor (see pages 84-85), with production licensed to a company called Tongxin. The motor was too wide for the unusually narrow Brompton forks, but it was small in diameter, and for the time, extremely light. The motor was squeezed in by expanding the forks, and in a brilliant bit of lateral thinking, the battery was put in the detachable front pannier, powering the bike through copper contacts on the tapered frame-mounted pannier block.

At around 19kg, the Nano-Brompton wasn't astonishingly light, but when folded, it made two packages: the battery and bag weighing 4.4kg, and the bike itself around 14.4kg. This was quite practical to carry, at least over short distances, and it was in a completely different league to conventional folding electrics, most of which weighed 25kg or more in one lump. It was also extremely compact, and well up to carriage by train, or even by bus. With a light, ridable frame, efficient low-geared motor, and high pedal gearing, the range of the Nano-Brompton could be quite striking. With care, the bike could easily be coaxed for 40 miles or even more, giving it a greater range than most full-size electric bikes, albeit at a lower speed. Unfortunately, Tony Castles was effectively hand-building the power kits, and when orders began to flood in, he was unable to build the kits fast enough, a problem compounded by sporadic delivery of motors, price increases, and a few technical problems with motors and batteries.

By early 2009 a couple of hundred kits had been sold, but with a big and increasingly rancorous queue of waiting customers, Tony finally threw in the towel and ceased production. As it turned out, the design was too good to lie dormant for long, and in June that same year, the Nano rights were transferred to the Electric Wheel Company, also in Wiltshire, and kit manufacture restarted later in the year. Today, the Nano is available either as a kit or a ready-to-run folding bike, production being made a great deal easier by the introduction of a narrower 80mm motor that will squeeze between the Brompton forks without major adaptation. The weight of the modern Nano-Brompton bike depends on the weight of the recipient Brompton. Using the latest, lightest, 1- or 2-speed titanium bike, the complete machine can weigh as little as 15kg.

Following on from the success of the Nano, others have produced their own Brompton-based electric bikes. Perhaps the most interesting is the Freedom, sold as a complete bike or conversion kit by a small company is Israel. This is a technically simpler conversion, with the same Tongxin motor but with a basic plug in place of the Nano's clever pannier block power connector. The battery is a tiny A123 pack of only 91Wh, which fits with the power controller into one of the Brompton pannier bag back pockets. Range is only seven miles, but the packs are so tiny several can be carried with ease. The A123 packs charge quite quickly (under two hours) and – developed in America for the tough world of battery-electric hand tools - are said to have a relatively long service life.

These Brompton-based kits are not cheap. A super-lightweight titanium Nano would cost just under £2,000 (the Freedom a little less) but they are certainly at the cutting edge in terms of weight, foldability and performance. In late 2010 all eyes were on Brompton. Would the company capitalize on the success of this design with an electric variant of its own?

This Nano-Brompton, from the Electric Wheel Company, features a large 370Wh battery that is quite sizeable in relation to the folded bike. It is housed in Brompton's own front luggage pannier (omitted on this photo for clarity). The advantage of this is that when carrying the bike you have two lighter packages, rather than one heavier one.

Electricity Made Easy

Harnessing electron power

In order to understand why electric bikes have become successful and practical machines, whereas electric cars and delivery vehicles have yet to make any real impact (other than in very specific areas), we need to go back to basics and get to grips with what electricity is, and how and why it can provide propulsion.

An electrical current is a flow of electrons. Electrons are little particles (or perhaps not, but we won't go there) that are an essential part of the atoms that are the building blocks of us and everything around us. Without going too deeply into the science, an atom likes to be in electrical balance, with a large, positively charged particle at the centre, balanced by lots of little negatively charged electrons whizzing around it, rather as satellites spin around the earth.

Sometimes in nature, an electron gets stripped from an atom, leaving the atom with a positive charge, and a desire to attract another electron in order to restore the balance. If many millions of electrons are removed from millions of atoms, you can be fairly confident that something big will happen, as it does in a thunderstorm, where the charge on part of a cloud eventually becomes so high in relation to the ground (or other clouds, or parts of the same cloud) that a lightning strike momentarily connects the two, restoring equilibrium. In practice, there are many different types of lightning, and they can go up as well as down, but all we need to know now is the basic principle.

The gradual build-up of energy and its cataclysmic release in the lightning strike occur because the air is a relatively poor conductor of electricity. In other words, electrons do not readily flow through it. When a small number of electrons are jumping about trying to bridge the gap, they can't, but when millions are massed to jump across, the resistance of the air is overcome, and the electrons travel together, heating the air to a very high temperature, producing the familiar flash and bang.

The breakthrough in harnessing these formidable natural forces came with the discovery that electrons could hop from one atom to another and flow very easily through certain materials (principally metals such as copper), but they found it very difficult to move through others, such as glass, waxed cloth, rubber, or later, plastic. So for example, a source of electrons might be isolated in a glass jar, and led out through a copper wire when required. In this way, our Victorian forebears discovered that the simplest electrical circuit comprised a generator of electrons, a loop of a suitable conductor, a device where the electrons could do useful work, and another conductor to lead them back to the other end of the generator.

Several means were discovered for producing a flow of electrons. The primary means, then as now, involved moving a conductor rapidly through a magnetic field. At first this effect was little more than a curiosity, but once steam or water-powered rotary devices had been invented to turn many conductors very rapidly through a strong magnetic field, the electrical age had begun. This primary form of power generation is still with us today, and nearly all power stations produce electricity in this way, whether they are powered by atomic energy, energy from the sun fossilised as coal, gas or oil, or the weight of falling water. As nearly all hydro-electric power plants use rain water, which has been lifted into clouds by the warmth of the sun, hydro power plants are really just another way of harnessing the energy from the sun.

It had already been discovered that a flow of electrons could be produced by chemical means. Early electrical cells contained two plates, or electrodes, separated by a liquid or gel 'electrolyte' that allowed electrons to flow through the cell. With the right electrodes and electrolyte, electrons tended to mass at one plate, so if you connected an external circuit from there to the other plate, you could harness the energy of the electrons as they jostled with each other to return to the cell. Unfortunately, when the chemical reaction between the electrodes and the electrolyte had run its course, the cell was dead and had to be thrown away. The next big breakthrough came with the discovery that some chemical reactions were reversible, so that electrons could be pumped backwards through the cell to 'recharge' it. Electricity could now be stored in the cell and used as required.

The first practical rechargeable cell was invented in 1859, using 'lead-acid' technology. This sort of cell remains by far the most common rechargeable chemistry even today, powering everything from budget electric bikes to milk floats and emergency lighting systems. The lead-acid cell contained plates of lead and lead oxide, surrounded by an electrolyte of dilute sulphuric acid. The difference in voltage between the two plates was about two volts, and as this small voltage flowed around a circuit, the battery discharged, gradually turning the lead and lead oxide to lead sulphate and the acid to water. When you recharged it, by forcing two volts (or a little more in practice) back through the cell, the water turned back to acid, and the lead sulphate back to lead or lead oxide. In the Victorian age, this was quite an awe-inspiringly magical conjuring trick, and although lead-acid cells are still very widely used today, they do have their disadvantages, being heavy and dangerous (as well as containing acid, they can vent explosive hydrogen), with quite a limited life. We shall come back to this!

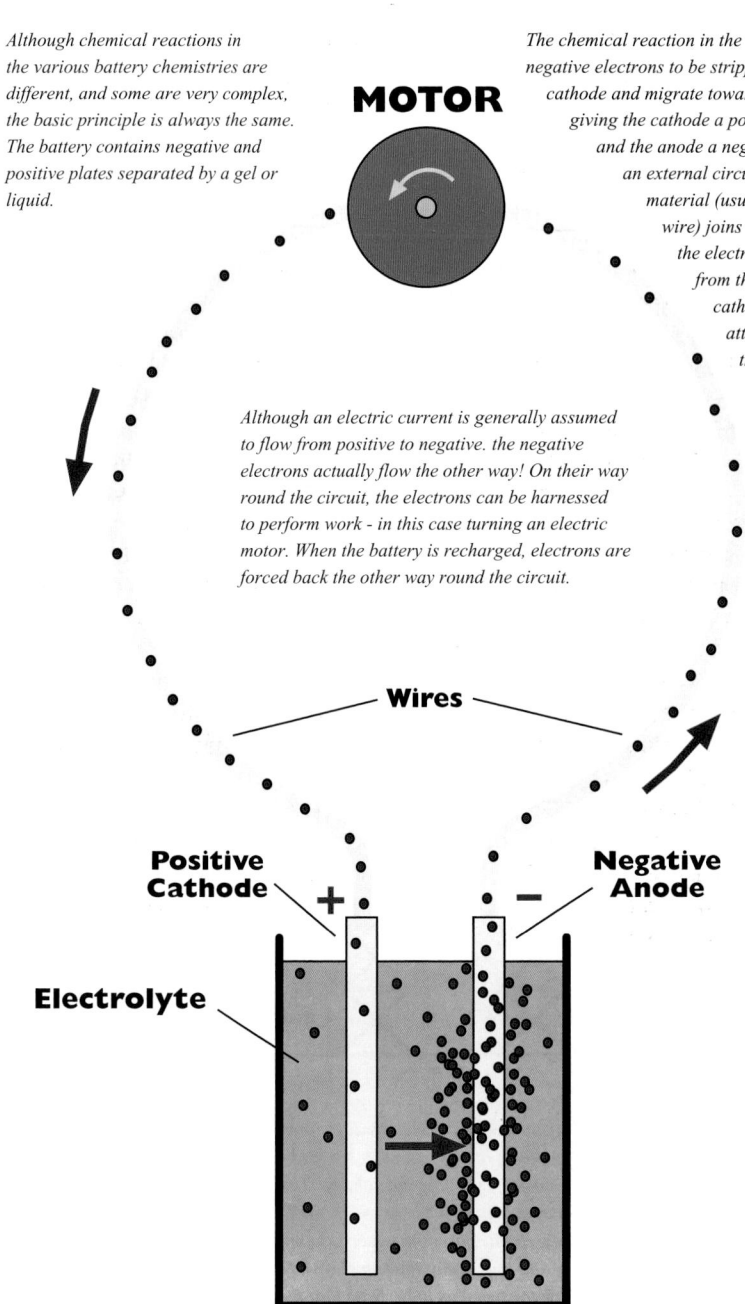

Although chemical reactions in the various battery chemistries are different, and some are very complex, the basic principle is always the same. The battery contains negative and positive plates separated by a gel or liquid.

MOTOR

The chemical reaction in the battery causes negative electrons to be stripped from the cathode and migrate towards the anode, giving the cathode a positive charge and the anode a negative charge. If an external circuit of conductive material (usually copper wire) joins the two plates, the electrons will flow from the anode to the cathode as they attempt to restore the balance.

Although an electric current is generally assumed to flow from positive to negative. the negative electrons actually flow the other way! On their way round the circuit, the electrons can be harnessed to perform work - in this case turning an electric motor. When the battery is recharged, electrons are forced back the other way round the circuit.

Wires

Positive Cathode **+** **−** **Negative Anode**

Electrolyte

BATTERY

Fact from spin – measuring electricity

Electrical energy has two components: the 'vigour' or 'pressure' of the electrons is known as the voltage, and the volume of the electrons is the 'current', measured in amperes, usually abbreviated to amps. If atoms and electrons are a bit hard to envisage, a watery analogy might be helpful. A rechargeable cell is a bit like a tank full of water. Open a tap at the bottom and water will flow down a pipe to do useful work, although in this case the water doesn't complete a circuit, as it does with electricity. Recharging the cell is a bit like pumping water through the pipe back into the tank, and the higher the tank the greater the pressure or voltage. The analogy works better if we apply it to an electricity generator, which is very like a water pump, forcing water down a hose at pressure, through a device where the pressure is utilised to do work, and back at low pressure along another hose to the pump. Using two pumps arranged in series will double the pressure, making it possible to do twice as much work. Arrange two pumps in parallel, i.e. side by side, and the pressure (i.e. voltage) will be the same, but the volume of water (i.e. current) will double. Put two or more cells in series and you have produced a 'battery', a term commonly, and quite erroneously, used for single cells too.

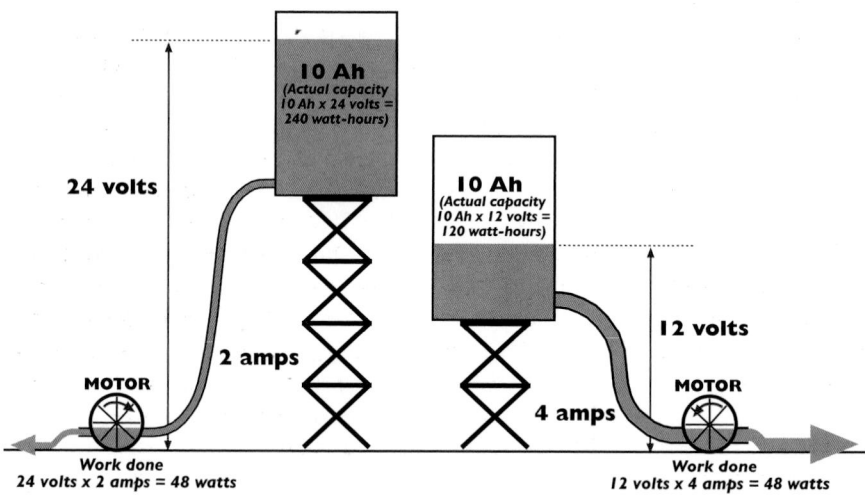

THE WATER ANALOGY The current and voltage of electrical power can be thought of as a flow of water with the supply tank being the battery. In this example, the tanks both have a capacity of 10Ah, but one is twice as high as the other, making it double the voltage. This means that in falling under the force of gravity, the water in the high tank can do twice as much work as the water in the low tank - 240 watt-hours against 120 watt-hours. In this case, the water is being delivered at half the rate from the top tank (2 amps against 4 amps), and thus doing the same work (48 watts). The water/battery in the high 24 volt tank will run the motor for twice as long. Note that the high tank can use much thinner pipes, making the pipework, lighter and cheaper, but the stand supporting the tank is more complex! Choosing the voltage of an electric bike raises exactly the same issues.

Battery basics

To make any sense of the information and misinformation put out by electric bicycle manufacturers, we need to get to grips with the basic principles of electrical power. A small flow of very energetic electrons (low current and high voltage) can do the same amount of work as a large flow of less energetic electrons (high current and low voltage). Both options have their advantages and disadvantages. High voltage will flow easily through thin wires, making conductors, switches and motors lighter and cheaper, but a high voltage (100 volts or more - much higher than normally found on an electric bike) will also flow through people, making it very dangerous. Individual cells in a battery produce a very low voltage (the two volts of the lead-acid cell is typical), so to develop a higher voltage, several cells must be connected in series. For example, to produce the standard 36 volts of a modern electric bicycle, a manufacturer could link together 18 x two-volt lead-acid cells. That level of complexity won't be an issue when everything is shiny and new, but it's an important principle that the battery will never perform better than the weakest of those 18 cells. So if one fails, or weakens significantly, the whole battery will start to fail, even if 17 cells are perfectly all right. That's a big disadvantage, and one of the main problems with rechargeable batteries.

Manufacturers could use a few large cells to create a system with a high current and low voltage. This would result in a simpler, more reliable battery, but there are several downsides. A high current needs thicker wires, which are expensive and heavy, and electronic circuits for high currents tend to be bigger, heavier, more expensive and less efficient. Motors, which contain quite a lot of wire, are usually bigger and heavier in high-current form too. So a low voltage bike will have a simpler, cheaper battery, but it will be less efficient elsewhere. For this reason, batteries of 12 volts (six lead-acid cells for example) are generally considered to be the practical lower limit for small electrically-powered machines. For some reason, American electric bicycle manufacturers such as ZAP and Izip were initially drawn to the rugged simplicity of 12-volt lead-acid technology, but such machines are now quite rare. With advances in electronics and battery construction, it is conceivable that ultra-low voltage, even single cell, batteries might make a comeback in the future, but at the moment the trend is towards higher voltages and ever more complex (and troublesome) batteries. Early 12-volt electric bikes soon gave way to 24 volts, then 36 volts, and a few recent higher powered machines have utilised 48 volts, with even higher voltages under consideration. These very high voltages make sense on a powerful machine like a motorcycle, but are quite unnecessary on a legal electric bicycle, so the upward trend is really just a matter of fashion. In some ways, it's a positive trend, but high voltages are not universally good news.

Measuring power and range

Multiplying the flow of electrons (the amps) by the vigorousness of the flow (volts), gives us watts, a universal measure of electric energy, and indeed all other kinds of energy. Where an electric motor is being specified for use on a factory production line, it's useful to know the 'continuous rating' – the amount of work the motor can do day-in and day-out without a break. This continuous rating is usually specified in watts, and it is used to indicate the power of electric bike motors, but a continuous rating is rather meaningless in this case, because what you really want to know when you're climbing a hill on a bicycle is the peak output that the motor can deliver for, perhaps, ten minutes. This is rarely shown in advertisements, but will typically be two to three times as much as the nominal continuous rating.

On an electric bicycle, the legal continuous rating in Europe is 250 watts, but the continuous ratings of bikes on sale in the shops can vary from 200 to 400 watts, and the peak rating can be anything up to 1,000 watts, but not for very long. By way of comparison, a reasonably fit human can supply 50 to 100 watts for an hour or two, a fit cyclist 200 watts or more for long enough to climb a hill, and a trained athlete in excess of 1,000 watts for very short periods. So the capabilities of a typical battery and motor on an electric bicycle are broadly similar to those of a human. Both can supply a low level of power for quite long periods and a much higher level for short periods. This match might help to explain why the 'human scale' concept of the electric bicycle has proved so successful.

As watts are a measure of instantaneous power, we can multiply watts by time to get a measure of battery capacity. This is watt-hours - the number of watts the battery can produce for an hour - and it's one of the least well understood measures in the electric bike world. Most of the Far Eastern manufacturers and Western importers measure battery capacity in amp-hours, or Ah, but this only gives an indication of the 'breadth' of the electron flow, not the voltage, making it rather meaningless. It may be misleading, but it's not a conspiracy to deceive, and if you know the voltage of the battery, you can easily calculate the true battery capacity.

For example, a common battery size these days is 10Ah, but this tells us nothing about the work it can perform. A typical lithium-ion cell has a voltage of 3.7 volts, and there will typically be ten cells, giving a voltage of 37 volts, and a capacity of 10 amp-hours x 37 volts = 370 watt-hours. Similarly, a seven-cell Li-ion battery will produce 26 volts, giving a capacity of 10 x 26 = 260 Wh, and a single cell 10 x 3.7 = 37Wh. In the literature, all three will be described as 10Ah capacity, but the first battery has ten times the capacity of the single cell.

So a ten watt/hour battery will produce ten watts for an hour, and presumably 20 watts for half an hour, or 100 watts for six minutes? In theory yes, but in practice no. The efficiency of batteries falls as current increases, and every battery will be slightly different in this respect, so the capacity measure can be no more than a guide. Different motors, control systems, riders and terrain will result in different peak loads on the battery and a different range. And as a battery ages, its capacity will gradually fall.

Our final indicator is watt-hours per mile, or if you like to think in metric, watt-hours per kilometre. This is an indication of the power from the battery (usually measured in terms of the power put into it, which is always more than the power taken out) divided by the mileage achieved. Like Wh, this is a really useful and meaningful measure, because it gives a guide to the efficiency of the motor, battery and control systems, and the rolling efficiency and wind cheating capabilities of the bicycle. The fewer watt-hours a bicycle needs to travel a mile at a set speed, the further and/or faster it will go for a given size of battery. Batteries are expensive and have a limited life, so this indicator of overall efficiency can have a big effect on the running costs, which can be quite high with an inefficient machine. As a very rough guide, the most efficient machines, ridden carefully with gentle pedal assistance, can achieve about 8Wh/mile, and the least efficient and/or faster bikes will consume 18Wh/mile or more. Obviously with a hybrid vehicle of this kind, it's impossible to give a precise figure, because the mileage will depend on the degree of human assistance, which can vary a great deal with some machines.

These power consumption figures are very small, and it's because the light and relatively slow electric bicycle uses so little power that it has rapidly developed into a practical means of transport, whereas electric motorcycles (drawing at least 100Wh/mile) and cars (drawing as much as 1,000Wh/mile) are having trouble making the step from 'concept' vehicles to practical everyday transport. These higher demands necessitate larger cells and a higher voltage, which means a lot more cells. As the battery gets bigger and more complex, the viability of the machine tends to recede. That is why the electric bicycle works so well.

Measuring - a summary

If you remember no other electrical formulae remember the following - they will help you to understand electric bikes and their performance:

Measurement of power: volts (pressure) x amps (volume) = watts or **W**
How is this useful? The legal limit for a motor in the UK is a continuous output rating of 250 watts - anything above this is not road legal. However, peak outputs above 250 watts are allowed (and not specified) so be clear which is being referred to.
Measurement of battery capacity: volts x amps x time = watt-hours or **Wh**
How is this useful? Batteries range from the tiny, around 100Wh or even less, to nearly 600Wh.
Measurement of bicycle efficiency: volts x amps x time ÷ distance = watt-hours/mile or **Wh/mile**
How is this useful? Modern electric bicycles tend to range from a bit below 8Wh/mile (superb) to well above 15Wh/mile (poor). These figures are based on standardised *A to B* magazine road tests. Different riding styles and weight of rider will alter these parameters.

Electric Bike Systems

Types of electric bicycle

Electric bicycles are widely misunderstood. It's true that some can be ridden like a moped, using electric power alone, but most models - in Europe and the UK at least - are hybrid vehicles utilizing both human and electrical power in varying proportions. Different countries have different rules on the amount of electrical energy that can be added to the mix, but the machines can be divided into two broad families:

Electrically Assisted Pedal Cycles or EAPC's (also known as Pedelecs)

These machines have found favour on mainland Europe, particularly in countries where there is a strong existing cycling tradition. In appearance and function, these are conventional bicycles, generally designed along European roadster lines, but with 'top-up' electrical assistance available when the rider pushes on the pedals. In other words, you must pedal to activate the 'top-up' power, although on most pedelecs you can still switch the power off and ride as you would on a 'normal' bike. This may be a little harder than normal, because the electric bike will be a little heavier, and the motor usually adds a little extra pedal resistance in one way or another.

Various systems are used to sense when the pedals are turning, or in more sophisticated designs, how hard the rider is pressing on the pedals. This information is translated into electrical energy to power the motor and assist the rider. The best designs, such as the Panasonic crank motor, produce an instant electrical surge that exactly matches your push on the pedals, giving the strange and rather magical feeling of having bionic legs. Less satisfactory designs generally measure crank speed with an optical or magnetic system utilizing a little castellated plastic disc revolving with the chainwheel. The worst offenders introduce a lag of several seconds before giving a crude full power surge that can continue for a second or so after the rider stops pedalling, which can be very disconcerting.

The motor can be mounted in the front or rear wheel, the pedal crank or, rarely, mounted on the frame, driving the wheel through a separate chain or belt. All have pros and cons, but there are many practical benefits to the crank motor, which puts the pedal sensor, motor, control unit, and sometimes the battery, together in the same waterproof housing. Being designed primarily for the European market, where this type of control system is the norm, pedelecs are mostly limited by law to 25km/h (15.5mph) top speed.

EAPCs - pros and cons

✚ Pedelecs are by far the easiest electric bikes to use and are much favoured by non-technical riders who simply want to 'get from *A to B*' as easily and cheaply as possible. They tend to have fewer electrical problems than other types, and on crank-drives the weight of the unit is concentrated in an ideal position. A crank-drive EAPC

CRANK MOTOR PEDELEC When the rider pushes on the pedals (the crank is bottom right), their effort passes through the torque sensor just behind the chain ring, then out through the chain ring and into the chain. The torque sensor sends a signal to the control unit (also in the casing), and motor power arrives at the motor drive sprocket, highlighted in green. So within a matter of milliseconds both muscle and motor power are on their way to the rear wheel.

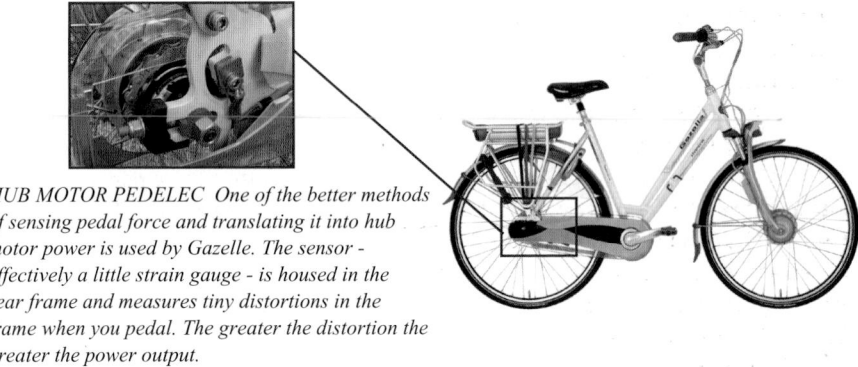

HUB MOTOR PEDELEC One of the better methods of sensing pedal force and translating it into hub motor power is used by Gazelle. The sensor - effectively a little strain gauge - is housed in the rear frame and measures tiny distortions in the frame when you pedal. The greater the distortion the greater the power output.

is also the best machine for climbing really big hills, because both the human and electrical power is fed through the rear gear hub or derailleur, multiplying the effort available more effectively over a wider range of speeds than EPVs. We'll go into this in more depth in the section on crank-drives below.

▪ Pedelecs are less suitable for those with serious medical conditions who need the option of riding without pedalling and those who simply don't want to pedal. Pedelecs also tend to have smaller batteries, although this can be partly negated by their greater efficiency. With crank-drive EAPCs in particular, gears, sprockets, chains and rear tyres have a tough time, which can add to maintenance costs, particularly where hub gears are concerned.

Good examples: Giant Lafree (2000-2006), Kalkhoff, Monark, Raleigh Dover, E-motion, Swiss Flyer, Kettler, Gepida, Sparta, Gazelle.

Electrically Powered Vehicles or EPV's (also known as E-bikes)

EPVs have become the standard amongst cheaper machines, which are generally made in China and designed for the American market. They tend to be heavier and cruder than EAPCs, with a simple twist-grip throttle to control the output from the motor, although many are 'hybrids' that can be switched to a (usually crude) EAPC sensor linked to pedal rotation.

The motor can be mounted in the same positions as on an EAPC. There are a few crank-drives and belt or chain drives to the wheels, but by far the most common arrangement is to put the motor within the front or rear wheel hub. There are advantages and disadvantages to both: a rear hub motor usually has a shorter less vulnerable electrical cable run, but this tends to put rather a lot of weight on the rear of the bike, and the gearing options are severely limited by the position of the motor. Rear-wheel drive EPVs cannot be fitted with hub gears, and usually only have space for a cheap 6- or 7-speed derailleur. This is a big disadvantage, and there is no after-market means of rectifying it.

A front motor effectively creates a two-wheel drive machine, giving better traction on loose or slippery surfaces and more even tyre wear. Weight distribution tends to be better, and with the electrical components separate from the rear wheel, any sort of gearing can be fitted. The disadvantage is a long cable run, and a cable that has to twist and turn with the steering, which will sooner or later result in a broken wire.

A clear advantage with an EPV is that the twistgrip throttle gives a faster, sportier response, particularly in heavy traffic, where a pedelec can feel quite slow and ponderous. The throttle can be flicked straight open when the lights change, and full power can be maintained through gear changes, making for quicker acceleration.

Many US-spec machines and kits capable of 18mph-20mph or more have been sold in the UK in recent years, even though their maximum speed is above that permitted by European law. Some manufacturers fit an 'on road/off road' switch to provide a nominally legal option, but this probably isn't enough to protect the rider from prosecution. Having said that, there don't appear to have been any prosecutions for riding an EPV at above 15mph, except where other offences have been committed. But at the time of writing, it looks likely that EPVs may be outlawed in the UK. For a full picture of the law see the chapter *Electric Bikes and the Law*.

EPVs - pros and cons

+ The greater speed and instant response of the throttle system makes an EPV the best choice for faster riding on switchback country roads or negotiating busy traffic. The option to ride without pedalling makes it the best system for those with medical conditions, or the seriously unfit! At the top end, a small, unobtrusive front hub motor can be fitted into a near conventional racing bike to produce what is in effect a conventional bicycle with the benefit of extra hill-climbing power. The Cytronex is one of the best examples, and there are bound to be more as this market expands.

▬ EPVs look simple to use, but they can be difficult to master in traffic, and ridden badly they can be very inefficient, limiting the range. With the motor in the wheel, gearing is effectively fixed, and cannot be adjusted to suit local conditions. This problem is made worse with a rear wheel motor, which will usually be fitted with cheap derailleur gears too, resulting in a very limited range of pedal speeds. In some cases the weak hill-climbing is overcome with a more powerful motor, which is fine in territories where powerful motors are allowed, but could cause problems elsewhere.

Good examples: eZee, Wisper, Heinzmann, Cytronex, Nano (Electric Wheel Co.).

HUB MOTOR E-BIKE: COMMON FEATURES

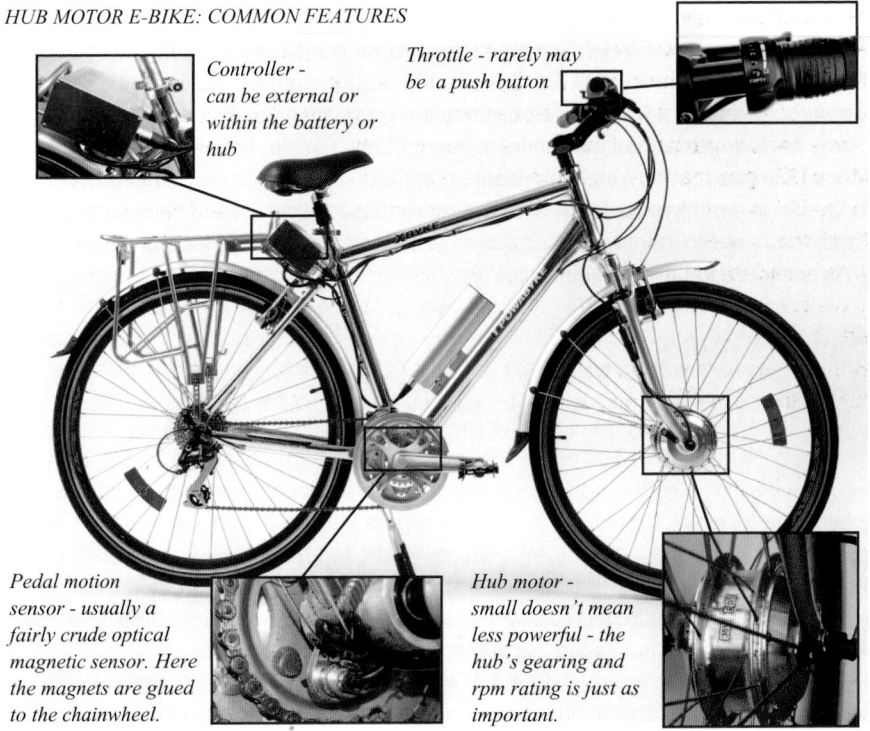

Controller - can be external or within the battery or hub

Throttle - rarely may be a push button

Pedal motion sensor - usually a fairly crude optical magnetic sensor. Here the magnets are glued to the chainwheel.

Hub motor - small doesn't mean less powerful - the hub's gearing and rpm rating is just as important.

Control systems

Electric bicycles need sophisticated control systems for two reasons. On a typical bike destined for the European market, the motor will be designed to push the machine along at 15mph when fed with 36 volts from the battery. Obviously, if you want to go slower than that, the motor will need to run at a lower speed, and in practice, that generally means supplying it with a lower voltage and less vigorous electrons. Thus a means must be found to reduce the voltage from the battery.

But there is a second very important reason for giving the cyclist control over the voltage supply to the motor, that might not be immediately obvious. Electric motors only run efficiently at a given speed, which is usually quite close to maximum, so a typical 15mph machine will run most efficiently at perhaps 13-14mph. Take the motor out of this comfort zone and efficiency can drop quite rapidly, until at walking pace the motor is drawing a high current, but providing little in the way of propulsion. Some crude EAPCs switch the motor straight to full power at low speed, which is not only dangerous, but very inefficient, effectively throwing precious electrical energy away.

A machine with a twistgrip throttle is much more controllable, and can therefore be ridden more efficiently. For example, by twisting the throttle open gradually at low speed, rather than straight round to full power, the rider can accelerate almost as fast, but use much less energy.

On most crank-drive motors, like the sophisticated Panasonic drive fitted to many European and Japanese EAPCs, there's no twistgrip, but the voltage to the motor, and thus the motor power, is controlled by the pedal pressure the rider applies, giving an even more intuitive control system. In this design, the motor drives the rear wheel through the gears, so it can be started in a low gear at a speed at which the motor is comfortable. We will look in more detail at this system later on.

Firstly, we need to identify the sorts of motors used on electric bikes, and these can be broadly divided into three families.

Types of motor

Brushed DC Motors

Direct Current, or DC, motors are the simplest type, and they have been in production for well over 100 years. Power is delivered from battery to motor along a wire, where it is fed through a carbon brush into a copper 'commutator' on the rotating motor shaft, then through a coil of copper wire, and back via another brush and a return wire to the battery. Without going into too much detail, the theory is exactly the same as the 19th century electrical generator in reverse, and these motors can in fact function perfectly well as generators if an outside force turns the shaft faster than it wants to turn as a motor.

The windings fixed to the rotating motor shaft act as magnets which interact with permanent magnets fixed to the casing, of which there are usually two. When power is passed through one of the windings, the magnetic forces generated try to turn the shaft away from the fixed magnets. Without the commutator, the motor would turn a little way and stop, but the commutator acts as a high speed switch, so that when one winding has gone beyond the magnets, power is fed to the next, producing another jerk of movement and so on. At very low speed, these individual movements can be felt, but once the motor is running at several thousand revolutions per minute the motion becomes completely smooth. A toy motor might only have two or three rotating windings from the commutator, but a traction motor on an electric bike will have many more.

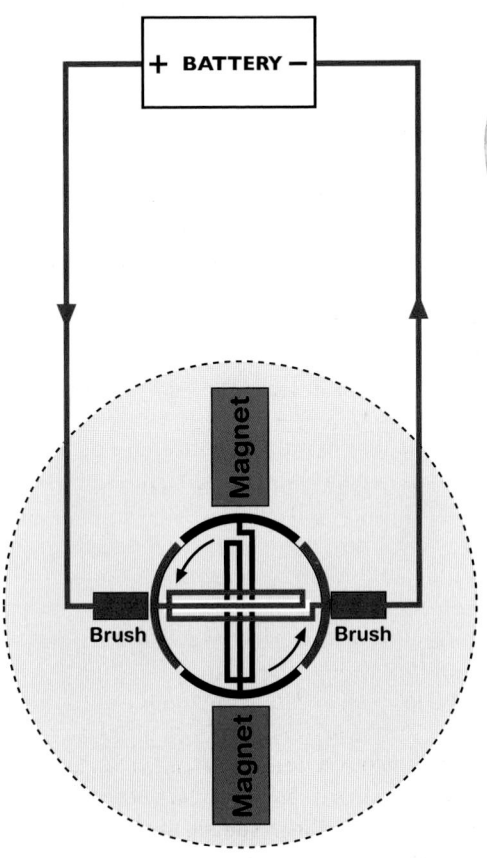

POWABYKE MOTOR The Powabyke motor is unusual in being DC (the two wires exit from the other end) and using a train of gears rather than an epicyclic gear set. The motor is inside the central casing, and fitted with a small output gear beneath the central shaft, driving the spur gear on the right. This in turn transfers the drive back to a large centrally-mounted gear capped by the freewheel, both omitted for clarity. Note the greased gears which have straight cut teeth and are very noisy. It's also a large and heavy motor by modern standards. A plate covers this gear assembly, and drive is transmitted to the outer rim and - via the spokes - to the wheel.

DC MOTOR Electric current runs from the battery to a brush which transfers the current to a segment of the commutator, then via a coil to another segment and via another brush back to the battery. The current in the coil reacts against the field of the two fixed magnets, causing the coil, commutator and shaft to rotate.

There are a couple of major disadvantages with this sort of motor. The brushes, and to a lesser extent the commutator, wear down in use, so occasional maintenance is required. More seriously, the action of the brushes rubbing on the commutator absorbs some power, so this simplest of switching systems tends to result in a less efficient motor, and one that functions less well away from its ideal speed.

On the positive side, DC motors are simple, rugged and reliable. They can be connected to the battery in reverse, shaken, soaked and generally abused without serious issues developing. Very few manufacturers use them today, but amongst the major brands Powabyke has remained loyal, and the staying power of the Powabyke is testament to the reliability of their DC motors. A big advantage is that there are only two wires going into the motor, making it easy to put a joint in the wiring loom. Some manufacturers do this, so that the wheel can be removed quickly and easily to mend a puncture, or to replace the motor or control box.

It's worth mentioning in passing that more complex versions of the DC motor use electro-magnets in place of, or together with, permanent magnets, but these are not generally used on electric bikes.

The simplest way to control the speed of a DC motor is to insert a resistor between the battery and the motor. A resistor is simply a small piece of metal or other material that holds back the passage of electrons, taking some of the vigour out of the electron stream. But a resistance is a clumsy, inefficient device, and it needs to be well cooled, because under certain combinations of road speed and throttle setting, it will be turning most of the valuable battery output into heat. In practice resistors were only fitted to very early machines, because by the time electric bikes were being produced in large numbers in the 1980s, transistor control had arrived. In its simplest form, transistor control does exactly the same job as an old-fashioned resistance, throwing away some of the electrical energy to slow the motor.

A much better system involves turning the electrical current on and off very rapidly, known as PWM or Pulse Width Modulation. If the current of electrons is turned on for 10% of the time, the average output will be 10% of full power; if it flows for 50% of the time, output will be 50% of full power, and so on. The switching speed is usually so fast (thousands of times a second) that the individual pulses are impossible to feel, although the motor and wiring may vibrate and emit a whine at certain throttle openings.

Direct current electronic controllers of this kind can be extremely efficient (90% or even higher). Until recently the control units were heavy and expensive, but advances in miniaturisation have resulted in very small, very cheap controllers for such things as radio-controlled aircraft. Although not yet used on electric bicycles, these cheap, lightweight electronic speed controllers may yet result in a return to DC motors.

The Raleigh Select (below), launched in 1997, used a brushed DC motor, like most electric bikes at the time. DC motors tend to be bigger, heavier and less efficient than modern BLDC units, and the dinner plate-sized Sanyo motor used by Raleigh was no exception. The vintage helmet in this rather dated marketing brochure suggests moped-like speed, but in reality the Select ran out of steam at 11mph and had a range of less than 15 miles. Electric bike performance has improved out of all recognition since then, but simple, rugged DC technology still has a role to play. The Powabyke (left, climbing out of Slaithwaite in the southern Pennines) is a good modern example.

Select empowers you with the freedom to sidestep congestion or discover your rural retreat. It is the pleasure of cycling with all the effort removed. **Turn the key** and for every turn of the pedal to power you effortlessly along. **Freewheel and the Select** control system recognises there is no need to assist, conserving charge to extend your range. **At the end** of your ride another turn of pack, to plug in, recharge and be ready for your next journey. Select is simple, efficient and a new generation of transport design, by Raleigh.

81

Brushless DC (BLDC) motors

The brushless motor works rather like the DC motor, but in this case the permanent magnets usually rotate, while the windings powered from the battery are either placed around the casing or inside the rotating magnets. This arrangement brings the immediate benefit that there are no carbon brushes to transmit power to the spinning part of the motor, which more or less eliminates maintenance and makes the motor run more freely.

Some household motors in washing machines and other appliances are fitted with similar motors, in this case utilising alternating current (AC) from the mains electricity supply to replace the switching function of the commutator in the DC motor. As the name suggests, the electrons in alternating current change direction very rapidly – typically 50 times a second with mains electricity. Interestingly, this means the electrons never actually travel very far, because they are continually being sent back where they came from, but that doesn't matter, because it's the motion of the electrons that counts, and although they change direction, they're still nearly always moving. True AC motors may appear on electric bikes in the future, but as they haven't yet, we'll ignore them for the sake of simplicity.

Unfortunately, our electric bike will generally be powered by a battery supplying direct current, so some form of electronic switching is needed to switch power from one motor winding to another, and generate the rapidly rotating magnetic field needed to pull the permanent magnets around, and make the motor shaft spin. The difficulty (and it's a big difficulty) is instructing the different windings when to fire up. This problem can be solved by placing little position-detecting sensors inside the motor, linked by tiny wires to a control box elsewhere on the bike. The sensors (commonly known as 'Hall' or 'Hall-effect' sensors) tell the control box where the motor shaft is, the motor sends a pulse of power down winding A (there are usually three), the motor kicks around a few degrees, the sensor updates the control box on the new position, winding B fires, and so on. As with the brushed DC motor, the movement of the shaft can be quite jerky at very low speed, but once it's whizzing around the output becomes completely smooth and almost silent, because with a BLDC the only contact points are in the ball bearings that support the shaft.

An advantage of this type of motor is that its characteristics can be tailored by altering the precise firing points of the windings, which can help produce a wider efficiency band than a DC motor. In practice, this means that a good BLDC motor will pull cleanly and efficiently from perhaps 3mph to 15mph, which is quite impressive for an electric motor, which is often regarded as a constant speed device.

The disadvantage is the extremely complex electronics required to make the motor work, and without which it will be completely useless. And as the control box is usually quite big (and vulnerable to water, extremes of temperature and vibration), it tends to be positioned high up on the bike frame, some distance from the motor.

82

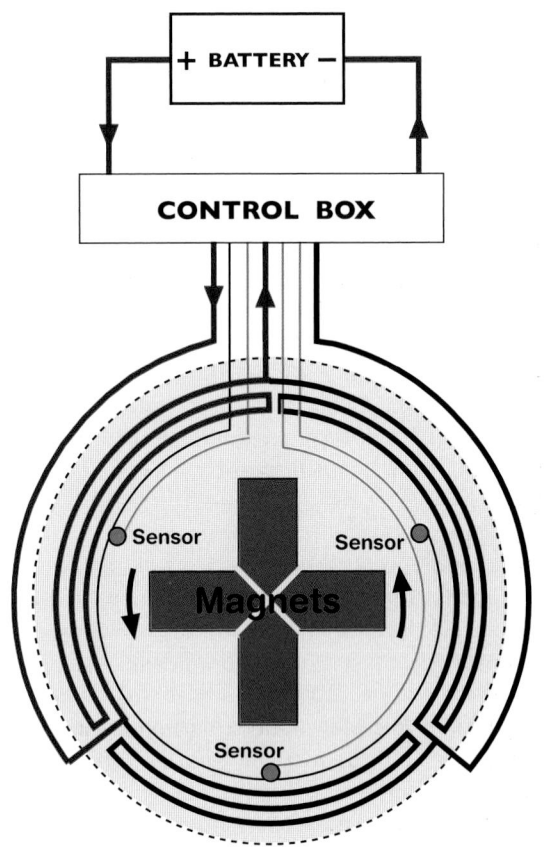

BLDC MOTOR Electric current runs from the battery to a control box, where it is switched into one of three coils positioned around the outer (or inner), stationary part of the motor. In this design it is the permanent magnets that rotate and there is thus no need for brushes. The three coils are fired in sequence by signals from little sensors which feedback the position of the rotating magnets.

This means that the three chunky power wires (and typically five tiny sensor wires) from the controller to the motor, will be quite long. If the motor is in the front wheel, this big, clumsy wiring loom has to run along the frame, then twist and turn with the steering. Bearing in mind that failure of a single sensor wire will generally render the motor completely dead, it's not surprising that wiring problems are one of the most common causes of failure with these systems. The second most common is control box failure, and once again, if a single component goes pop, it will probably kill the whole machine.

So the sensor-controlled motor eliminated the noisy, maintenance-heavy DC brushes, but brought it's own problems of delicate electronics and even more delicate wiring. Because there are so many wires feeding into the motor (and a loose connection or dampness on any one of them will disable it), these bikes usually have wiring connectors close to the control box in a drier, less hostile environment. This is very bad news on a bicycle, because removing the wheel will mean stripping out most of the wiring loom, which can turn into major surgery. And if something goes wrong it can be almost impossible to trace, let alone fix, without replacing the entire system - motor, loom and sometimes the control box too. As this operation can cost more than the bike is worth, a simple failure of a single tiny wire can mean a scrap bicycle.

Despite these reliability issues, Chinese manufacturers have taken to sensor-controlled motors in a big way, and in 2010, the vast majority of bikes produced in the Far East were thus equipped. Speed is usually varied by adjusting the voltage sent to the motor, and on most systems, this is done with a twistgrip throttle on the handlebars.

If buying an unknown electric bike take a look at the thickness of the wiring loom to the motor – if the outer insulation is quite thick (up to 10mm), the motor is almost certainly a BLDC machine. Check the wiring loom for vulnerability - it should be well secured and protected everywhere except where movement is needed, as on the steering, and here there should be plenty of room for the cable to twist and turn. If in doubt, buy something else, because failure will be troublesome and expensive. A rear wheel motor is generally a safer bet where reliability is concerned, but it brings all the disadvantages outlined elsewhere in this chapter.

Manufacturers have a tendency to change spec without notice, but typical front BLDC-motor bicycles include eZee and Byocycles, and machines with rear BLDC motors include many familiar names, such as Wisper, Urban Mover and Powacycle. BLDC systems are also fitted to most of the hundreds of cheaper brands. Ironically, a BLDC motor can also be found in the top-end Panasonic crank-drive, but in this case the motor and controller are almost integrated, so the cabling issues do not apply.

Sensorless BLDC motors

Through a brilliant bit of lateral thinking, someone somewhere realised that the three power wires to the motor feed back tiny generated impulses to the control unit as the magnets spin past the windings. As only two of these wires are carrying power at any one time, the temporarily redundant wire can provide positioning information to the control unit, thus entirely eliminating the complex and troublesome sensor system fitted to most electric bikes. The issue here, of course, is that the motor is completely 'blind' when stationary. The answer was to give it a little exploratory electronic 'kick' when the throttle was first opened. This got the shaft rotating, enabling the motor to feed back its position, and run as smoothly as a sensor-controlled device. The disadvantage is that the blind kick may push the motor in the wrong direction briefly, so pick up isn't always entirely smooth, and clearly the electronics have to be very clever indeed.

This is the sensorless BLDC motor, and its big advantage is a lighter, simpler, more elegant package than any of the alternatives. The control box is complex, but the wiring loom to the motor contains only three chunky wires, so a connector is generally fitted, making maintenance easier. Fewer wires entering the motor, and fewer components inside, enable it to be made smaller and lighter than a sensor-controlled motor.

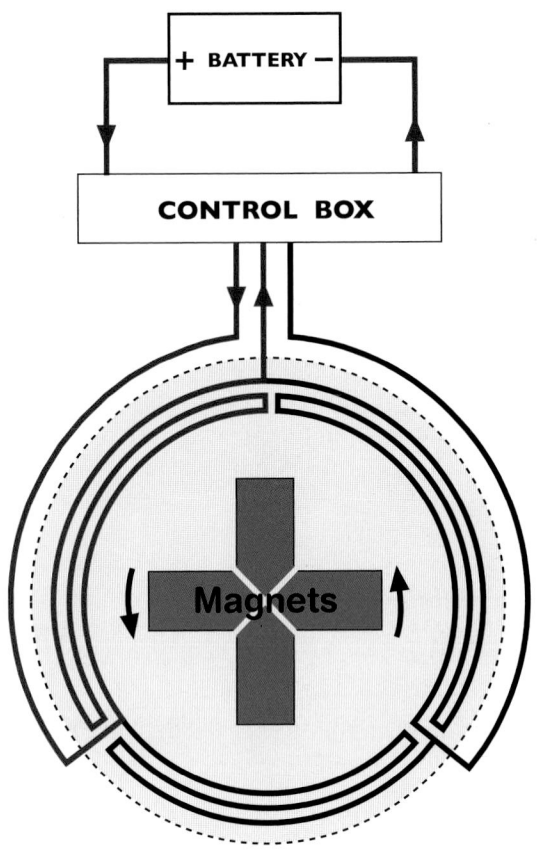

+ BATTERY −

CONTROL BOX

Magnets

SENSORLESS BLDC MOTOR
As on the BLDC, electric current runs from the battery to a control box, where it is switched to one of the three coils, fixed to the stationary part of the motor. But in this case, the control unit senses tiny feedback currents in the three power wires to 'fire' the three coils in the correct sequence and turn the motor.

The only real disadvantage is the characteristic kick to get the motor running. This is less of a problem on a pedelec machine, especially where the motor doesn't cut in until the bike is underway. But if the motor is asked to pull hard from a standing start, it may stall, causing some nasty jolts and vibrations, rather like stalling a car engine, making it more than usually important to select an appropriately low gear before starting.

Like the sensor-controlled motors, sensorless designs can be controlled either by turning the pedals (most crank-drive systems work like this) or with a twistgrip throttle. As with other designs, speed can be altered by simply adjusting the voltage sent to the motor.

At the moment, sensorless BLDC motors are considered state of the art, but that is already changing. One thing that is becoming very clear is that the relatively heavy and fragile sensor-controlled BLDC motors are fundamentally unsuited to the arduous bicycle environment and long-overdue for replacement... it's a shame that almost all the machines on sale today use it!

Good examples: Cytronex and Nano-Brompton (both using the Tongxin front wheel-mounted motor.

	Pros	Cons
DC motors	**+** Reliable, widely understood	■ Heavy, relatively inefficient, complex motor, needs some maintenance
BLDC motors (brushless direct current)	**+** Efficient, fairly simple	■ Complex control unit, vulnerable wiring, especially in front hub examples
Sensorless BLDC motors	**+** Light, compact, reliable, very simple motor, simple, reliable wiring	■ Starting can be awkward, complex control unit

Types of drive

We've looked at the three main types of electric motor. How is the motor's power transmitted to the bike's wheels? As you might expect, there is a variety of different systems, each with their pros and cons.

Friction drives

One thing most electric motors have in common is a desire to rotate very fast, and as a rule maximum efficiency is not achieved until the motor is spinning at several thousand revolutions or more per minute. As a typical 26-inch bicycle wheel needs to spin at around 200rpm to maintain a road speed of 15mph, the speed of the motor must be geared down by at least 20:1. With a friction drive rubbing on the tyre, altering the gearing is a simple matter of choosing a suitable friction roller diameter. For example, a 1.3-inch roller will give a 20:1 reduction to a 26-inch wheel, and this will result in a suitable road speed for a motor running at 4,000rpm. Friction drives were quite popular in the early days of electric bikes, and the ZAP in particular stayed in production for a number of years. This 12-volt American device (usually sold as a bolt-on kit) first appeared in the late 1990s. It sat above the rear tyre, and could be fixed to most bicycles, provided they didn't have a rear mudguard and had relatively smooth tyres.

With a steel roller rubbing on the rubber tyre, the ZAP was fairly quiet, and could be locked completely out of engagement for non-assisted riding. The simple DC brushed motor (a single motor on the SX, but dual on the more powerful DX) was well made, and relatively gentle in operation, so it could be controlled by a simple on-off switch, rather than a complex speed controller. Power came from a cheap and easily obtainable lead-acid battery, making the whole package quite attractive. The only real problems were slipping in the wet (particularly with unsuitable tyres) and drive roller wear. The fine-toothed steel roller was later changed to a harder stone finish, but by that time, drive technology had moved on, and the ZAP was already out of date. Manufacture was outsourced to the Far East, but the ZAP gradually disappeared from the shops.

While friction drives were briefly in vogue, several other weird and wonderful systems came and went. The ETC was a sort of saddle arrangement with a motor and drive roller on top of the wheel driving the tyre tread, and panniers either side to hold the twin lead-acid batteries. The Viking also plonked the motor and drive roller over the rear wheel, but in this case the heavy lead-acid batteries were up top too, which didn't do the handling any good.

The distinctly oddball Bikit put the battery on the frame, with a pair of motors driving rollers spring-loaded to clamp against the sidewalls of the front tyre. This was a rather elegant solution to the problem of drive roller slippage, and it worked with knobbly tyres, but the Bikit rapidly went the way of all friction drives as better technology came along.

Both the Bikit (left) and the ZAP (above) attempted to popularise the friction drive but both ultimately faded away. This well-worn ZAP has the later stone roller.

Crank-drives

Crank-drives are by far the best system for most purposes, and to understand why, we need to look in more depth at gears for a moment. Just as electrical power is a combination of amps and volts, your pedal effort and the motor's effort are transmitted to the road with two components: speed and 'torque', or turning force. The gears, whether they are hidden in a hub, or part of an exposed derailleur system, are a simple mechanism for varying the proportions of speed and torque. A large cog driving a small cog will give a high speed/low torque output, and a small cog driving a large cog will give a low speed/high torque output. This can be seen very clearly with an exposed derailleur gear system, where you can actually see all the cogs.

The power output will always be the same as the power input in all the gears (slightly less in practice, because some power is always lost in gear systems), but the proportions of speed and torque will vary. Pedal at normal speed in a 'low' gear and the bicycle wheels will turn slowly, but the trade-off is that the torque will be multiplied for climbing hills. So hills are easiest in a low gear, but you will have to go slowly. Pedal at normal speed in a 'high' gear and the road wheels will turn fast, which is great for bowling along on the flat, but torque will be low, so a high gear is of little use on a hill.

A good bike has a wide variety of gears to suit different road conditions, but on most cheaper electric bikes the motor is fitted inside one of the wheels, so although the rider has the benefit of the gears, the motor will be stuck with one. Like leg muscles, electric motors work better through gears, which enable them to spin close to their most efficient speed, whatever the gradient.

A crank-drive puts the motor 'upstream' of the gears, allowing it to take advantage of their torque/speed balancing act, just like your legs. Crank-drive systems tend to be more expensive, but they work much better on hills than hub-mounted motors. Where there is a legal top speed for power assistance, as in Europe, this maximum speed is set by keeping the top gear quite low, usually by fitting a large rear sprocket to the bike. This simply means the motor (and your legs) run out of steam at about 15mph, so that you can't pedal or power the motor any faster.

Because the motor drives through the gears with this system, it's easy to fine tune the assisted speed by changing the rear sprocket. Fitting a larger rear sprocket will improve hill-climbing (useful if you live somewhere with extremely steep hills), while a smaller one will raise the overall gearing for a faster and more relaxed cruise in flatter country. Raising the gearing for more speed may be technically illegal, but as these machines are not usually very powerful, the increase in speed tends to be quite small (remember that an increase in speed means a reduction in torque), but the pedal and motor action will be more relaxed.

Usually a crank-drive motor is controlled by pedal effort, so as a rule you will have to pedal for the motor to function. But this obligation to apply a certain amount of effort to the pedals can give these bicycles a considerable range - the rider's effort makes life easier for the battery.

Several early crank-drive designs lasted into the modern era, notably the British-made TGA Leisure Electrobike and Electrotrike, which utilized a motor (according to legend, a commercial vehicle windscreen wiper motor) fitted behind the pedal crank. However, with the rise and rise of better Japanese systems, the Electrobike and its brethren have faded from the scene.

The first modern crank-drive system was produced by Yamaha in the late 1990s, but the Panasonic that followed soon afterwards proved commercially more successful, and Yamaha threw in the towel in 2002. Jealous of Panasonic's domination of the market, Yamaha has recently returned, and new crank-drives have been introduced by both Daum and Bosch of Germany. In 2010, Panasonic was still by far the most common crank-drive, fitted to the majority of better quality bikes, but this will probably change as the market expands. The main retrofit crank-drive kit, the Sunstar, appears to have been discontinued, but in any case fitting a crank-drive to a previously non-assisted bicycle can raise all sorts of technical issues.

新駆動ユニット
New Drive Unit
DC Brush flat motor

Putting all the components together in the middle of the machine, crank-drives are an excellent solution to the problem of powering an electric bicycle, but feeding human and motor power through gears designed for human power alone can result in rapid gear failure unless the system is carefully designed. An answer is to put the power through a continuously variable transmission (CVT) such as the NuVinci. With no gear changes to worry about, these give a much smoother drive, but they tend to be heavy and inefficient.

All in One, In Drive, DC Brushless

This modest announcement in a 2004 Japanese trade journal heralded the arrival of the revamped Li-ion Panasonic crank drive that is still in widespread use today. Developing this technology must have involved a great deal of research and funding, but the reward for Panasonic was a virtual crank-drive monopoly until new designs arrived in 2010. Note that this drive claims to be 12% lighter than its predecessor and 3% more efficient.

Weight
重さ   4.1kg   3.6kg   12%ダウン(down)
Efficiency
効率   85%   ▶   88%   3%アップ(up)
Noise
ノイズ 57db   3.6kg   3%ダウン(down)

軽く高効率を達成したモーターユニットの中核を担うDCブラシレスモール
ドモータ。重量36kgの超軽量モータだ
The DC brushless molded motor is the hub of the motor unit that is
both light and efficient. The ultra-lightweight motor weighs only 36 kg.

Hub motors with conventional gears

As we've seen, most electric bike motors drive through the centre of the wheel rather than the rim, and thus need to be geared down through a compact set of gears to achieve the same sort of gear reduction as a friction drive. Some (like the Powabyke) utilise a little group of reduction gears, but the majority are fitted with an 'epicyclic' gear set, often described as a sun-and-planet gear. This is a clever system, found in most bicycle hub gears, car automatic gearboxes, powered screwdrivers, and other machines that need to achieve a large gear reduction in a small space.

Epicyclics can gear up too, but on an electric bike motor, power is fed in through a small central gear wheel (the sun) via a set of larger gear wheels (the planets) to a large diameter outer ring called the annulus. The planet carrier is often combined with a freewheel that locks to the axle when drive is being transmitted, but can spin freely when the bike is coasting, and the teeth of the annulus are either formed on the inside of the motor shell or on a hardened ring pressed into the shell. This arrangement - with the reduction gears fitted on the end of the motor - makes for a very small overall package.

The bad news with any type of gearing is noise and friction. A well designed brushless motor will run almost silently, but the sun-and-planet gears can make quite a loud whine, particularly when working hard. Efficiency is relatively high, but turning the gears and the motor does take quite a lot of energy, and that's why most hubs include a freewheel or 'one-way clutch' to allow the motor and gears to have a rest when power is not required. If you want to feel the motor and gear friction, push the bike backwards, which will lock-up the freewheel and cause the gears and motor to rotate. Some machines are actually quite hard to push backwards for this reason. Incidentally, don't push the bike backwards too fast, because the motor will act as a generator, and it can easily generate enough voltage to destroy the electronics in the controller.

The epicyclic gears in a typical hub only provide one ratio, and this will (or should be) set to give a maximum speed to suit local legal requirements. In practice, most hubs are designed for American and other markets where the maximum assisted speed is higher than 24km/h, and they may or may not be fitted with a 24km/h electronic speed limiter when sold in Europe and other restricted markets. Being destined for America, some have a great deal more power than they should too. This extra performance may be just what you're looking for, of course, but bear in mind that unlike a crank-drive, the gearing cannot be fine-tuned to improve hill-climbing or make the bike faster on the flat, because the characteristics of the motor and drive are fixed. The exception to this rule is the Tongxin motor fitted to such bikes as the Nano-Brompton and Cytronex, which is available with different internal gears, allowing the user to swap motors and make coarse adjustments to the road speed and hill-climbing ability.

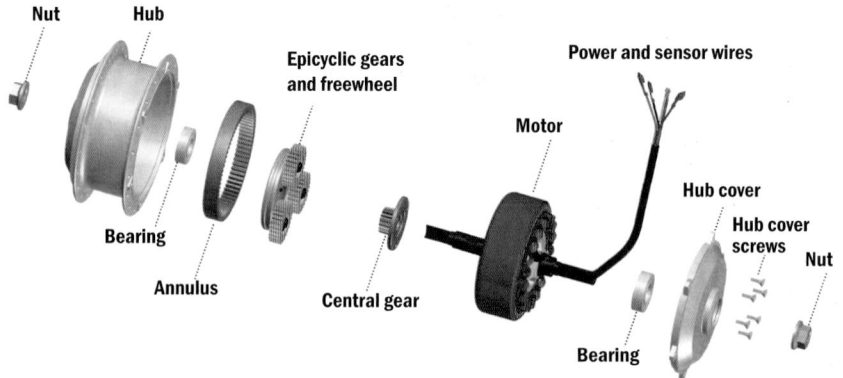

Nut Hub

Epicyclic gears
and freewheel

Power and sensor wires

Motor

Hub cover

Hub cover
screws

Nut

Bearing

Annulus

Central gear

Bearing

HUB MOTOR - A simplified diagram of a hub BLDC motor (above). The electric current flows into the motor coils which are fixed to the axle. This causes the ring of magnets (yellow in the picture) to rotate, driving the central 'sun' gear, which in turn drives via the 'planet' epicyclic gears to the annulus on the casing.

Above: Hub motor disassembled.
Right: Epicyclic gears mesh at their centre with the central 'sun' gear and at their outside edges with the annulus.

Above: Freewheel and gears in place in the motor, ready for the hub casing and annulus gear to be refitted.

Left: Hub casing and annulus gear.
Right: The freewheel forms part of the planet gear carrier and allows the motor to stop turning when the bike is coasting with the motor turned off.

Hub motors with friction roller gears

One way round the noise problem is to use friction rollers in place of toothed gears. These can be arranged in exactly the same sun-and-planet layout, but with the drive transferred through smooth rollers pressed hard together, rather than through gear teeth. This technique was pioneered by Yamaha in the 1990s and is used today by Tongxin on its excellent sensorless, brushless motors. These friction drives are near silent in operation, but have to be built to very fine tolerances to endure the stresses and strains of everyday use, and if abused, they can begin to slip. Frictional losses are probably a little less than a conventional geared system, and the sun wheel can be smaller, reducing the size and weight of everything else too.

Hub motors with direct drive

Some manufacturers have solved the noise and friction associated with gears by eliminating them altogether, most commonly with a 'direct drive', gearless BLDC motor in the centre of the wheel. The obvious disadvantage here is that the motor has to run at wheel speed, which may only be 200rpm with 26-inch wheels, or 300-400rpm on a small-wheeled bike. This is very slow for an electric motor, but with careful design it can function quite efficiently at such a low speed.

A less easily soluble problem is the lack of brute twisting force or 'torque' available at the wheel. By making the hub large in diameter and fitting it to a wheel of relatively small diameter, torque can be increased to a reasonable level, but short of a remarkable breakthrough, gearless bikes will never be great hill-climbers. That said, the technology is tempting. Low speed gearless motors are almost frictionless, completely silent, and they can provide equally silent regenerative braking with little extra complication. The most successful to date, in terms of sales, is probably

the Dutch Sparta, which sells very well in the flat Netherlands. Another interesting design, available as a kit, or fitted to a few production bikes, such as Trek, is the BionX, a French-Canadian design offering four levels of power and four levels of regenerative braking.

Direct drive motors tend to be big in diameter, but they can be narrow, leaving room for a derailleur gear set, as on this Dutch hub fitted to the Sparta Ion and other bikes, including the high quality Koga E-light shown here.

The commercially successful Sparta Ion direct drive technology is fitted to Koga electric bikes (here on the E-light) as well as Sparta's own models. Both companies are part of the Accell group.

The Sparta and BionX have rear wheel motors, the Sparta powered by NiMH batteries hidden inside the frame, and the BionX by Li-ion batteries mounted with the control unit in a mid-frame battery/control unit. Both employ very sophisticated electronics. The BionX has recently been adopted on two folding bikes too: the Airnimal Joey Move and Birdy BionX. It is no coincidence that both have relatively small wheels, the system working rather better on such machines.

The BionX direct drive motor system was originally a bolt-on kit, but is now being fitted as original equipment on an increasing number of bikes. This is the Airnimal Joey Move.

Belt drives & Velocity series hybrids

Another interesting, if rather Heath Robinson, drive system utilizes an external motor linked to the front or rear wheel by a belt or chain. British company TGA Leisure fitted a front-mounted motor to some tricycles in the 1980s and 90s, but these have since been superseded by more modern designs. The USA has long been the home of belt-driven electric bicycles, perhaps because exposed belts on motorcycles are relatively common there, and weather-proofing is not seen as a major issue in a country where electric bikes are primarily leisure toys. Motors have sometimes been mounted on the frame, driving to the crank, putting such devices into the crank-drive category, but the general arrangement is to link the belt or chain direct to the back wheel.

Frame-mounted motors came into vogue because they offered an easy route for after-market fitting, but there are many disadvantages: the duplicate chains and cogs weigh more and add friction, and exposed belts can be a serious danger unless carefully shielded.

The Currie company produces an interesting variant, the Electro Drive, with a partially enclosed chain driving to the non-derailleur side of a custom-made rear hub (on early models it drove directly to the spokes of a normal rear wheel). The motor sticks out some distance from the bike, and is thus potentially vulnerable to damage, and the older spoke drives can munch their way through the already hard-pressed rear spokes, and so need needed to be fitted to a solidly constructed rear wheel a with strong hub and spokes.

With the arrival of better protected, lighter, safer hub motors and other systems, external belts and chains have largely followed the friction drive into extinction, although one or two survive. Notable examples include the Swiss-made Dolphin, and the American Izip Express, both developed from the Velocity, built by Swiss engineer Michael Kutter in the 1990s.

The Velocity family is unique because although these machines appear to use two separate drive systems for human and electric power (technically as a parallel hybrid), torque from both sources is actually combined in the rear hub (a series hybrid). The mechanism involved, although simple in principle, is quite hard to follow. The human power is fed into the planet carrier of an epicyclic 'sun and planet' gearbox, while the electrical power turns the sun wheel. Both inputs are fitted with one-way clutches to prevent them rotating backwards. Power input from either source will push the bike along at a modest speed, but power input from both has the effect of boosting speed and/or torque depending which gear the pedal drive-train is using! In practice, the device feels rather like a crank-drive, but with the advantage that torque from the motor doesn't flow through the gears. The Velocity can, however, run a lot faster than a crank-drive in hybrid mode, and is currently only legal in Switzerland, where a special 'fast Swiss class' has been created to cater for them, and in other countries where top speed is not strictly limited.

The Currie Electro Drive powers the rear wheel with a short chain. Note this is the newest version; older versions clamped around the spokes rather than coming ready-built into a wheel, and used a micropitch chain instead of a conventional Reynolds one.

The early Velocity hybrid system (right) combined human and electric power in a special geared hub housed in the rear wheel. On later models, the motor was moved to a housing just behind the seat tube, as on the Swizzbee (below), but the system is basically the same, with a belt drive from the motor and traditional chain and derailleur gears for the pedals (left).

Eneloop - something for nothing?

The first question asked by many people new to electric bikes is, 'Does it recharge the battery going downhill?' As most motors are fitted with a freewheel to prevent the motor spinning when it isn't needed, power 'regeneration' of this kind isn't usually possible, because to regenerate power, the motor must be driven by the wheel, rather than vice-versa. With a freewheel, as soon as the twistgrip throttle is closed, or the pedal-movement sensor detects that the pedals are stationary, the motor will stop turning. Eliminate the freewheel, and regeneration is possible with most electric bike motors, the extra drag created by generating power acting as a handy auxiliary brake, so systems are generally called 'regenerative braking'. Sanyo's Eneloop system eliminates the freewheel. This part is easy of course. The clever technology has gone into reducing the friction in the motor and gears, because on most electric bikes the extra drag while riding on the flat would far outweigh the usefulness of regenerating a little power going downhill.

Both Giant and Panasonic have experimented with motors of this kind in the last few years. Giant, oddly enough, failed to take advantage of the technology and fit a useful regenerative braking system, but the Panasonic (now called Sanyo following the 2009 merger between the two companies) Eneloop is claimed to regenerate power to a high degree of efficiency. Initially only available in Japan, this power system is now rolling out into other markets, and promises to make regenerative braking an everyday reality.

In use, the spinning Eneloop motor is barely audible, and the frictional drag is little more than that of a high quality bicycle dynamo lighting system, so a bike like this can be ridden on the flat with much the same effort as a conventional bicycle. But of course, power is also available to help you up the hills, and braking force is available to reduce your speed going down the other side.

Is it worthwhile? Whatever Sanyo might claim, regenerative power is of marginal benefit on a bicycle, because in most circumstances, the amount of power that can be put back into the battery is very small. To help explain why, we need to think about the size and weight of a bicycle, and the forces that are constantly trying to slow it down.

A railway locomotive and train of carriages might weigh 1,000 tonnes. It takes a very large amount of energy to accelerate a 1,000 tonne train to 100mph, but once that energy has been expended, relatively little energy is required to keep the train moving at that speed, because the frictional resistance of steel wheels running on steel rails is very small, and with a small frontal area in comparison to its size and weight, the 'drag' of cutting through the air at 100mph is of little consequence. The train has a great deal of stored 'kinetic' energy, and it can coast for some miles without losing much speed, before a great heave on the brakes is needed to stop it again. For locomotive engineers, regenerative braking is very worthwhile, because a high proportion of the energy used to accelerate the train can be tapped to stop it again, which saves overall energy consumption, and reduces wear and tear on the braking system. In smaller vehicles it is less useful, but still worth fitting, and most electric cars and motorcycles have a regenerative capability.

A bicycle and rider, by contrast, will probably weigh less than 100kg. The good news is that very little energy is needed to accelerate the bicycle to the much lower speed of 15mph, but this also means there is very little energy to recover. And even before we start thinking about the rolling resistance of the motor, the bicycle suffers from relatively high drag from its rubber tyres and large unstreamlined frontal area, so it loses speed quite rapidly of its own accord. Even going down hill, so much speed is scrubbed off in the form of wind resistance and tyre rolling resistance that relatively little can be recaptured.

An electric locomotive can easily regenerate 20% or more of the energy put into it, but a bicycle might struggle to achieve 5%, and with a very languid style of riding, the level of regeneration will be virtually nil. With these sorts of figures, the extra complication and frictional losses just aren't worth the trouble, unless the cyclist is descending from a mountain range, where the reduced heat build up in the braking system will be extremely welcome. For city cyclists, and those towing heavy loads, this reduced reliance on the brakes might well tip the balance in favour of regenerative braking, even if the additional battery range is barely detectable. Practical or not, the public are keen on the concept of regenerative braking, and the Japanese are very adept at fulfilling a public need, albeit a perceived one.

Eneloop technology was used in Sanyo's own Eneloop bikes. It appears such bikes haven't sold in any great quantity outside of Japan.
The Japanese home market targets young women in particular and their electric bikes often feature very small capacity batteries.

DRIVE SYSTEM SUMMARY	Pros	Cons
Friction drive	**+** Light, easy to fit, can provide limited regenerative braking	**−** Inefficient, poor hill-climbing, slippage in wet weather, rapid wear
Crank-drive	**+** More efficient, better hill-climbing, reliable, usually quiet, easy to use	**−** Can be slower where lots of gear changes are required, tough on gears, expensive, cannot provide regenerative braking.
Geared hub motor	**+** Cheap, simple, lightweight. Front hub gives two-wheel-drive. Can be designed to provide regenerative braking.	**−** Relatively inefficient, poor hill-climbing unless low geared, can be noisy
Friction roller hub motor	**+** Very light, very quiet, efficient. Front hub gives two-wheel-drive. Can be designed to provide regenerative braking.	**−** Manufacture requires fine tolerances, can slip in use, relatively poor hill-climbing unless low geared
Direct drive hub motor	**+** Very quiet. Front hub gives two-wheel-drive. Can easily provide regenerative braking.	**−** Big and heavy, poor hill-climbing
Velocity series hybrid	**+** Fast, easy to use, relatively quiet, efficient	**−** Complex, relatively heavy, cannot provide regenerative braking

The Battery

A quick battery guide

There are four battery chemistries in common use on electric bicycles: lead-acid, nickel-cadmium (NiCd), nickel-metal hydride (NiMH) and lithium-ion (Li-ion). We will look at these common types in a moment, but first it's worth discussing a few characteristics that are common to all of them, and indeed other more exotic chemistries.

The first rule is that a battery is not an empty receptacle like a fuel tank. It's a complex and sophisticated mixture of solid and liquid chemicals, some of them quite dangerous, so don't ever dismantle any of these cells. As a general rule, a cell will have two solid or gelatinous plates, one negative and the other positive (known as the anode and cathode respectively). The plates are immersed (or wrapped) in a liquid or gel 'electrolyte', which allows electrons to pass from one plate to the other. The chemical reactions that create electrical power are reversible with all these battery chemistries, but unlike a fuel tank that can be refilled again and again for decades, the number of 'charge cycles' a battery can endure is strictly limited, particularly in the case of lead-acid and lithium-ion. And whereas a fuel tank will be 100% efficient (as long as it doesn't have a hole in the side!) rechargeable batteries always take in more power than they give out. With some chemistries, battery designs, and uses, efficiency is so high it can be ignored, but in other examples, it can be a major limiting factor.

There are several key characteristics common to all rechargeable batteries:

● Like you, batteries have an optimum operating temperature and lose efficiency if asked to work outside this 'comfort zone'. For most common batteries, the ideal is around room temperature. Output and efficiency can fall rapidly at colder temperatures, so it makes sense to charge the battery indoors in very cold weather, and keep it indoors until the last second to keep the cells warm. Some chargers will refuse to operate if the battery or charger are too hot or cold.

● All batteries will be damaged if persistently over-charged, although some are more tolerant than others. Most battery chargers cut off at (or close to) full charge, but you are in the hands of the control systems in the charger, and all are set to slightly different parameters. With lithium-ion, the control circuitry is usually in the battery itself.

● Similarly, all batteries will have their life shortened if over-discharged, and lithium-ion may shut down permanently if left flat for a while. How do you know when a battery has been over-discharged? Again, it's very difficult to say. Some (principally lithium-ion) will shut down when the voltage gets dangerously low, but others can be driven to complete exhaustion. The only safe advice is to try turn the battery off before it is fully discharged: an almost impossible job.

• All batteries have a finite life in terms of the number of charges they will accept, and this life is affected by numerous things, including over- and under-charging. With lithium-ion, the manufacturer will generally have preset the cut-outs for charging and discharging. A cheap battery with suspiciously high capacity has probably been set to the extremes, giving it a short and eventful life. Better quality batteries are usually rated more conservatively, and can live much longer.

You can, of course, turn off the charger before it cuts out, and stop riding the bike before the battery is flat. With older chemistries, this sort of battery care is entirely up to the user, but there's no simple answer: if you avoid over- and under-charging, you'll need to charge the battery more frequently, accelerating the ticking clock of battery life (there can be other complications too – see below). If you get the most out of each charge, you risk reducing the life by going too far with the charging and discharging cycles.

• As a general rule, if the battery gets warm, it's probably not happy. After the charger has cut off, it usually continues to give the battery a gentle trickle charge. The advice here varies with the chemistry: generally lithium-ion batteries should never be left connected to the charger, because even a very gentle over-charge can do damage, but recent batteries from Koga Miyata are designed to be stored with the charger connected and powered up. The Koga warranty will be invalidated if the battery is over discharged through *not* being connected to the charger, but most batteries will be damaged if left connected! Read the small print carefully. Other chemistries are less critical - nickel-cadmium and nickel-metal hydride may benefit from being left connected for a short time, and lead-acid will positively welcome a *very* gentle over-charge.

• Some batteries will last for a few years if kept charged, but not over-charged, whereas others (typically lithium-ion) will deteriorate whether you use them or not, so storage can be expensive. If you have to store a lithium-ion battery, aim for a lowish state of charge (topping up occasionally to prevent it discharging completely) and keep the battery in a cool place. Nickel-cadmium batteries are the only type that can be expected to survive a long period of storage while discharged.

• Finally, all batteries are affected by vibration and shock to differing degrees, so it makes sense to treat them gently, as they are expensive things! Never buy a battery-powered machine without checking the replacement battery price in advance... you may be in for a shock (not the electrical kind). Replacement batteries can cost anything from 25% to 50% of the initial purchase cost of the bicycle. After the depreciation of the bike itself, battery depreciation is far and away the biggest running cost.

So remember: comfortable temperature, avoid shocks or vibration, no over- or under-charging, try to avoid storage, but if you have to do it, keep the battery cool, and never let it go flat.

Lead-acid

General characteristics & battery care

For almost a century, the lead-acid cell was the pre-eminent rechargeable device, and all early electric bicycles used this sort of battery. Inside each cell are alternating plates of lead and lead-dioxide suspended in a bath of dilute sulphuric acid. As the battery runs down, both plates are converted to lead sulphate, and the sulphuric acid to water.

The useful life of a lead-acid battery can vary enormously. A cheap battery working hard, and subjected to the sort of temperature variations, shocks and vibrations prevalent on an electric bike, might last less than a year, and few will be guaranteed for more than three months - perhaps 100 charges. Better quality batteries can last much longer if treated with care, maybe 300 charges or more, and a life in excess of ten years is quite common. But if left discharged, particularly in very cold temperatures, the battery can be destroyed in a matter of weeks.

In the traditional lead-acid battery, the acid is free to slosh around, and any build-up of gas – principally hydrogen and oxygen released during charging – is simply allowed to escape through a vented cap. There are two principal problems with this design: acid spillage through the caps, and the need for regular top-ups with distilled water to replace that lost through gassing. Several recent developments have sought to deal with these problems, and it is these newer batteries that will usually be found in an electric bike.

In the Valve-Regulated Lead-Acid battery (VRLA), vented hydrogen and oxygen are recombined into water and returned to the electrolyte, so the cell can be partially sealed. However, over-charging can cause an excess of gas to be produced, and safety valves are fitted to allow this gas to vent to the atmosphere.

In the Sealed Lead-Acid (SLA) battery, the electrolyte is in the form of a gel, but it plays exactly the same role as the liquid electrolyte. Because the gel cannot be lost through spillage, cells can be sealed, but as with the VRLA, there will always be a safety valve of some kind to prevent the battery exploding if misused. SLA batteries can spend long periods upside down without the gel escaping, but mechanical damage or over-charging can result in acid venting from the safety valve and causing havoc with wiring, paintwork, clothes or carpets.

These modern lead-acid variants should last for several years without problems, but it's worth bearing in mind that they contain corrosive chemicals, and these do occasionally find their way out. In normal use they lose little water or acid, but there's no way of replacing it, so if they are regularly over-charged, gas or electrolyte will escape, and the battery will start to fail. After prolonged use, the gel will start to dry out, however carefully the battery has been treated, reducing its capacity.

As any battery is charged and discharged, some cells inevitably get out of step with their fellows, reaching a fully discharged state a little earlier. If a cell drops to zero volts and the machine continues to be used, power will effectively be forced backwards through the weak cell, a process known as 'reverse polarity'. Lead-acid batteries are less vulnerable to damage in this way than other battery types (see below), because they can be given a very gentle and prolonged 'equalising' or 'balancing' charge once in a while, allowing the weaker cells to catch up with the strong ones.

The chemical reaction in lead-acid cells is reversible, but the number of times the trick can be performed is strictly limited, and the cells are vulnerable to physical damage through vibration or heavy knocks, low temperatures, high charge or discharge rates, and standing unused in a discharged state. Leaving a lead-acid cell discharged for even a short time will cause some of the lead sulphate to become permanent, a reaction that is not reversible, although hard use may cause some of the sulphate to be shed from the plates leaving a fresh layer available for use.

Lead-acid batteries can be made more rugged by using a smaller number of thick plates, and other techniques, but the resulting batteries (often called Deep Cycle batteries) are more expensive, have a lower output for a given weight, and are unable to produce high current. These days, most electric bikes are fitted with other chemistries altogether, but in the days when lead-acid batteries were the norm, manufacturers generally used Deep Cycle cells. Cheap and cheerful electric bikes today tend to be fitted with mass-produced multi-purpose Far Eastern cells, better suited to static applications like burglar alarms. These may have a very limited life in traction applications.

Advantages

Lead-acid batteries require comparatively little energy to manufacture and can be easily and cheaply recycled, a process that consumes less than a quarter of the energy required to produce a new battery. Most local authorities make collection arrangements for this purpose and with the price of lead currently quite high, the batteries have a high scrap value, discouraging inappropriate disposal.

Despite the weight disadvantage and limited life, the simplicity of the lead-acid battery makes it very appealing. With output of two volts per cell, only 18 are required to generate a typical electric bike voltage of 36 volts, which helps a bit with reliability, reducing the tendency for cells to go into reverse polarity on discharge. Whilst lead-acid batteries certainly have many disadvantages, their simplicity and low-tech construction has made them great favourites in China where, ironically, the electric bicycle industry is consuming enough lead to inflate the global price.

Despite recent price increases, lead-acid batteries remain by far the cheapest technology, watt-hour for watt-hour, and they have the big advantage that the batteries (usually three 12-volt batteries on a 36-volt electric bike) can be exchanged for readily available replacements by anyone who can handle a screwdriver. Where weight is not a major issue, they remain an excellent battery technology.

Downsides

We've already mentioned the heavy weight of these batteries (output is typically just 25Wh per kg), but there are other more subtle disadvantages too.

Lead-acid batteries are peculiarly well suited to being trickle charged, and providing a very high current for short periods, which matches particularly well with cars, where the battery is called on to start the engine, but otherwise (generally) stays fully charged. They are less well suited to being completely discharged on a regular basis, as on an electrically-powered machine, such as a bicycle.

Charge rates can be quite slow. A lead-acid battery is usually charged at a constant voltage, and this simplest form of charger are cheap and efficient, with little or no electronic circuitry inside. This type of charger gives a high output for a few minutes, but as the battery voltage starts to rise, the charge rate will automatically fall over about six hours. After this, the battery will be taking a so-called 'trickle' charge, which will need to continue for another six hours or even more. Traditional lead-acid batteries can tolerate long periods of trickle charge, but with the SLA batteries fitted to electric bikes, prolonged charging will cause the electrolyte to dry out prematurely and should be avoided.

More complex charger technology can reduce the charge time, but if the battery charger attempts to push this envelope with an inappropriately fast charge, the battery simply turns some of the water in the electrolyte to hydrogen and oxygen, which are vented to the atmosphere. Modern batteries use various chemical and mechanical techniques to reduce this emission of explosive gases, but charging remains a long, slow process, despite claims and counterclaims over the years.

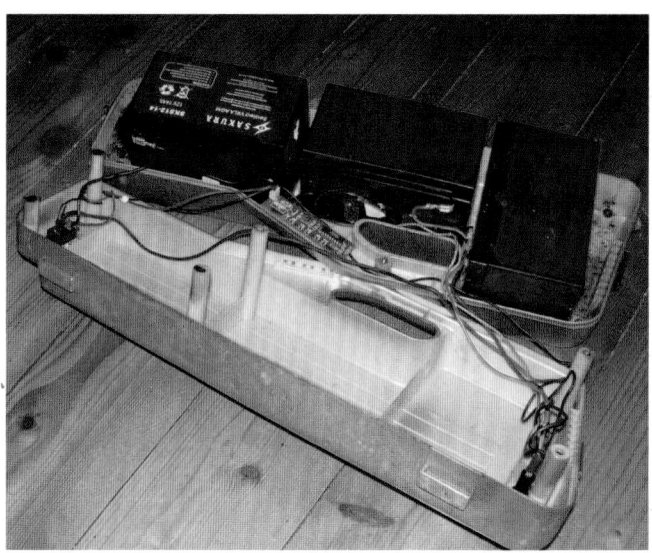

The Powabyke battery is typical of older lead-acid battery packs. This one contains three 12 volt Sakura VRLA batteries with Lucar connectors, making a battery change very straightforward. The small circuit board is the capacity meter, and the external fuse is bottom right. This example weighs 13.9kg... a kilogram more than the ENTIRE Cytronex Cannondale Super Six, said to be the lightest electric bike available!

The future for lead-acid

Developments continue, with many claimed breakthroughs, but most bring disadvantages of their own. For example, thinner, more porous plates allow the battery to store more energy weight for weight, but such batteries tend to have a shorter service life. The Guangdong Jiangmen Yuyang Special Battery company in China markets the Silicon Power Battery, claiming it to be a completely new technology. In fact, the low-sodium silicate compound in the gel simply serves to reduce the rate at which the electrolyte dries out, although it is also claimed to give a reduced charging time and increased cycle life. As so often with battery technology, sexy-sounding acronyms and chemical formulas are deliberately bandied about to suggest a step change in technology. They may well be better, but they are not a completely new technology.

Several Western manufacturers are pumping development funds into lead-acid batteries, principally to reduce the weight and cost by reducing the lead content, and increasing the surface area of the plates to increase power output, without weakening them or reducing service life. If a breakthrough does take place - and it certainly can't be ruled out - lead-acid could well come back into vogue.

Lead-acid battery terminology - a summary

VRLA (Valve regulated lead-acid) - Liquid electrolyte in a sealed battery fitted with safety valves.

SLA (Sealed lead-acid) - The electrolyte is in the form of a gel, and again, the battery is sealed and fitted with safety valves.

AGM (absorbed glass mat) - The electrolyte is held in a glass fibre mat.

Deep Cycle - Rare today. A heavy duty battery designed for traction transport applications.

Nickel-Cadmium (NiCd)

General characteristics & battery care

Relatively uncommon today in electric bikes, nickel-cadmium cells have been around for more than a hundred years, but were held back for a variety of reasons – principally because lead-acid was cheaper and reasonably effective. However, the chemistry began to replace lead-acid in the 1990s, mainly because of its lighter weight (typically 50Wh/kg) and reduced sensitivity to temperature and vibration. Unlike lead-acid cells, which are usually rectangular, nickel-cadmium cells are generally made from large flat plates rolled into a cylindrical casing.

Despite its many advantages, NiCd technology fell out of favour quite quickly, partly because cadmium is a dangerous heavy metal, more difficult and dangerous to recycle than lead, but primarily because more recent chemistries such as NiMH offered better performance and safer disposal. As a consequence, NiCd batteries are rare today in transport applications.

Nickel-cadmium batteries require slightly cleverer charging systems than lead-acid, because it's more difficult to sense the rising voltage of the battery, and they are easily over-charged. Both charge and discharge rates can be quite high though, and several manufacturers, notably Heinzmann, have developed fast charge systems for nickel-cadmium batteries. As with the lead-acid battery, over-charging will cause oxygen and/or hydrogen to be liberated through a safety valve, and although the cells usually remain cold as the charge progresses, they can warm very rapidly as they reach a full charge. This heating can give an accurate guide to the well-being of the battery during charging, and some fast chargers monitor battery temperature, cutting the charge off when the temperature reaches a pre-determined level.

Advantages & downsides

Unusually, nickel-cadmium exhibits a 'memory' characteristic, whereby a battery subjected to repeated partial discharges will 'learn' to discharge to this level and refuse to discharge completely when required, permanently or semi-permanently limiting the battery's capacity. Another disadvantage in some applications (but an advantage in others) is that the cell voltage remains near constant as the battery discharges, before failing in a matter of seconds. On an electric bike, this helps to keep speed up, but means there is little warning that the battery is almost flat and about to give up completely.

Nickel-cadmium batteries are better able to tolerate deep discharge cycles than other types, and can be stored in a completely discharged state, unlike most other chemistries. This ability to tolerate deep discharge and withstand storage helps to give nickel-cadmium a very long life, often claimed to be in excess of 1,000 charge cycles.

All the same, performance can deteriorate at high or low temperatures, as it can with all batteries, and charging at low temperatures will cause gases to be released, as if the battery were being over-charged. To avoid problems, some chargers will refuse to start, or will charge at a reduced rate, if the temperature is above or below the cell's typical 'comfort zone' of 10°C to 40°C. In very cold weather, the battery is best stored and charged indoors, which will maximise the range.

Ironically, considering that individual NiCd cells can tolerate being fully discharged without damage, the same is not true of a battery of cells. With output of only 1.2 volts per cell, 30 are needed to power a typical 36 volt electric bike. The problem with this long string of cells is that it's hard to judge when one has fallen to zero volts, making damaging reverse polarity very likely if one cell is weaker than its neighbours. As over-charging is a potential problem with nickel-cadmium batteries, the cell voltages cannot easily be 'equalised' as they can in a lead-acid battery. The reverse polarity problem can be eased if the battery, or control circuitry of the bike, is equipped with a sensor to cut power to the motor when voltage falls below a pre-set level. This should at least save the weakest cells from further damage, but they are likely to get further and further out of step with their fellows unless some clever charging and discharging techniques are employed.

If you're riding a bicycle fitted with a nickel-cadmium battery that does not cut out completely when nearly discharged, it's important to stop using it as soon as the performance begins to weaken, and not keep riding with the power on, which will damage the weaker cells. Over-charging or reverse polarity will result in gas being released from the cell safety valves, which is not only dangerous, but will soon dry out the cells rendering them useless.

Nickel-cadmium batteries have disappeared from modern electric bikes, replaced by the similar, but 'cleaner' NiMH, or the 'technology of the moment' Li-ion. For older bikes, replacement NiCd cells are becoming hard to find, but they can be fitted to most battery packs by a competent electrician. The cost of this tricky operation is likely to be quite high, and used cells or batteries must be properly disposed of.

Nickel-metal hydride (NiMH)

General characteristics

The search for a cadmium-free nickel battery resulted in nickel-metal hydride or NiMH in the late 1990s. These batteries require even more intelligent charging systems, because the cell voltage actually drops slightly as full charge approaches, and complex circuitry is required to detect this. They are however, more weight efficient than their older cousins, storing 55-70Wh/kg, and have now largely replaced nickel-cadmium. In most other respects, the cells are very similar, but NiMH cells cannot tolerate being completely discharged, so it's important that a NiMH-equipped bicycle is not ridden when the battery is almost flat. Some will cut-out to save the battery, others won't.

On the positive side, gases produced during charging are generally reabsorbed, so a NiMH battery has no need for venting systems, other than in an emergency, and is less likely to lose capacity through loss of electrolyte. Replacement cells are quite widely available, but the cost of the cells and fitting can be high and may not be worthwhile in practice. Not all replacement cells are designed for high current applications like electric bikes, and may give disappointing performance, so if a complete replacement battery is still available at a reasonable price from the manufacturer, this may make more sense than refurbishment.

Bikes produced with NiMH batteries are getting increasingly rare. Heinzmann and BionX hung on until very recently, but these companies have now gone down the Li-ion road, and at the time of writing (in late 2010) only the Dutch Sparta, British Cytronex and GoCycle plus a few American Izip bikes still use the older, but more reliable NiMH technology. It's worth noting that stocks of NiMH batteries for out of production bikes are still available through dealers - the Giant Lafree (the 2000-2006 remodelled version, not the early lead-acid powered one) and the Yamaha PAS are two such examples, making purchasing these second-hand bikes a much more feasible option. Both these machines come up for sale at reasonable prices. NiCd and NiMH batteries can last for a considerable time, and many five- or even ten-year old batteries continue to give good service, albeit with reduced range.

Lithium-ion (Li-ion)

Advantages

On paper, the Li-ion battery has many advantages over the alternatives. At about 3.7 volts per cell (the different chemistries vary a bit), the cell voltage is unusually high, so only ten cells are required in a typical 36-volt battery. Lithium, in marked contrast to lead, and even nickel, is a particularly lightweight metal, so the cells are very light, giving a typical capacity of 90Wh/kg to 150Wh/kg, and the figure is rising all the time. Li-ion cells can be made in rectangular rather than tubular cases, which effectively reduces the overall volume, so the packs can be made quite small, as well as strikingly light.

Downsides

Although Li-ion sounds like the consumer's dream technology, it has proved to be an engineering and chemical nightmare, and there remain many complications with these batteries.

Soon after introduction, it became clear that lithium-ion batteries suffered from most of the issues that had affected earlier battery chemistries, but they were also more sensitive to maltreatment, and less forgiving when things went wrong. Unlike lead, which is a particularly unreactive metal, lithium is very corrosive, and highly reactive, notably with water. So if things do go wrong (they occasionally did in the early days), spraying water onto a lithium fire will make matters much, much worse.

As with most other battery designs, lithium-ion cells consist of negative and positive plates of active material sandwiching a liquid or gel 'electrolyte'. In this case, the electrolyte obviously can't be water-based, so other solvents may be used, such as ether, which doesn't react with lithium, but is itself combustible.

Early laboratory experiments with lithium cells used anodes made of pure lithium metal, but this simple chemistry proved too unstable for commercial exploitation. Further development resulted in the use of other materials, such as porous graphite, in which the lithium could be suspended in a safer ionic form, hence the name.

The first practical lithium-ion battery was launched by Sony in 1991 using a lithium-ion anode and a cathode of lithium cobalt oxide. This chemistry also proved somewhat unreliable in real world conditions, and in the early noughties laptop and mobile phone batteries caused a number of spectacular fires. Relatively few electric bikes caught fire, but when they did, the bigger batteries caused havoc, and several house and garage fires have been attributed to lithium-ion batteries running amok in the middle of the night. The problems are caused by the same sort of issues that upset older battery types, but with lithium cells, mechanical damage, over-charging or heavy discharge can cause a fire, rather than simply venting a bit of oxygen or hydrogen.

The unreliable nature of lithium batteries resulted in two strands of research: a search for more stable chemistries, and an improved electronic Battery Management System (BMS) to prevent the dangerous conditions developing. All multi-cell lithium-ion batteries will have some form of onboard BMS. A typical system will control the maximum current output to neutralise an accidental short circuit, terminate charging when the battery is full, shut down the output when the battery is empty, and constantly monitor the well-being of all the cells. In the early days, these complex fail-safe mechanisms were bigger than the cells themselves, adding considerably to the weight, size and price of the battery, but improved miniaturisation has resulted in smaller, cheaper and lighter management electronics.

Unfortunately, the sheer complexity and fail-safe nature of the management systems has given lithium cells an unenviable reputation for poor reliability, with many batteries failing within weeks of purchase, in some cases because of a single component failure in the BMS rather than the actual battery cells. Like the sensor-controlled brushless motors, the problem only came to light when these complex, high technology devices were let loose in real world conditions of sudden temperature changes, physical damage, and careless charging and discharging by users.

Meanwhile, the search for improved chemistries able to deal with the often conflicting requirements of safe operation, long life and cheap manufacture has yielded all sorts of exotic cathode materials, including manganese and iron, but in late 2010 none has completely cracked the problem.

An offshoot of the lithium-ion cell is lithium-polymer. Often treated as a distinct chemistry, the lithium-polymer cell differs primarily in construction. Because the electrolyte is in plastic form, the polymer battery cannot leak, and can be made without a reinforced case. This makes it possible to produce very slim batteries, but the pros and cons are broadly the same as for lithium-ion.

We don't want to rub this in, but it's worth knowing that even with a 100% reliable BMS, cells will (very rarely) develop an internal short circuit. If this happens, temperature climbs rapidly until a safety valve opens, spraying combustible ether out of the cell. If the ether ignites, we have a situation called, rather obliquely 'venting with flame', or in everyday language, a serious fire, and one that will get much worse if quenching with water is attempted. If the fire really takes hold, the lithium itself will begin to burn and matters can become quite serious. For this reason there are strict controls on the size of lithium-ion battery that can be carried by air (see *Electric Bikes and the Law* chapter).

As well as preventing dangerous situations from developing, the BMS can perform many other functions. It can record the number of charges and discharges, monitor the owners' use and abuse of the battery, and provide a read-out of individual cell condition. Some feature simple diagnostic systems, flashing lights at the user to indicate various failure modes, but others can download a great deal of information via a laptop computer. As well as storing data on the way you use your battery and your bicycle, some BMS systems are designed to permanently shut down (in a benign way!) after a set number of charges, even if there's still some life left in the battery. Presumably this would be explained away as a safety system by the manufacturers, but it could also be regarded as a bit of a con trick. How many other products self destruct when the manufacturer decides you should buy a new one? Unlike most batteries, lithium-ion does not self discharge over time, but the BMS itself draws a little power, so after a few months storage, the battery will be completely flat. In these circumstances - or perhaps for example when the ignition has been left on for a few days or weeks - an awkward catch-22 situation develops where the voltage drops too low to fire up the BMS, yet without the BMS the battery cannot accept a charge. In these circumstances the battery will appear completely dead and it may be damaged beyond repair. Better quality batteries, such as the Panasonic unit fitted to many European pedelecs, will automatically go into 'storage mode' after a couple of weeks without use. Hopefully, the BMS will fire up as soon as a charger is connected and the battery will return to life. This sort of technology will no doubt become more common, but at the moment few batteries are protected in this way.

To its ultimate cost, eZee was one of the first companies to develop a Lithium-ion battery. In this example the rectangular cells are squeezed together in two packs of five, with a BMS circuit board out of sight alongside the top pack. Unusually for Li-ion, the battery has an external fuse at the top, and the two power output wires (oddly black and blue!) exit from the small plate at the bottom. This battery weighed 4.3kg and had a claimed output of 370Wh, a great advance for 2005, although the best modern batteries have nearly double the capacity weight-for-weight. The cycle life of these early Li-ion batteries was extremely short.

Even where the battery has been treated with great care, life can be disappointing compared to nickel-based chemistries in particular. Optimistic early forecasts suggested a battery life of 1,000 charges or more, but although this has been achieved in some applications, the cycle life of electric bike batteries has gradually been downgraded through experience to 300 or so, suggesting typical battery life of one to three years of regular use. This wouldn't matter too much if the batteries were cheap, but in the last few years, the price of Li-ion batteries has risen sharply, apparently because of a shortage of lithium.

The search for new Li-ion chemistries has yielded some good results, and a great deal of investment continues today. For fundamental chemical reasons, iron is probably the most suitable cathode material, and the current 'state of the art' material is Lithium Iron Phospate (LiFePo4). If this proves stable, the thrust of development will move to the carbon anode, possibly using nano technology to yield a greater surface area to improve output, while maintaining the strength to give an acceptable life. The performance of lithium batteries is rising fast, and management systems are becoming more reliable, but at the time of writing, the Li-ion cell remains hampered by its short shelf and cycle life. All this might change, of course, but the claims of long life and low prices seem as far away as ever.

Lithium-ion batteries designed for electric cars and motorcycles have replaceable cells, but the norm with smaller batteries is a sealed and unserviceable unit. When one component or cell fails, the entire pack, including the expensive BMS must be scrapped and/or recycled, an appalling waste of resources, particularly when the technology is supposed to demonstrate a 'green' alternative to fossil fuels. Replaceable cells would go some way to reducing the long-term cost and environmental impact of these batteries, but with cell chemistry and BMS design evolving so fast, manufacturers can see little commercial advantage in developing a system to keep current technology on the road, when newer, better batteries are being developed almost every week. Eventually, the pace of development will calm down and manufacturers may turn to 'plug in' cells, making the long-term prospects for Li-ion much more attractive.

Despite the drawbacks, lithium batteries are astonishingly light (and getting lighter), and have gone from being an exotic chemistry to everyday technology in just a couple of years. Far Eastern manufacturers have largely standardised plugs and chargers, which are now generally interchangeable and give a typical charge time of four to five hours. For several years, battery have settled at 37volts, with a capacity of 10Ah, giving a nominal battery capacity of 370Wh, but during 2010, newer designs began to emerge with capacities of 518Wh, then 650Wh. Even including the weight of a rugged battery case, that's an energy density of 140Wh/kg, more than four times the performance of a typical lead-acid battery from a decade before. Is it any wonder the electric bike world has gone lithium crazy? Today virtually every electric bicycle sold in the western world will be fitted with a lithium-ion battery.

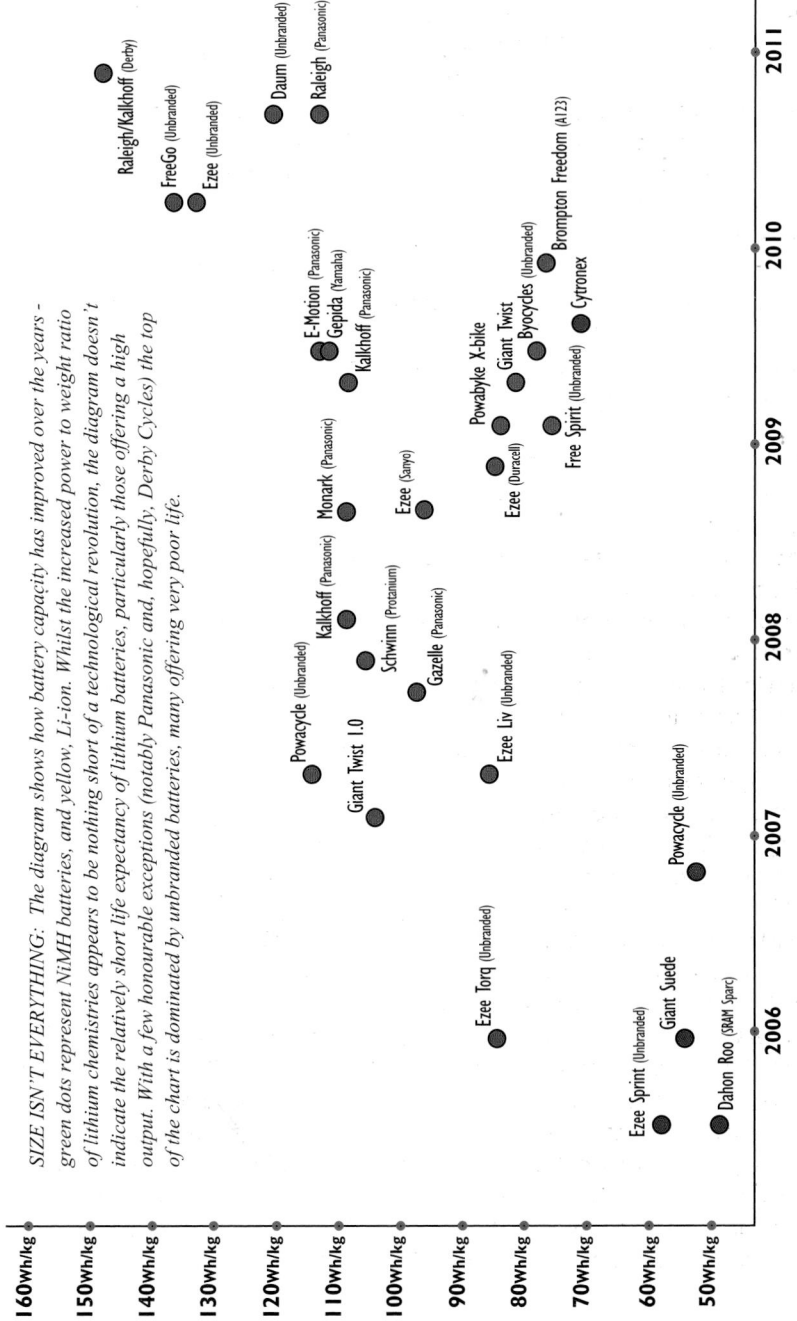

Battery capacity - increase over time

SIZE ISN'T EVERYTHING: The diagram shows how battery capacity has improved over the years - green dots represent NiMH batteries, and yellow, Li-ion. Whilst the increased power to weight ratio of lithium chemistries appears to be nothing short of a technological revolution, the diagram doesn't indicate the relatively short life expectancy of lithium batteries, particularly those offering a high output. With a few honourable exceptions (notably Panasonic and, hopefully, Derby Cycles) the top of the chart is dominated by unbranded batteries, many offering very poor life.

	Power density	Pros	Cons
Lead-Acid	25Wh/kg	+ Easy to maintain and replace * Low cost * Easily recycled * The technology is still being developed	- Heaviest chemistry and therefore poorest range * Contains corrosive acid which can spill * Slow charge rate
Nickel-Cadmium	50Wh/kg	+ Tolerates deep discharges * Reasonably fast charging	- Cadmium is a dangerous heavy metal * Cells are generally cylindrical * Very rare nowadays * Can suffer from 'memory' effect
Nickel-Metal Hydride	70Wh/kg	+ A long lasting chemistry - battery life can be five to ten years	- Requires intelligent charging and should not be fully discharged * Becoming rare
Lithium-ion	90-150 Wh/kg	+ Very power dense so generally lighter and with longer range than other battery types * Relatively fast charging * The technology is improving all the time	- Limited charge cycle life * Complex battery management system prone to failure * Expensive * Not generally recycled * Lithium very volatile particularly if exposed to water

Alternatives to batteries

Fuel Cells

Despite all the issues of safety, price, weight and limited life associated with chemical batteries, they continue to be the primary means of supplying electrical energy to vehicles and other machines that cannot be linked to a mains supply. A considerable effort has gone into perfecting fuel cell technology, but writing in 2010 the commercial applications have yet to leave the aerospace and defence fields where cost is not considered a major drawback.

Hydrogen fuel cells sound ideal for vehicle use: they produce no emissions other than water, and the fuel is light and readily produced from water (given the required energy input), but hydrogen brings complications that make lithium-ion batteries look relatively harmless. Propelling a vehicle with uncompressed gas is impractical, because the tank needs to be very large – as demonstrated by experience with coal gas, used briefly to power vehicles during World War II. Some gases, such as butane, can be liquified at low pressure, making them suitable for fuelling vehicles, but hydrogen requires more pressure than any other gas: an unimaginable 800 bar or 12,000lbs per square inch. The compression process itself takes a lot of energy, and the tank must be immensely strong, not only to resist the pressure of the fuel, but to withstand accidental damage. In a road vehicle (including of course, a bicycle) a heavy reinforced tank is a major drawback, and it is this problem that has held back fuel cell acceptance.

In practice, it would be impossible to compress hydrogen to these enormous pressures mechanically, but it can be turned into a liquid at extremely cold temperatures close to absolute zero and either kept in a very strong tank at room temperature, or very, very cold and unpressurized.

So instead of a strong fuel tank able to contain the gas as it warms and expands, hydrogen can be carried in an especially insulated tank to keep it cold. This sort of thing might work in a space craft, but in day-to-day use on the ground, the hydrogen will begin to warm up, and the gas will have to be vented to prevent a dangerous pressure build up, which is all rather impractical in a vehicle. Even if these seemingly insoluble problems could be solved, liquid hydrogen only contains one third as much energy as the same volume of petroleum, suggesting rather limited range, litre for litre.

Storing the fuel is just the start of the complications. The fuel cells that turn hydrogen into electrical power are vulnerable to impurities, both from the air and the fuel, and even such things as moisture levels have to be carefully controlled.

Environmentally, there are many issues. The hydrogen fuel itself has to be produced, transported and stored, and at present, all these elements of the hydrogen story result in the burning of fossil fuels one way or another. So the cells may be emission-free at point of use, but they can leave a trail of pollution in their wake. Overall efficiency,

Left: In 2003 Jorg Weigl equipped this Optima recumbent trike with a hydrogen fuel cell system. Compressed to 5,000psi in big carbon fibre tanks, the hydrogen fuel was claimed to give the machine a range of 550 miles. This prototype cost €32,000, but the project went no further.

Right: Built by John Turner, this prototype hydrogen fuel cell bicycle was exhibited at the Tour de Presteigne in 2008. By this stage, the technology had become cheaper and more compact, but these smaller, low-pressure tanks were only claimed to give a range of 35 miles. For various reasons, hydrogen fuel cell technology seems to have stalled.

113

In a further attempt to solve the hydrogen storage issue, energy company SiGNa showcased a fuel cell-powered electric bike in 2010. The hydrogen generator in the 'water bottle' canister uses

sodium silicide to which water is added to produce hydrogen. Older readers may recall that acetelyne lamps worked in a similar way a century ago! The technology is not available to the public yet, but the company claims 60 miles on a single cartridge of sodium silicide and says it is taking 'pre-orders' for the cartridges. The reaction results in sodium silicate, a safe and easily recycled product, plus nearly 10% hydrogen weight for weight (this, apparently, is better than it sounds), but the cost of the returnable fuel cassettes has yet to be announced, and the reaction is fundamentally a rather explosive one, although SiGNa claims the new process is completely safe.

from water, through hydrogen production, distribution, fuel cell power generation and back to water is currently very poor indeed, with only a few percent of the energy input being available to power the vehicle.

In many ways, the direct-methanol fuel cell sounds a more likely candidate for transport applications, as the fuel is liquid at room temperatures, but it is also corrosive and poisonous, and the exhaust contains carbon dioxide as well as water. So direct-methanol cells don't actually reduce CO2 pollution, they simply move it around. Methanol can be produced by brewing wheat and other crops with yeast, and distilling the resultant broth, but as with hydrogen, processing and fuel transport generate a lot of pollution, and with CO2 being released at point of use, the technology is arguably little better than a modern, clean-burning internal combustion engine in practice. Another option involves generating hydrogen and mixing it with atmospheric carbon to produce easily transportable methanol. This sounds a neat carbon recycling trick, but it remains very much the stuff of science fiction at the moment.

Despite all the problems with methanol, it is conceivable that a small fuel cell might find a practical application as a range extender for an electric bike, and on such a very small scale, the disadvantages become less marked. Cells of this kind are already under development for use in mobile phones and laptop computers, and as all the battery chemistries have come up by this route, this suggests that methanol may be the next big advance.

Direct solar power

Solar energy sounds ideal for powering an electric bicycle. Bright sunlight provides around a kilowatt of power per square metre, suggesting that a solar panel of about a quarter of that size could power a 250-watt electric bicycle. A panel measuring

50cm x 50cm is an awkward thing to carry, but manageable enough: unfortunately, it would provide nowhere near enough power for an electric bike. That 1,000 watt figure assumes a completely clear day, and a panel aimed continuously directly at the sun - difficult to do on a building, let alone a vehicle. Even in bright sunlight, the average strength of solar radiation hitting a flat panel is rather less than 350 watts per square meter at all latitudes, and much, much less when the sun is obscured by cloud or fog. To make matters worse, with current technology, very little of that energy can actually be turned into electrical power. Solar panel efficiency rarely exceeds 20%, and can be less than 10%, so even where clear skies and strong sunlight are guaranteed, several square metres of panel would be needed to power an electric bike without battery back-up, and the machine would be useless when shielded by tall buildings, trees, and so forth. Laboratory tests have claimed around 40% efficiency for multi-junction solar cells, but whether this figure will ever be replicated in real-world conditions remains to be seen.

For a bicycle, direct solar energy is simply not realistic because of the sheer size of the panel array required. On the other hand, panels are already starting to appear on rickshaws in the Far East, where there's plenty of sunlight, a large roof to carry the panels, and weight is less of an issue. And with improvements in panel and battery technology it's conceivable that - in the tropics at least - a panel of perhaps 100 watts, backed up by a modest battery might eventually appear on a bicycle. Whether it ever happens depends partly on battery technology. In 2010 the best lithium batteries can supply in excess of 600watt-hours from a compact package weighing less than 5kg. If battery technology improves, the appeal of direct solar power will inevitably continue to wane.

Author Richard Peace's trip through Southern France in 2006 was an experiment in direct solar power. Richard used cutting edge technology (a folding, military grade panel) and travelled in a near perfect climate, harnessing sun power on the move. The panel was very useful for extending daily range, but could not replace the need for a spare battery and mains supply at night.

Solar powered charging stations

Solar power generated en route might have little future, but a solar power station at home makes a lot of sense. There are several ways to do this. The easiest and most practical method is to keep one battery on the bike and another continuously on charge. A roof-mounted panel can be positioned clear of obstructions and aligned with the sun, and in this application, the size and weight of the panel is not a major issue. Panels for boats and caravans are widely available, usually with an output of 12 volts, so two or three would have to be wired in series to produce the 24 or 36 volts needed to recharge a typical electric bike battery.

The size of the panels depends on the sort of bike, and the use it gets. A very efficient bike, used occasionally, would require about 40 watt-hours a day. Typically, that could be supplied from a ten watt panel array costing £50, with a battery swap every week or so. In July, the battery might recharge in as little as three days in UK latitudes, but solar radiation more or less disappears for days on end in winter, so some sort of back-up would be required. A more powerful bike, commuting 20 miles a day, would need a much more expensive 100 watt array, with the same seasonal proviso.

With a very low power system of just a few watts peak output, a lead-acid or NiMH battery can be charged directly without the need for a control system. Care must be taken to avoid over-charging, and the battery disconnected as soon as any warmth becomes apparent, because even a low level of over-charging is bad news in the long run. Direct charging might also be possible with a lithium-ion battery, but much depends on the characteristics of the onboard BMS. This device should be able to regulate the output from a small solar panel and cut the charge when the battery is full, but it will not be designed to do this, and it may not work properly - the last thing you want with an expensive and potentially explosive battery.

A more complex, but more reliable system involves feeding the electricity from the solar panel to a 12 volt battery, then through an inverter to produce mains voltage to power a conventional charger. This arrangement is more predictable, because the car battery absorbs the peaks and troughs of solar production, releasing the power only when you want it (even after dark), but it's an expensive, complicated and relatively inefficient option. Easier still is to fit your own grid-linked solar panels, so that recharging from the 'mains' on a sunny day effectively means recharging from the sun.

The cheapest, and by far the easiest, method is simply to buy power from a green energy supplier! Most conventional suppliers offer a 'green' tariff, but to date, none of these are quite what they claim to be. Some provide only a proportion of the energy from renewable sources, with the remainder coming from the sort of technology you might not want to buy into, such as waste incineration or nuclear power. Others do little more than make vague promises to plant trees to offset energy bought on conventional markets. At the time of writing, in the UK only Good Energy (www.goodenergy.co.uk) offers 100% renewable power and builds its own renewable stations, typically wind farms.

Unless you have a very strong desire to make your own 'green' energy point, producing power at home is not really cost-effective, but for all the downsides, it's much more practical than producing the energy required to run an electric car, or even an electric motorcycle, where the panel array and control systems would run into many thousands, or tens of thousands, of pounds.

Solar charging technology might not be cost-effective on a very small scale, but it is already becoming a reality commercially. Sanyo has developed a range of solar-powered 'parking canopies' designed for electric car, motorcycle and bicycle charging.

For Sanyo, a company that produces both solar panels and electric bikes, there is of course some useful synergy here. The panels are mounted on the roof, which also serves to protect the parked machines from rain and sun. These units can be grid-connected or free standing, and are being targeted at corporate users as well as 'green' local authorities. The biggest problem, apart from cost, is dealing with the sheer variety of charging systems, plugs and voltages across the electric vehicle spectrum, although some standardization is now starting to emerge. It is quite conceivable that such charging stations will soon become commonplace in Japan, and the more cycle-friendly western cities such as Freiburg in Germany.

In November 2010 Japanese company Kyocera launched its Solar Recharging Station. Designed for six electric bikes, it claimed a maximum daily output of up to 1,140Wh of electricity. With each recharge requiring around 300Wh, the back-up grid connection is essential, particularly in cloudy weather and at night. The launch price was the equivalent of around £14,500.

Choosing, Using & Maintaining

Choosing a bike

Choosing an electric bike depends on several key factors:

1 How hilly is the terrain?

If the bike is to be used on really steep hills (in excess of 1:7 or 14%), the only practical option is a crank-drive machine, because hub motors are not usually geared to climb this sort of hill without considerable extra input from the rider. There are a few exceptions: some small-wheeled bikes, such as the eZee Quando and some versions of the Nano-Brompton, are fitted with hub motors designed for bigger wheels, giving them low effective gearing. This means they can be very good hill-climbers, but the top speed will be seriously compromised. Most crank-drive bikes will deal with gradients of 1:6 with ease, and with the right gearing will tackle any gradient anywhere, although range will obviously be quite limited if you live at the top of a 1,000 foot hill. Until recently, a crank-drive meant a Panasonic drive, but alternatives have now proliferated, with new units from Yamaha and Sunstar in 2009, Daum in 2010 and Bosch due in 2011. The cheapest start at about £1300 in the UK, but increasing competition is bound to drive prices down. Most crank-drive bikes are produced by European bicycle manufacturers, and are fitted with relatively high quality electrics and good cycle components.

2 How much boost do you need?

The answer depends on many factors. In the past, crank-drive machines tended to provide a fixed ratio of electric to human power, and so the muscle input required was often too high for a weak rider or too low for a strong rider. Modern designs usually offer two or three preset assistance levels, and some can be tuned by the dealer to give *exactly* the level of assistance required. This has helped increase the flexibility of crank-drives over a wide range of applications. For hilly rides, pulling a large load, or simply topping up your muscle power with a bit of extra oomph, the crank-drive is by far the best system.

For the very unfit, or those with serious medical conditions, a hub motor bike with a twistgrip throttle can be more practical, because the twistgrip allows the rider to choose precisely how much power they wish the motor to supply, from nil to 100%. This capability means the motor can be used as a 'get you home' device where, for example, a medical condition might limit your ability to pedal. Machines with a twistgrip throttle vary a great deal in price, from £400 to £1400. Because these bikes are classed as mopeds in much of Europe, they are mostly made in the Far East, with the sort of reliability and component quality one might expect from relatively cheap machines.

3 How much range do you need?

An electric bike allows a typical cyclist to commute over a much greater distance, and at a much higher speed, than they would contemplate if riding a 'normal' bike. Obviously this is particularly true in hilly areas, but the greater speed and more consistent journey times (electric bikes are less affected by head winds) will be useful anywhere.

Over longer distances, other factors come into play. An electric bike rider is less likely to stop for a drink or for a rest, and at journey's end there is less need for a shower. Many electric bikers regularly ride long distances, but for most, the practical maximum commuter range will be about 15 miles, taking just under an hour with most machines, largely irrespective of the terrain.

Try calculating your proposed daily range. In general, it makes sense to double this figure when choosing a bike. This gives an allowance for forgetting an overnight charge (with a new battery at least), the option of making longer or hillier trips (very common when changing from a conventional bike to an electric) and it will give some surplus capacity as the battery deteriorates with age. Whatever the salesmen might claim, all electric bike batteries start to deteriorate from the day they are manufactured, so range will gradually fall. There is also some evidence that lithium-ion batteries have a longer life if they are charged and discharged more shallowly, so a large battery will have an easier life than a small one in this respect. The bottom line is that a battery manufactured to high standards should last longer than a budget model, especially Li-ion ones, but of course you will pay a premium for this. More battery advice is on page 99.

Taking the example of a 10 mile commute and 20 mile daily round trip, the ideal would be a bike with a 40 mile range. Most Raleigh and Kalkhoff crank-drive bikes fitted with the new Derby Cycles 486Wh battery can easily exceed this, and most other crank-drive bikes (and a few hub motors) should be good for 30 miles on full power, and rather more on reduced power, so this sort of daily mileage is certainly achievable. If in doubt, it makes sense to either carry a spare battery or keep a charger at work.

Unfortunately, the mileage figures put out by electric bike manufacturers range from the cheerfully optimistic to the downright bogus, and can be largely ignored. The reality is that most electric bikes consume between 8 and 16Wh/mile, according to top speed and general efficiency, so if you know the size of the battery, you can calculate the range with some accuracy without even seeing the bike. For example, the Kalkhoff Pro-Connect draws 8Wh/mile and has a 270Wh battery, giving a range of about 33 miles. Fit the same bike with the 486Wh battery and range (if the manufacturer's figures are reliable!) will be just under 60 miles. The eZee Forza draws 16Wh/mile and has a 370Wh battery, giving range of about 23 miles. Again, there is now a long range option – 518Wh in this case – giving 32 miles. These are typical figures, and can vary a great deal, but they give a guide. Steep hills, heavy-

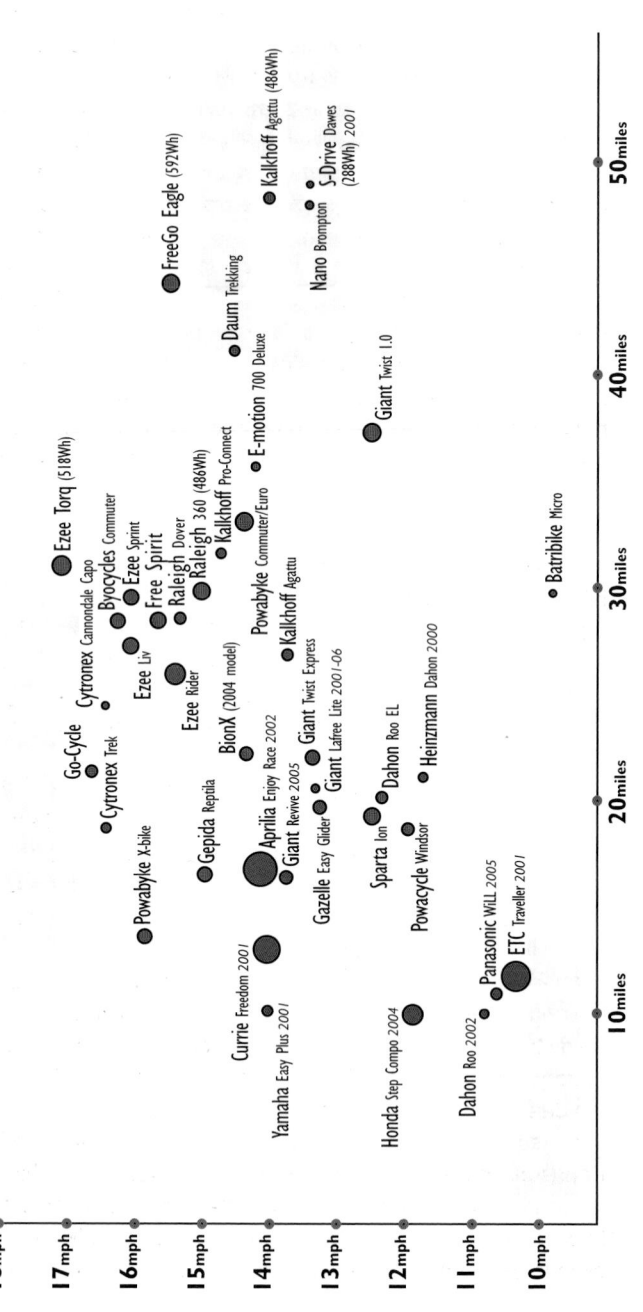

Bikes tested for range and speed

It can be instructive to plot the range of electric bikes against their average speed, those highest and furthest to the right performing best, and those lowest and to the left performing worst. In this case, the efficiency in Wh/mile is also shown - the larger the blob, the greater the fuel consumption. Perhaps not surprisingly, the bikes now out of production (shown in green) tend to be power thirsty, and poor performers in terms of speed and range. But not all... the distance record is still held by the S-Drive Dawes, a long forgotten NiMH bike tested ten years ago. Inefficient bikes can be forgiven if, like the eZee Torq family, they are impressively fast, but remember that bikes this high up the graph are illegal in most countries! Similarly a very slow bike may be acceptable if it is impressively economic. The technical characteristics of the bike can make a huge difference. The Raleigh 360 and long-range Kalkhoff Agattu share the same 486Wh battery, but because the 360 is geared to run faster and uses a relatively inefficient NuVinci transmission, its range is much reduced. All figures – range, average speed and fuel consumption – come from A to B magazine, which tests all bikes on the same road route.

120

handed use of a twistgrip throttle or powerful motors can easily halve the predicted range, while cycling on a low power setting (very effective with crank-drives) and gentle fuel saving techniques can more or less double the range.

Because electric bike range is quite limited, you'll need an efficient machine if you intend to ride a long way, particularly if loaded up with touring gear. Once again, the crank-drives tend to do better, although a good hub motor, like the sensorless BLDC Tongxin can do just as well if ridden sensitively. The least efficient machines tend to be heavy Chinese bikes with hub motors, crude 'on-off' pedelec control systems and a limited pedal gear range leaving the motor to do most of the work. The golden rule is to look for a bike that's easy and pleasant to ride with the power off. A free-running, pleasant bike suggests that the rolling efficiency is good and the seating position and general geometry allow the rider to add muscle power efficiently. If the bike feels heavy, slothful and unresponsive with the power off it will never break any records for economy with the power on. The good bikes, not surprisingly, tend to be good conventional bikes that have been converted to electric assist, such as the Cytronex range or the Nano-Brompton (both fitted with the Tongxin motor).

4 Reliability

Reliability, as you might expect, is closely linked to price, and once again, European bikes and Japanese or German electronics tend to do better than Chinese equipment, but there is no direct correlation. A £1400 Chinese bike will certainly perform better than a £400 Chinese bike, but in terms of reliability, it can't begin to compete with a £1400 European bike. If you're commuting in all weathers, you'll want to be sure that the bike starts every morning and is covered by a reasonable guarantee.

Frame guarantees vary a lot, and are pretty meaningless, because frame failures are rare. With an electric bike, you want to know that the electrics are covered for at least 12 months, because failures often occur early, but once bedded down, electronics should last for many years. Lithium-ion batteries are very different. These batteries have a finite life even under laboratory conditions, and they can fail at any time, either dramatically or gradually. A guarantee is important because they are very expensive - £250 to £450 being typical. Some manufacturers guarantee their batteries for three to six months – acceptable enough for a cheaper, more predictable, lead-acid battery, but not for an expensive and delicate lithium-ion battery. Look for a no-quibble guarantee of at least 12 months, and make sure the dealer has batteries in stock at a reasonable price. As with so much else, the Japanese manufacturers do better than the Chinese, with both the Yamaha and Panasonic batteries guaranteed for two years. Some Chinese bike distributors are responding by offering 18 month guarantees, and a few have risked two years. Try to choose a company that will be still be around in two years! Some distributors sell electric bikes until the warranty claims start rolling in, then melt quietly away.

The better European manufacturers are now thinking of stepping up to a three -year battery guarantee, and Koga has taken the bold step of offering an additional three years on a two-year guarantee for £165. As its batteries cost £800, this is probably worthwhile, but only because it's a lithium-ion battery... NiMh batteries should last five years without complications. Improved warranties of this kind will put pressure on those offering short or restricted guarantees to follow suit, and that in turn will encourage manufacturers to put reliability at the top of their research agenda.

With NiMH technology, the guarantee period is less of an issue, because battery life should be much greater than other types, but the availability of NiMH batteries is now very restricted. Lead-acid batteries tend to have a short and cheerful life, so guarantees of less than 12 months are common. But the cells are easily and cheaply replaced, and that may tip the balance in favour of such old technology, if the weight of the battery is not a big issue.

The availability of spares, and dealers able to service electric bikes, are still major issues. Small dealers selling cheap Chinese bikes are unlikely to hold spares, yet these are the machines most likely to have problems. On the other hand, the big manufacturers with numerous local dealers tend to be very good. Giant continues to take electric bikes seriously, providing spares for all its machines, and the arrival of Raleigh and Trek is very good news.

Cycle shops often look suspiciously at electric bikes, and with good reason. Fault-finding on a sensor-controlled BLDC motor can baffle even an experienced electrical engineer, and external (let alone internal) wiring can be fiendishly complex. The crank-drives tend to score points on servicing, because all the electronics and unfamiliar mechanical items are in one unit, so the rest of the bicycle is effectively a normal machine that can be repaired and serviced by any cycle shop. Mechanical problems with crank-drives are quite rare, but they can usually be repaired by a competent engineer. Electronic problems are even rarer, but generally terminal, resulting in replacement of the complete drive unit. This is very expensive, but once again, it's a simple mechanical task that can be carried out by any competent cycle shop.

With a hub motor bike, failures tend to be confined to the control electronics, switches or wiring, as motors rarely go wrong. Repair is generally a matter of swapping components until the source of the fault is revealed, but this approach is only practical for an experienced service centre with all the parts to hand, and examination beyond a general search for loose wires or blown fuses is unlikely to be worth attempting for a conventional cycle shop.

If buying a bike, ask the dealer what will happen if it goes wrong, and don't accept the promise that it won't, because compared to a normal bike, failures are relatively common, especially on cheaper machines. If buying from a small distributor, many of whom are one-man businesses, ask to see their service centre. That one man may, of course, be an electronics genius and expert on the brand, but many are general wheeler dealers who have got into electric bikes for the money. These sort of people may not even know how to change a fuse, leaving you high and dry if the simplest fault occurs.

5 Foldability, weight and convenience

Almost all folding electric bikes are Chinese in origin, and like most conventional Chinese folding bikes, they are heavy, inconvenient, hard to ride and poorly geared. Some are better than others, but few of these machines are worth considering. As a rule, the best folders are conversions based on existing high quality folding bikes, such as the Brompton or Dahon. Even then, the machines can be quite heavy. The best at the time of writing is undoubtedly the Nano-Brompton, because the battery is in the quick-release front luggage, reducing the weight of the bike itself to around 14kg, according to model. That's still heavy in folding bike terms, but lighter and more compact and convenient than most of the opposition. Other clever European designs include the GoCycle at 16.7kg complete with battery, but this bike takes apart rather than folding, so it's hardly a train/bus commuter.

This a typical budget folder - 20-inch wheels with a rear hub motor and rather crude pedal motion sensing device. First impressions on riding may be favourable (especiallly if the price is right!) - this example was speedy and comfortable.

However, unless you are only going to be folding the bike infrequently, the folded package is a true handful. All but the better models such as Brompton and Dahon are unwieldy with a tendency to unravel unless secured with bungees or similar.

123

Whether an electric bike folds or not, the question of weight is important. In terms of performance, the real difference between a very heavy bike weighing 40kg and a very light one weighing 20kg is actually just 17%, rather than the 100% you might expect. This is because we need to look at the gross weight of the machine when analysing performance. The gross weight of a 40kg electric bike, with a 70kg rider and 10kg of luggage on board will be 120kg. Removing 20kg from the bike will probably make it handle better, but it will have a barely discernible effect on range and acceleration.

Weight reduction makes a considerable difference in other ways. The UK's stated legal maximum weight limit for an electric bike is 40kg, a weight that some people couldn't tilt onto the centre stand, let alone carry up a flight of steps. For the first 15 years, most electric bikes weighed close to this legal maximum, but the machines have become much lighter in the last decade, a trend started by the superb 2000-2006 Giant Lafree, which weighed 22-26kg according to model.

After the Lafree, the downward trend continued, with the Kalkhoff Pro-Connect hitting 21kg in 2007, the Cytronex Trek 17kg in 2008, and the (admittedly single-speed) Cytronex Capo just 14kg in 2009. Another Cytronex, the carbon fibre Cannondale Super 6, tips the scales at a claimed 12.9kg, and in 2010 cost a staggering £4400. These are cutting edge figures, but such weight reductions are not confined to the top end: in the same period, the weight of a typical low-tech Chinese bike has come down even more. In 2002, the 40kg Powabyke Commuter was not unusual, but by 2009 its replacement, the X-byke, raised few eyebrows with a weight of 24kg, and today even the heaviest, clunkiest electric bike will weigh 28kg or less.

Whatever your perceptions, you will enjoy a lightweight electric bike much more than a heavier one. Lighter bikes may not be much faster, but they're more agile, more responsive, easier to manoeuvre, and generally much more fun to own and use. They cost more, but they also hold their value much better.

Buying secondhand

Buying a secondhand electric bike requires a degree of caution. The cheaper Far Eastern machines will have limited warranty cover and low quality components, so even a three month-old bike can prove a bit of a gamble. Remember to check out the battery warranty before buying the bike, and find out whether there are problems transferring it to a new owner, because a bike without a warranty is worth a lot less and may be hard to resell. Always insist on a ride, and try to find a hill, because even the ropiest secondhand bike can feel smooth and powerful with a freshly charged battery on the flat. If the seller claims to have forgotten to charge the battery, be very suspicious. If they're selling the bike, the chances are they've detected premature battery failure, and discovered how much a replacement will cost.

The consequence of all this uncertainty will be (or should be) a very low sale price. Cheaper Far Eastern machines selling for up to £800 brand new a year or two ago, are changing hands for just £200 secondhand. Of the older bikes, only the crank-drive Giant Lafree commands a high price, and good ten year-old examples can cost £500 or more. Giant keeps stocks of key spares, including batteries, chargers, chain rings and power switches for the Lafree, and indeed all its machines, and this after-sales care has done much to keep the bikes popular secondhand.

Amongst the modern bikes, the evidence seems to point towards the current UK best sellers, such as the Kalkhoff, Raleigh and E-motion, being the best buys of the future. These mid-range crank-drive European bikes seem to be keeping their value, but with few coming up secondhand (always a good sign) depreciation is hard to judge. Much will depend on the longevity of the Sanyo and Derby Cycles Li-ion batteries, and it's still too early to say how long these will last.

There are few ten year old electric bikes still in regular daily use. The Giant Lafree is one of the better performers secondhand, thanks to its reliable Panasonic crank-drive, and Giant's policy of stocking spares, even though the bikes went out of production in 2006. This example is fitted with a replacement battery from a different Lafree and new front forks and head light.

Using an electric bike

Commuting

For many people the classic raison d'être of the electric bike. Mileage can be higher than for a typical conventional bike commute and improved speed and reliability are key factors. In an urban or suburban situation, an electric bike will get you to work faster than almost any other form of transport. Journey times can be as precise as a Swiss watch, with the extra power making light work of hills and headwinds. At journey's end the rider may be hot, but will rarely be sweaty, so the shower and change of clothes preferred by conventional bike riders may be unnecessary, saving even more time.

Load carrying

From small child trailers to heavily-laden cargo trailers, load carrying or hauling is something that electric bikes excel at. An electric bike can tackle a whole range of tasks that might previously have seemed the prerequisite of the car: taking two, or even three, children to school, riding to an out-of-town supermarket for a hatchback-sized shop, hauling wood, coal, tools, smallholding produce, recycling, the list is endless. A good electric bike will haul up to its own weight (including rider) at a reasonable speed, so with the right trailer, expect to carry up to 70-100kg. Range with this sort of load might be cut by half, but in urban areas, it's usually adequate. Provided there are no big hills involved, a good solid Chinese bike with plenty of power and a twistgrip control is ideal for towing. With a trailer behind, weight is a positive advantage, especially over the rear of the bike, so a rear hub motor plus a handful of derailleur gears are probably adequate. A twistgrip is ideal for getting the power on in advance of a hill - essential for keeping a big load moving at a reasonable speed. If steep hills are involved, a crank-drive may be the only option, but the rather slow gear changes can make life difficult.

Loaded touring

A good electric bike can make light work of a heavy touring load, even in hilly country, but again, battery capacity can be an issue unless you have the willpower to keep the motor switched off most of the time, and that can be quite hard. Most cyclists can ride a laden bike 40-50 miles in a day, and the really fit can expect to double that. The best electric bikes now have a range of 40 miles or more, so power-assisted touring has become a practical proposition. By carrying two or even three, batteries, considerable distances can be covered.

Charging three batteries overnight may just be possible with the better machines, but in the end, the amount of equipment needed to provide assistance over long daily rides may rather spoil the simplicity and purity of the cycle touring concept for some. That said, even with a spare battery and charger, electric bike cycle touring can make longer challenging tours more of a pleasure than a toil for riders with basic fitness, previously put off by the sheer effort of moving all their kit with them over long distances and hilly terrain.

Electric bikes make all sorts of strange loads practical. This hub drive Byocycle belonging to one of the authors has hauled heavier loads, but this pair of five-foot by six-foot fence panels has to be one of the biggest. Too big for a car or small van, the panels were strapped into a child trailer, with the weight well forward over the rear tyre of the bike. The load weighed around 60kg, the trailer 10kg, and the passenger (sitting on the rack, while the rider stood up) 30kg - a grand total of 100kg, and a graphic example of the sort of loads these bikes can haul.

One possible line of development is the Gruber Assist. In this very lightweight system, the motor is safely hidden away in the frame tube driving the bottom bracket with external wiring kept to a minimum. Assistance is relatively slight, but enough to make life significantly easier. This simple (and more importantly to some, hidden!) means of power assistance would seem particularly suited to off-road touring up long steady gradients that would normally sap the energy, especially when carrying a touring load. Power-assisted cycle touring is a relatively new phenomenon, but all the pointers are that it will be a big growth area in the future, if battery range continues to improve.

Off-road

Front hub motor electric bikes have much to recommend them off-road, because with pedal effort to the rear wheel and electrical effort to the front, they are less likely to lose traction on rough or steep surfaces, and they can be fitted with a wide range of gears. But although electric bikes perform well on tracks and fire trails, they are not really suitable for rough off-road use. Heavy batteries can work loose, delicate wires snag on obstructions, and even the lightest bikes are difficult to lift over, or guide through, obstacles. On the other hand, power assistance is very liberating off-road, making such rides exhilarating and fitness enhancing without the feeling of having trained for the marines!

Steve Punchard of Electric Mountain Bikes fits powerful Heinzmann motors (oddly enough, usually in the rear wheel) and a battery carried in a rucksack on the rider's back. This helps to keep the weight of the bike down, making it more manoeuvrable and reducing shock loads on bumps. The battery pack has a quick-release connector should the rider be thrown off!

Once again though, the real obstacle is battery range. Riding off-road requires anything from two to ten times as much power as riding at a steady speed on good tarmac surfaces, and electric bikes have limited battery capacity at the best of times. Once the battery is flat, they can be heavy and awkward to ride home unassisted. As with cycle touring, assisted off-road riding is set to explode as and when the battery technology improves.

The Heinzmann hub motor is one of the few that has successfully been adapted to off-roading. This example is by Electric Mountain Bikes and features a high torque version of the motor, especially useful for steeper, rougher tracks. The battery is in a small backpack and the power lead can be seen leading to a controller under the seat.
Should rider and bike part company the 'bail-out' connector comes apart automatically to avoid damage.

Riding techniques

Pedelecs

Electric bicycles are hybrid vehicles, meaning that they draw power from two sources - usually electrical and muscle power - and mix these two forms of energy in various proportions to drive the machine forward. With some electric bikes, like the more sophisticated pedelecs, the power mixing is carried out entirely automatically, the machine sensing pedal effort and feeding in electrical power in the same - or greater or lesser - proportions according to the position of a small switch on the handlebars. The switch usually adjusts motor power, but it can also adjust the level of muscle power at which the electrical power cuts in, which isn't quite the same thing, but has a similar effect.

Typical examples are the crank-drive models from Kalkhoff, Monark, E-motion, Raleigh, Daum, Gepida, Scott and Sparta, and hub-motor bikes such as the Gazelle and Giant. Pedelecs of this kind are the easiest to ride because all you have to do is pedal and change gear as normal, but they provide limited opportunities for riding creatively to get the best from the bike.

With hub motor pedelecs, the motor speed is linked to road speed, so the motor will start weakly at low road speed, gather power rapidly at mid-speed, and grow weak again at higher speed. This motor/road speed relationship is fixed and cannot be altered.

With the crank-drive bikes, the motor speed is, of course linked to pedal speed, so assistance is weak at low pedal speed, strong at medium pedal speed, and weak again at high pedal speed. This brings in a new variable, because the way you use the gear change will have a major effect on the way the motor works. A common mistake by those used to a conventional bike is to spin the pedals too fast, known as a high 'cadence'. If the pedals spin too fast, the motor never quite catches up, and the bike can feel weak and ineffective. Some modern designs have been tuned to work quite well with a high pedal cadence, but as a general rule, crank-drive bikes need to be ridden at a lowish cadence to get the best from the motor. Counter-intuitively, the slower you pedal, the harder the motor works, although *very* low cadence will cause the motor to run too slowly, which will reduce efficiency and again give weak assistance. With practice finding the best pedal cadence soon becomes second nature.

The only other thing to watch is the way you actually make the gear changes. Crank-drives are quite tough on geared hubs, which are often the weakest part of the design. To give the hub a slightly easier life, avoid pedalling during gear changes, even if the hub seems willing to take the punishment. The most common hub gear fitted to electric bikes is the Shimano Nexus 8-speed, a hub which changes very well under load from the pedals, but on an electric bike, the stress can be just too much for it, resulting in some nasty noises. An exception are the bikes built with the Velocity Series Hybrid system (see page 94), where the gears are not affected by the motor torque, so power can be kept on through the gear changes without doing any harm.

What crank-drive electric bikes have been waiting for is continuously variable gears, or CVT, which give a completely smooth progression from a standing start to top speed. The first American-made NuVinci automatic hubs were slow to be adopted by manufacturers because they were heavy and relatively expensive, but the lighter, cheaper NuVinci N360 is expected to be fitted to an increasing range of electric bikes from 2011. This hub matches a crank-drive well, but the gear twistgrip becomes stiff to move when the motor is working hard (on a normal bike, you can reduce pedal effort momentarily when changing gear), and the inefficiency of the hub means a disappointingly short battery range, especially in hilly terrain.

E-bikes

Throttle-controlled E-bikes are hybrids too, but in this case the rider usually has complete control over the level of electrical assistance. This can be useful for all sorts of reasons: precise control makes life much easier off-road, and the ability to stop pedalling and run the bike entirely on electric power is helpful when your legs are feeling weak, for whatever reason. It can also keep your feet high and dry riding through a flood, or allow you to keep power on while leaning steeply into a corner, where a cyclist would normally have to stop pedalling. Another real advantage - as when taking off from traffic lights - is that the electric assist can be kept on full power whilst changing gear.

There are various useful techniques on hills too. On a very shallow hill, it makes sense to attack the climb on full power, riding as fast as possible to keep the motor speed in the most efficient area for as long as possible. On a series of smaller switchback hills, the technique, again, is to ride as fast as possible, getting as much impetus behind the bike as you can to rush each hill.

On a long steep climb, the opposite is true, because speed will soon fall whatever you do, and low motor speed is bad news in terms of power and economy. Allow the speed to fall gradually and naturally, changing down through the gears and pedalling fairly hard. If speed falls to the point where the motor is straining, gradually reduce the throttle setting. Because power-assistance is becoming inefficient at such a low motor speed, reducing it doesn't have the negative impact you might expect, and with care you can climb the hill *and* save a lot of battery capacity. Climbing a hill this way requires some effort from the rider, and it might seem odd to suggest this, but with an E-bike a steep hill needs input from both motor and rider - you can always get your breath back on the flat.

Other fuel-saving measures with a twistgrip throttle are perhaps more obvious, but no less important. In stop-start traffic, it's very tempting to take advantage of the bike's reserves of acceleration, but you should keep the throttle closed. It really makes little sense to waste power in this way, except at road junctions and roundabouts, where the extra acceleration can be a great aid to safety.

Maintenance

What maintenance? There is a very little regular maintenance to be done with an electric bike, but a number of small, simple tasks will make the bike much more reliable. If the battery or bike has an exposed fuse (rare these days), it's worth removing it every few months, checking the fuse and holder for signs of burning or overheating and cleaning the contacts with very fine emery paper or wire wool. The same goes for the battery-to-bike contacts, which can be exposed to the weather, and often cause problems, especially in the wet. An occasional clean with very fine abrasive, followed by a polish with a solvent such as petrol, will keep the power flowing smoothly.

With electronics and handlebar switches and controls, water ingress can be a major issue. If rain can work its way in it will, and just a couple of drops is enough to disable sophisticated electronics. Modern switches are generally sealed, but this wasn't so with older designs. The power switch on the Giant Lafree was a frequent offender, although this can be completely cured by working a little Vaseline into the gap between the rotating and stationary parts. If water has already got in, the switch will have to be dismantled and dried first - a delicate and tricky job. Make sure that the tiny ball bearing doesn't escape!

Many modern bikes are fitted with a diagnostic system. The most basic simply use the existing Li-ion battery management system to provide information on battery faults. The Panasonic battery, fitted to many pedelecs, will give an indication of cell capacity rather than state of charge if the test button is held down for more than five seconds. More complex onboard computers put diagnostic circuitry on the bike itself, enabling many more faults to be diagnosed. Some, such as the Gazelle and Sparta, allow the bike to be plugged into a laptop computer, where all sorts of parameters - such as top speed, maximum and minimum power and pedelec assist ratios - can be adjusted. The bike can also be disabled to prevent theft, and the Daum can even be instructed to report its whereabouts in the event of theft!

Any diagnosis system is better than none, of course, but as a general rule, all the simpler ones do is tell you what you already know. The bike doesn't work, and the chances are the control unit or battery needs replacing. On the more sophisticated versions, the ability to fine-tune the bike to suit local conditions and rider preference sounds useful, but with strict legal limits on speed and power, there is relatively little scope for big changes, unless the dealer is willing to break the law. A downside you might not expect is that these systems can 'crash' like any other complex computer system. If this happens, the power-assistance is generally put out of action until the bike has been taken to a dealer and 'rebooted'. On the Sparta Ion, the computer needs to be rebooted every time the rear wheel is removed... as if punctures weren't already tedious enough!

There is another slightly un-nerving side to all this gathering and dissemination of information. On some systems, the technician can download information on your riding style, daily mileage and even your movements, and you might feel there are civil liberty issues involved here. As we saw in the previous chapter, Koga Myata will declare the warranty invalid if the battery has been stored without being trickle charged, and the dealer will be able to interrogate the BMS to prove that you are the guilty party.

Motor & controller maintenance

The motor gears, whether situated on the crank, the hub or elsewhere, are usually pre-packed with grease. After a considerable mileage this grease will dry out, making the hub noisy, although excessive noise and rough running can also point to something more serious. It makes sense to top-up or redistribute the grease around the gearbox when the motor is off the bike for some other reason, but take care – hub motors and crank-drives are complex and sophisticated machines and heavy-handed maintenance can prove very expensive. The motor itself should need no maintenance.

Older DC motors like those on the Powabyke are fitted with brushes. Sometimes these are accessible beneath an external panel, but in many cases the entire motor and gearbox will need to be dismantled. Either way, brush wear should be very gradual, but it's something worth checking when fault finding as a possible cause of intermittent running or complete failure.

If kept dry and handled with reasonable care, electric bike controllers should work for years, which is lucky because only the very oldest designs (Powabyke again) are economically repairable by an engineer with a soldering iron.

Battery maintenance

Batteries should never be dismantled unless you know what you are doing, and they should preferably be fully discharged, with any external fuse(s) removed. Older lead-acid battery cases can be easily dismantled, checked, cleaned and reassembled. The casing will usually contain three SLA 12-volt batteries, each having 'Lucar' or screw terminals, so they can be replaced as and when they fail. The most common battery is the 12/14Ah family, measuring 150mm long by 100mm wide and tall. These are quite common, and cost from £20 for a basic type designed for burglar alarms and standby applications, to £30 for traction batteries, or anything up to £100 for a motorcycle version capable of turning over and starting a large motorcycle engine. The economy type will work well on an electric bike, but life will be limited compared to a proper traction battery which will be better able to withstand the vibration and temperature extremes on a bicycle. The motorcycle kind is not worth buying unless a good secondhand example is available. Barring mechanical damage, a lead-acid battery box can be dismantled and fitted with new batteries many times over.

More recent NiMH battery casings tend to be difficult to dismantle, and much more difficult to reassemble! Some contain sophisticated electronics, which must be treated with care, and there may be one or more 'car-type' fuses inside the casing - often one for charging and another for power output.

There will be anything up to 30 individual cells, which are usually spot-welded together, making replacement a difficult and dangerous task. But it's all quite practical for a competent engineer familiar with high-current electrics, and most of these batteries can be revitalised with new cells at a cost of around £6 to £10 per cell. Modern lithium-ion batteries should not be dismantled under any circumstances. There are no user-serviceable parts inside, and the electronics are complex, sensitive, and the main line of defence against a potentially catastrophic failure. A carelessly wielded screwdriver inside the casing could short circuit one or more lithium cells, with unpredictable results.

One thing you can and should do involves a pen rather than a screwdriver: keep a record of the range per charge, the number of charges (and the time taken to charge), and if you have a watt-hour meter, how much power the battery takes from the mains supply. If all goes well, and you sell the machine in serviceable condition, a user log will give the purchaser confidence that you have looked after the bike. If the worst happens and the battery fails prematurely, an accurate log will strengthen your case in the event of a dispute with the manufacturer. It also gives a clue as to when your battery has actually failed, because failure tends to be gradual rather than catastrophic.

The accepted industry standard for a failed battery varies according to the chemistry. NiCd are deemed to have failed at 60% capacity, NiMH at 75% and Li-ion at 80%, measured by discharging the battery at a carefully controlled rate at a set temperature. The problem for electric bike manufacturers and consumers is that although this relatively small loss of capacity might render the battery a failure in an industrial or military application, it's a high bar for an electric bike battery - which will still have plenty of useful life left in it after a loss of 20% of its capacity.

At the time of writing, there is no universally accepted failure criteria for electric bike traction batteries, but an agreement should come soon. This lack of guidance didn't really matter with cheap lead-acid batteries or relatively expensive but long lived NiMH, but it matters a great deal with today's unpredictable and expensive Li-ion batteries.

You can get a clue of the battery's capacity by logging the watt-hours drawn from the mains to give a full charge, but as older batteries discharge less efficiently, this method can give very optimistic results. Similarly, it's possible to fit a power meter to an electric bike, that will accurately record the watt-hours discharged, but, as this is working in 'real' conditions, it will generally give a pessimistic result. With batteries now costing £250 to £500, bike manufacturers and distributors are understandably keen to avoid replacing them under warranty, but if you keep a record of changes in the battery's behaviour from new, you will have a clue if and when to make a warranty claim, and be in a strong position should you subsequently need to make a legal claim. As a rule of thumb, if the battery is unable to charge or discharge beyond at least 70% of its new capacity, it should be considered a warranty failure.

Wear & tear

Electric bike frames have to handle a great deal more power than normal bikes, but the way the power is delivered is less stressful for the bike. A cyclist pulls and pushes on the handlebars and saddle in order to put power strokes into the crank. This can put a great strain on the frame and other components, but on an electric bike around half the power is generated very smoothly by the motor, so there can actually be less strain on the bike, unless it is ridden very hard. A front hub motor puts a little more stress on the forks and headset bearings, and there is some evidence that the headset and spokes may need to be adjusted more often, but there should be no other issues because the front wheel has little other work to do. A careful watch should be kept on the wheel nuts and anti-rotation washers with hub motors, because they will be under a lot more stress and liable to work loose, especially when the bike is new.

A rear hub motor is mounted in a stronger part of the bike, but in this case the spokes are carrying the weight of the rider, as well as transmitting torque from the motor and rider, which can cause problems. Ideally, these bikes should be built with tandem spokes, rims and other upgraded components, but no manufacturers seem to have gone down this more expensive route. If problems persist even after careful spoke tensioning, an upgrade to heavier spokes could be worthwhile.

Crank motors can put a lot of stress on the chain, but chain life doesn't seem to be badly affected. Hub and derailleur gears, on the other hand, can suffer. Either type is liable to wear out more quickly, and the only solution is to change gear carefully, by cutting pedal effort to zero before moving the gear lever, and not resuming until the gear is fully engaged.

Fault finding

Complete failure, no power or capacity lights, bike used regularly

Look first to see if there are any warning lights illuminated. If not, check for a fuse failure. If the fuse is OK, check with a voltmeter to see if there is any output from the battery. If there is no output from a lead-acid or NiMH battery, an internal fuse may have failed, which will probably mean dismantling the battery casing, not something to attempt unless you know what you are doing. Bear in mind that fuses rarely fail spontaneously, so a blown fuse may well be indicative of a problem elsewhere.

The BMS on lithium-ion batteries may shut down spontaneously if the battery is subjected to a heavy current drain, or other shock. A quick recharge may be enough to reset the battery, but again, the shut-down probably indicates a problem elsewhere.

If the battery has a healthy voltage output the problem will be on the bike. A loose or broken wire is a possibility, but sadly, such simple solutions are rare! Electronic failure is much more likely, and a control unit malfunction is not usually economically repairable.

Complete failure, no power or capacity lights, bike used irregularly

With older technologies showing these symptoms it could well be that the battery is flat, possibly because the 'ignition' or lights have been left on. If lead-acid batteries are left discharged for a long period, the cells will have been destroyed, and a quick attempt to recharge will confirm this. With NiMH, a recharge is much more likely to be successful, and with luck the battery may be fully restored to health after a few charges and discharges. With lithium-ion, a long period of storage can cause the BMS to shut down temporarily, and if the battery voltage gets very low, there may not be enough power to get it running again, causing a permanent failure. Sometimes, a recharge will work, but if the battery refuses to accept a charge, a few days storage in a warm place off the bike may get things working again. If not, you may need specialist help quickly.

Complete failure, power and capacity lights work as normal

A lot depends on the circumstances. If the bike fails suddenly while working hard, the most likely cause is a major control box failure. This is rare, but if it happens, there's very little you can do, except replace the control unit. Some batteries, control systems and motors are designed to spontaneously shut down when over-stressed, and this state may be indicated on the diagnostic system. In this case, it's usually enough to turn the power off, wait a few minutes for the controller to cool down and retry.

If the bike fails to work after falling over or being involved in an accident, check that the brake levers are returning properly. Many electric bikes have power cut-off switches in one or both brake levers that may switch the power off if the lever is depressed by just a few millimetres, a mechanical problem easily missed even by an electronics engineer.

If the failure occurs after a fall, or (with a front hub motor machine) after the handlebars have been swung round violently, suspect a broken wire, especially with sensor-controlled DC motors. Gently push the machine backwards. If there is a lot of resistance in reverse, but none with the ignition off, a broken sensor wire is very likely. This can't be repaired on the road, but sometimes the motor can be 'tricked' into spinning by knocking the wheel or casing, causing the motor shaft to jump round slightly and pick up speed. This may get you home if you can manage to keep moving and keep the throttle open! Wiring looms should be available, but fitting them can be a major operation, and some are integral with the motor. An experienced electrician will need to check each of the wires for continuity to find the broken one. Temporarily, another wire can be run outside the loom to get the bike running again. Not very pretty, but an effective and cheap repair. Complete or intermittent failure in the rain can be caused by water getting into the control box or wiring junctions. In some cases the bike appears to recover, but the water will continue to cause damage and the chances are the machine will fail completely a few weeks down the line. Early Chinese-made bikes (presumably designed for the Californian climate) had unprotected connectors beneath the crank, and this made them very susceptible to damp, especially with the delicate sensor wires. In an emergency a shot of moisture-repelling fluid such as WD40 may solve the problem, but in the longer term, the wires will have to be protected from water ingress.

Bike runs as normal, but with reduced power

There are all sorts of possible causes, from flat tyres to partially seized bearings, but by far the most likely cause is battery weakness - low speed and poor hill-climbing are the first signs of a low voltage and imminent failure. All battery technologies give out a lower voltage when worked hard, and this effect tends to become more and more marked with age. There's no cure, but you might find the bike goes further on a lower power setting, or, in the case of E-bikes, with a gentler touch on the twistgrip throttle.

Other faults are rare, but they can happen. The bike may have locked itself into a low power setting. Sometimes turning the power off and back on will cure this, but in many cases you will be stuck with low speed and extra effort. If the bike can be plugged into a dealer laptop, it's conceivable that one of the adjustable parameters can be reset.

Bike runs as normal, but with mechanical noise

Gear or bearing failures are rare, but they can happen, and this is by far the most likely cause of increased noise. Bearings are cheap and easy to replace, but failure of sun-and-planet gears will probably cost more to repair than the motor is worth.

Motor runs, but there is no drive

Most electric bike motors are fitted with a one-way clutch, and if this fails all drive will be lost. As with other gearbox failures, replacement or repair are unlikely be economical, unless spares are easily and cheaply available from the importer. The one-way clutch can also jam so that it transmits drive in both directions. If this happens, the motor will act as a generator and may well destroy the control unit too.

Motor runs continuously but on full power

On older DC machines, the electronic controls could fail on full power, making the machine shoot off whenever the key was turned. Though conceivable, this sort of failure is much less likely on BLDC or sensorless BLDC motors. Either way, it is almost certain that a new control unit will be needed.

Lithium-ion batteries are very expensive, and few (principally the family of bikes using the Panasonic system) are interchangeable. But because the monitoring electronics are inside the casing with this type of battery, any battery of the same voltage can be used, provided there is somewhere safe and convenient to mount it. Here, an eZee battery keeps a Byocycle on the road. This simple conversion has no ignition switch... the bike is turned on and off by removing a terminal!

Kits & Specials

Why kits?

Electric bike kits are packages of bolt-on parts that enable conversion of a conventional bike to an electric. Although sometimes cheaper than buying a complete electric bike, they represent only a tiny percentage of total electric bike sales. Perhaps the main reason is that manufacturers simply find it easier to sell electric-assist systems in large volumes to existing cycle manufacturers. Other contributing factors are, no doubt, the buyer's general preference for ready-to-ride electric bikes and the reticence of bike shops to sell, fit and maintain kits, when ready made bikes are easily and cheaply available.

Pros

However, despite their relative rarity, retrofit kits have several advantages over complete electric bikes:

- You might want a bit of power assistance on a cherished non-electric machine that fits you like a glove.
- The type of bikes you prefer may not be available in electric versions (folders and recumbents are cases in point, though more are gradually trickling onto the market).
- Kits can be swapped between bikes, giving the option of trying electric-assist on several different machines.
- Those who love fiddling with bikes may be intrigued by the endless permutations of motor kits and bikes - the performance of a kit will be affected by the bike it is fitted to. Hub motors are usually geared for a specific wheel size to ensure they stay within the speed limit set for electric bikes (usually 15mph/24km/h), but if you fit a hub motor geared for a larger wheel it will give excellent pulling power at low speeds, producing an excellent hill-climber or load-hauler.
- Several companies have started offering kits ready-fitted to popular wheel sizes, and the recent increase in competition in this area has meant a greater choice of kits for a wider range of wheel sizes.
- Kits can be great value for money. If you have a 'recipient' bike languishing in the shed or have picked up a decent quality steed at a good price, it can be converted quite cheaply. Careful secondhand purchasing should get you a nice quality non-electric bike for around £150. Add on the price of a decent electric kit and for around £800-£900 it's possible to create an electric bike of far greater quality than a new, custom made electric bike in a similar price bracket.
- Kits also make it possible to put together an incredibly lightweight electric bike - a total weight of 20kg is quite feasible with most of the kits detailed here, and if money really is no object (and you can live with a tiny battery) the remarkable Gruber Assist will produce an ultra lightweight system.

- You might also wish to build something faster or more powerful than the law allows. This would, of course, be illegal for use on public roads, but could be just the thing for moving heavy loads or even passengers around a private work site. Kits containing illegal motors and control units are now flooding the market from the Far East, and many people are using them on the road, either innocently or otherwise. A fast and/or powerful kit can be a lot of fun, but bear in mind that once you exceed the parameters set in the regulations, you are on your own. In most territories, your bicycle will be treated as a moped in the eyes of the law, and subject to the much more stringent penalties that come with motorcycle use. If you are found responsible for injuring someone, you will be in very serious trouble. The electric bike legislation is a safety net for your protection, and you leave it at your own risk.

Cons

- Some kits are easier to fit than others, but all require at least basic bike DIY skills.
- If you want a crank-drive system your choice is currently next to nil. With one rather expensive exception you are limited to hub motors (or a secondhand Sunstar crank-drive kit, which is extremely hard to find).
- Often kits will not look as neat as off-the-peg electric bikes. External cable runs secured with cable ties are the order of the day (the almost entirely concealed Gruber Assist kit being an exception), whilst most complete electric bikes come with cables hidden within the frame.
- Not all kits will fit all bikes. Attention needs to be paid to getting the correct speed of motor for your size of wheel and finding a suitable battery mounting point. Front hub motor kits are generally easier to fit than rear hub kits simply because they don't involve interfering with the gear system. Some kits, such as the Gruber Assist, must be fitted by a qualified fitter, and with other sophisticated devices such as the BionX, this is certainly recommended.
- As with complete electric bikes, quality varies from kit to kit: Heinzmann in particular stands out because of its high quality connectors and cabling giving you the confidence to produce smooth tight cable runs, minimising the kit's visual impact. Whilst there are no bespoke retrofit kits for specific kinds of bikes such as folders (with the exception of the Nano-Brompton kit), recumbents or cargo bikes, some stand out as being most suitable for particular applications and types of bike. The *Most likely users* heading under each kit gives an indication of its most suitable applications.

Smaller, lighter easier to fit kits seem to be an emerging trend, with many poised to come on the market. Shimano's STePS, announced in 2010 for a launch in 2011, could generate a huge rise in the popularity of retrofit kits, thanks in part to bike shops being familiar with Shimano products and after-sales back up. The Shimano batteries have a claimed recharge life of 800 cycles and the hub motor boasts regenerative capacity.

138

Existing electric bike companies such as Wisper, Urban Mover and Cytronex have also seen the potential of a 'universal' kit based on their respective products, but designed to fit the majority of bikes. Their 2011 launches are eagerly awaited.

Kit buying checklist

Buying criteria are as per standard electric bikes (pages 118-124) plus:

• How easy is the kit to fit yourself - or is it really a job for a specialist? Does it need specialist equipment or tools?

• If fitting a rear hub motor kit, how will this affect gearing? All rear hub motors use derailleur gearing of some sort, and they vary as to the size (i.e. number of gears) and type of rear sprocket cluster they will accept.

• How will the kit affect the bike's handling? Heavy lead-acid batteries mounted high up and at the rear - as in the Currie Electro Drive - can make the bike difficult to handle at low speeds and especially when dismounted.

This relatively easy conversion has given a new lease of life to a favourite bike. A secondhand 24 volt Heinzmann front hub motor and controller have been connected to two non-Heinzmann lead-acid batteries. A similar conversion could be done with a more modern 36 volt motor but would involve an extra lead-acid battery.

The kits

Note: kit specifications can change with little notice from manufacturers.

Model / type	Bike requirements	Weight / price / battery size
1 Alien / Suzhou Bafang Throttle with pedal sensor	Front hub motor ready spoked into 26" or 700c wheels. Mounting points required for rear rack which houses battery. Space also required for a small bag or box to mount controller and wiring loom.	Approx 9kg £599 plus carriage 370Wh
2 BionX Pedelec with regenerative braking	Ready spoked hub motor available in 24", 26" and 700c wheels. Rack-mounted and frame-mounted battery options (latter fits to bottle cage mounts).	5.5 - 8.9 kg £1099.99 - £1799.99 142/250/355/ 423 Wh
3 Currie Electro Drive Chain drive	Comes ready-mounted to a rear 26" wheel with battery on a standard rack. 700c fitting possible with respoking.	Circa 15.3kg inc. wheel (circa 12.3kg not inc wheel) £399.95 240Wh
4 Gruber Assist Push-button powered pedals	Larger than average (30.9mm or 31.6mm) seat tube required, which must be centred over the bottom bracket. Shimano external bearings required in bottom bracket.	1.9kg (larger battery option) £1750 plus £100 fitting 135/203 Wh
5 Heinzmann Throttle with pedal sensor option	Hub motor - front and rear options fitting most wheel sizes. Rear hubs have a standard screw-on thread to suit a 5-6-7-8 or 9-speed derailleur.	7 - 9.3kg £1155 - £1550 187 / 356 Wh
6 Tongxin Small yet powerful hub motor	Front wheel hub motor to suit most wheel sizes including folding bikes. 260, 210 and 190 rpm versions. The maximum road speed (for 190rpm and 260rpm respectively) will be: 16" wheel - 10-13mph 26" wheel -15-20mph 27" wheel - 15-21mph	5.2 kg Approx £750 370 Wh

1 Alien / Suzhou Bafang - note the complicated wiring loom.

2 BionX
The distinctive 'dinner plate' motor of the BionX. Regenerative charging is controlled by the handlebar console.

3 Currie Electro Drive
One of the simplest and neatest of kits to fit.

4 Gruber Assist
From the top you have controller, motor, gear unit, freewheel then bevel gear driving the crank in the bottom bracket. Fitting is a specialist, not a DIY job.

5 Heinzmann
The Heinzmann hub is comparatively large but very, very strong.

6 Tongxin
This version of the Tongxin is a narrower option that will fit Brompton forks. The controller is attached to the handlebars.

141

Alien / Suzhou Bafang

Suzhou Bafang is a longstanding Chinese manufacturer of hub motors that have appeared on bikes such as eZee. In this case the hubs come ready spoked into either a 26-inch or 700c front wheel. The other 'modular' components are a 36v lithium-ion battery housed in a substantial rear rack, handlebar mounted battery meter and thumb throttle, power cut-off brake levers and 'pedelec mode' pedal movement sensor of the plastic disc type (the last two can actually detract from the performance!).

Hub motor mounting is easy enough (a bit of grinding of the anti-rotation washers might be required), as is fitting the pannier rack to a bike with standard frame geometry and the appropriate braze-ons.

The hub motor has a smooth free-running 'freewheel', useful if riding with the power off. Open the thumb throttle, and the motor gives a nice steady, powerful pull once over about 6mph. It copes easily with extended gradients of 1:10, plus shorter, steeper gradients if you select the right gear to give a little extra pedal power. Alien also sell more powerful 36 volt and 48 volt kits that are not legal for road use.

Most likely users
The Alien seems to be a reasonably robust and powerful machine for daily use.

Kit weight 8.4kg
Battery type Li-ion *Capacity* Claimed 370Wh
Recharge time 4-6 hours
Replacement battery cost £279 *Guarantee* 1 year on all components including battery.
Bike requirements 36v kit ready spoked in 26-inch or 700c wheels. Check the dropout width and profile of your forks with the retailer to confirm they will not foul the hub motor. Compatible with disc brakes and V-brakes.
Price £599 plus shipping
Contact www.szbaf.com
UK availability www.alienbikes.co.uk

✚ One of the better hub motor kits at the 'budget' end of the market.
▬ Deciding where to put the controller and the spaghetti junction of associated wires can be a bit awkward and these may be hard to disguise neatly and keep out of harm's way. The main downsides of the motor are its relatively large size compared to the likes of the Tongxin and the buzzing it makes under load. The battery, mounted high up in the pannier rack, does make the bike rather top heavy, so a sturdy centre kick stand is a very useful feature for any converted bike.

142

The Suzhou-Bafang kit on tour and on test: the only problem was the need to rehouse the wiring loom after the very flimsy bag provided for it split. A conventional bar mounted bag proved ideal. The sturdy rack provided takes a reasonably heavy touring load and the battery slides out for recharging off the bike.

BionX

A very sophisticated, pedelec hub motor system designed, but no longer made, in Canada. This is a rare direct drive motor kit, and the lack of gearing makes it possible, at the touch of a button, to use the motor as a generator, putting electric current back through the battery to recharge it - so-called regenerative braking. The amount of power that can be generated in this way is relatively small but it certainly satisfies a demand from potential consumers - electric bikers will be quite well used to the question from curious onlookers, 'Does it put power back into the battery when you go downhill?'.

The kit consists of a large-diameter but thin hub motor, groovily-shaped frame- or rack-mounted battery and a small handlebar-mounted LCD console which allows you to control the level of power or regenerative braking. On the most powerful 'regen' setting you barely need to touch the brakes on all but the steepest of descents.

UK and Euro legal options are all 250 watt rated, but come in standard, light (smaller battery), and 'high torque' versions. The high torque motor was introduced following criticism of the poor hill-climbing performance of BionX, but direct drive motors are always weak in this respect. So expect only relatively high torque! Whilst earlier versions used NiMH batteries, BionX has now gone over to the industry standard lithium-ion batteries, reducing the weight of the kit, but probably reducing the battery life too. There will be a rather complicated choice of options for 2011 as follows:

•PL250S Frame-mounted, 142Wh battery with a claimed 22-mile range. Weight 5.5kg.
•PL250M Frame-mounted, 250Wh battery, claimed 40-mile range. Weight 6.9kg.
•PL250HT-RR-M High torque motor with a 236Wh battery built into rear rack with inbuilt rear light and claimed 37-mile range. Weight 7.5kg.
•PL250 HTL High torque motor, frame-mounted 355Wh battery, claimed 56-mile range. Weight 8.7kg.
•PL250 HT- RR -L High torque motor, rack-mounted 355Wh battery with inbuilt rear light. Claimed 56-mile range. Weight 8.9kg.
•PL250 HT-SL-XL High torque motor, 423Wh frame-mounted battery. Claimed 65-mile range. Weight 6.7kg.

All systems come with 26-inch and 700c wheel options. 24-inch option for the PL250S. Higher wattage versions are available for the US market, where they are road-legal, or for Europeans wanting a more powerful electric bike, in which case they are not legal on public roads unless registered as a moped. BionX is aiming to launch a new, smaller, lighter version of the high torque hub and a battery to fit inside the down tube.

Most likely users

Extended touring or commuting use in moderately hilly country. Low maintenance types who not keen on replacing worn wheel rims will appreciate the greatly reduced maintenance that is a side-effect of regenerative braking. BionX kits are a popular choice for recumbents and are also used widely by German manufacturers. For example Riese and Müller fit BionX systems to many models, including their popular Birdy folder. Systems can be fitted to Dahon 26-inch and Airnimal 24-inch folding bikes.

Kit weight 5.5kg – 8.9kg depending on option.
Battery type Li-ion *Capacity* Claimed 142Wh - 423Wh (nominal)
Recharge time 3-4hours
Replacement battery cost S £574.99, M £774.99, L £999.99, L Rack £1,049.99 *Guarantee* 1 year
Bike requirements 24-inch, 26-inch and 700c options available, ready spoked. It is also compatible with rear disc brakes.
Price £1099.99 - £1799.99
Contact www.bionx.ca *UK availability* www.zyro.co.uk

✚ Undoubtedly a high quality system. Silent, smooth power, and suitable for a variety of wheel sizes. Option of frame-mounted or rack-mounted batteries.
Virtually no friction in the drive system, so easy to ride without power
▬ Relatively narrow 'spread' of power, like all hub motors, compounded by the fact it is a direct-drive motor, resulting in poor hill-climbing. Not compatible with hub gear systems - 8 or 9 speed derailleur cassettes are the only options, although a 10 speed freewheel should be available soon. On all BionX kits, batteries are expensive and their life expectancy is still uncertain.

In 2009 BionX collaborated with hub gear manufacturer SRAM to produce the IGH3 combined motor and hub gear which was fitted to Trek models, but there don't seem to be any prospects of such retrofit kits on the horizon.

The BionX kit's telltale large diameter rear wheel hub motor and distinctive frame-mounted battery (rack-mounted versions are available too).

Currie Electro Drive

What the Electro Drive lacks in engineering and design sophistication it makes up for with raw power. The kit comes as a replacement 26-inch rear wheel with a 7-speed derailleur freewheel to which you need to add the sprocket cluster. The motor is clamped to the frame's chainstay with a metal plate and power is transmitted through a chain to the non-gear side of the hub (on older models an alloy block transmitted power directly into the spokes). Though geared for a 26-inch wheel the supplied hub could be respoked by a competent bike shop into larger or smaller wheels. Fitting into a smaller wheel would give more power at lower speed, whilst fitting to a larger wheel would give a higher top speed (though less torque at low speed). As probably the best selling kit of all time (certainly on the US market), the Electro Drive still crops up frequently on the secondhand market. In around 2007 a number of technical changes were made; a new brushless motor was introduced, the controller was placed outside the motor casing, allowing better cooling (though it means a larger battery case). The speed control was much smoother on this new design too (older options tended to jump very quickly to full power) and peak output power was greater. The current UK spec features a rack-mounted lead-acid battery, the rack allowing for the mounting of a second battery to effectively double the range. By 2010 standards, this is Stone Age technology, but the Electro Drive is simple, rugged and reliable.

Most likely users

If you live in a hilly area or regularly tow loads the Currie is well worth considering (though the standard lead-acid battery option means a rather limited range). It'll give at least some noticeable assistance up even the very steep climbs. Those looking for a budget kit need look no further, and it's worth noting that the price of the kit was £455 back in 2001, so quite extraordinarily the price has gone down even before allowing for inflation! But if you are intending to ride a lot without assistance or need to carry the bike about, the extra weight will probably rule the Currie out.

Kit weight excluding batteries Circa 13.3kg including wheel rim, hub and spokes.
Battery type Standard sealed lead-acid **Capacity** Claimed 240Wh.
Recharge time 5-7 hours
Replacement battery cost £140 **Guarantee** 3 months
Bike requirements 26-inch wheeled bikes with, or that can be adapted to, 8- or 9-speed derailleur gears in the rear wheel.
Price £399.95
Contact www.izipusa.com
UK availability www.moorelarge.co.uk is the UK distributor of IZIP electric bikes and should have details of a local retailer.

+ Easily fitted by a competent DIY mechanic. One of the most powerful options available in the UK. Extremely reasonably priced.

- Lead-acid technology is heavy, but UK distributor Moore Large say a lithium-ion option is under development. The previous frame-mounted battery option, which clamped into the middle of the frame, was a neat idea (though the mounts were a little flimsy) as it kept the heavy battery weight relatively low down and central. Secondhand models may feature this, along with other 'bespoke' options previously offered by specialist retailers, such as NiMH batteries and a twistgrip control.

The whole Currie kit fits to the rear of the bike. The large photo shows the motor and inset (top right) the removeable battery that comes with its own rack as part of the kit.

Old and new: the new motor is shown on the left. The older, slightly more powerful motor is on the right, with its distinctive cooling fins. It was larger and housed the controller.

Gruber Assist

Is the Gruber Assist the lightest power-assist motor for bicycles? At 900g, there doesn't appear to be any other motor coming close. It also appeals to those who don't want to appear to be riding an electric bike, as the motor is concealed in the seatpost tube (it needs a larger than average inner diameter of 30.9mm or 31.6mm, with the seat tube centred over the bottom bracket). During the 2010 Tour of Flanders, rumours began to circulate that some riders had cheated by using concealed Gruber drives, but there is no evidence this is anything more than Tour mythology!

With the 1kg battery slipped inside a saddlebag, the kit adds less than 2kg to the weight of the bike. Gruber says it hasn't done enough testing to know if the system works with carbon frames (some drilling is required), but it's fine with aluminium or steel.

Press the handlebar button and you get gentle assistance from the 200 watt motor, which drives the bottom bracket crank via a bevel gear, a truly unique system. It's designed to help only when needed, the bike looking and performing just like any other for the rest of the time, so unusually, it's aimed at existing riders with a basic level of fitness. The Gruber Assist was originally conceived in the Austrian Alps as a way of giving a small 'helping hand' to keen mountain bikers.

Because it's a crank-drive, the motor works through the gears and gives maximum assistance at a preset cadence level - in other words it works best when your pedal speed matches the speed at which the motor is most comfortable. This riding technique takes a bit of getting used to, and coming to a hill may even mean changing into a higher gear to get the best from the motor, rather than a lower gear as you would on a non-electric bike.

As the motor remains engaged all the time, the feeling is rather like riding a 'fixie' (fixed-wheel bike, in that you will not be able to stop pedalling when the power is on. But once the technique is mastered you have a small but very welcome electrical push up the hills. The Gruber Assist is available as a kit or ready fitted to a range of bikes from a step-through 'comfort' bike to trekking bikes, racing bikes and serious mountain bikes. The system has also been used successfully on recumbents, handbikes and trikes.

Most likely users

Designed for mountain bikers who want assistance up the steepest of gradients, but also suitable for most types of bikes in hilly terrain (assuming they have the correct seat post size). The Gruber suits riders with at least a basic level of fitness. If you want enough power to eat up the steepest of hills with little effort, the Currie or Heinzmann are better bets, but if you find hill-climbing just a little too hard the Gruber will turn hills into healthy exercise rather than a forbidding physical challenge and keep your bike nice and light too. The Gruber's mechanics are unsuited to 'stop-start' town riding, because the motor is always engaged with the crank when power is turned on, so it's not recommended to suddenly stop pedalling as this results in quite a jolt. To stop pedalling, you have to turn the power off using the handlebar button or *gradually* slow your pedal cadence (pedalling rate) to below 30 rpm. For the same reasons, the Gruber cannot be used with hub gears.

Kit weight Off-the-peg bikes from Gruber weigh from 13kg to 15.5kg - extremely light for electric bikes. Motor & controller 865g. Battery circa 1,000g for both options.
Battery type Li-ion *Capacity* 135Wh. Optional upgrade to 203Wh.
Recharge time 4 hours 35 mins for 203 Wh
Replacement battery cost 135Wh - £250 203Wh - £395 *Guarantee* 1 year
Bike requirements 30.9mm or 31.6mm) seat tube which must be centred over the bottom bracket. Shimano external bearings required in bottom bracket.
Price Gruber Assist kit including standard 135Wh battery and charger - £1750 Installation £100 (Upgrade to 203Wh battery + £145)
Contact www.gruberassist.com
UK availability www.electricgoatbikes.com / www.electricmountainbikes.com

+ Ingenious engineering gives a supremely lightweight and well hidden motor.
− Less power than you would get with a heavier motor (though it's clearly designed for low weight rather than power) and a rather small battery (though consumption is low). Manual on-off switch means the Gruber is not really suited to stop/start riding.

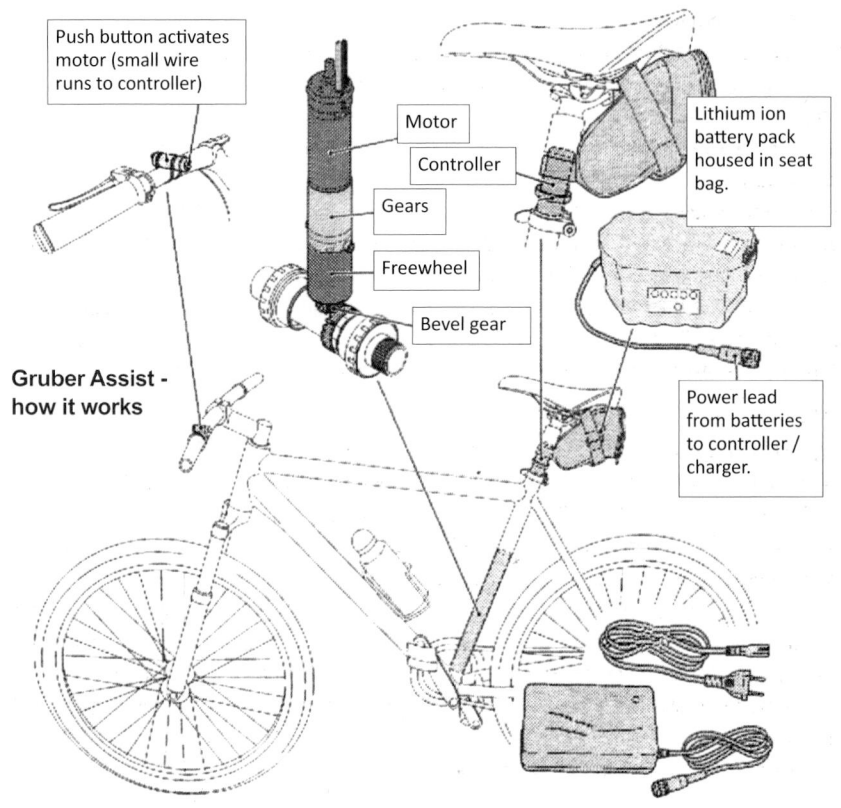

Push button activates motor (small wire runs to controller)

Motor

Controller

Gears

Freewheel

Bevel gear

Lithium ion battery pack housed in seat bag.

Power lead from batteries to controller / charger.

Gruber Assist - how it works

Heinzmann

The Heinzmann name is synonymous with quality. An initial inspection of the kit parts reinforces that; from the 'twist and click' style battery plug to the high quality cabling, it's clear that this German-made kit is the epitome of durability. The solidly built geared hub motors come in front and rear wheel versions, and have a high torque option, a good choice for fitting to mountain bikes, combining hill-climbing ability with sturdy construction. Like most kits, the Heinzmann uses a 'twist and go' throttle, but also includes a pedal sensor option which means the pedals must be turning to activate throttle power.

Installation involves fitting the motorised wheel, the controller and bar-mounted switch. The switch features an unusually accurate battery meter and an energy saving Eco-mode switch (thanks to the belated introduction of digital controllers), which is well worth having for less hilly runs and when you want more exercise or are keen to preserve battery charge and range.

Battery technology has also been upgraded, with lithium-ion replacing older NiCd and NiMH technology, although of course, this will probably mean reduced battery life. The current Heinzmann is available with 187Wh and 356Wh Li-ion options which will work with pre-lithium motors and controllers. The battery is mounted in a pannier style bag fitted to a pannier rack, giving the option of mounting an extra battery in a second pannier, or there are retrofit specialists who can customize Heinzmann systems (see *UK suppliers* section below).

Most likely users

Heinzmann power kits are suitable for a huge range of applications, and like all hub kits, they can be spoked into the wheel size of your choice down to around 16-inch, though bear in mind that smaller wheels mean better hill-climbing ability and lower top speed. The Heinzmann tends to be the first choice for heavy commercial use, in cargo bikes, pedicabs and the like. Retailers and retrofitters Electric Mountain Bikes of North Yorkshire produce a bespoke version for maximum assistance on the hills.

Kit weight 7 - 9.3kg according to the battery option.
Battery Type Li-ion *Capacity* 187 - 356Wh (nominal)
Recharge time Around 6 and 10 hours respectively.
Replacement battery cost £385 or £595 *Guarantee* 2 years from date of leaving factory (so maybe a few months less by the time it reaches a buyer - enquire about this!)
Bike requirements Hub motor - front and rear options fitting most wheel sizes.
Price From around £1100
Contact www.heinzmann.de
UK availability www.electricmountainbikes.com Bespoke systems with 'bail-out' connector for backpack-mounted batteries. Rack-mounting system also available. www.kinetics.org.uk Fitters of Heinzmann kits to a wide range of bikes.

✛ One of the highest quality and strongest kits around. Motors can be fitted into most wheel sizes and frames with standard width drop outs.
▬ Not the lightest kit and relatively expensive.

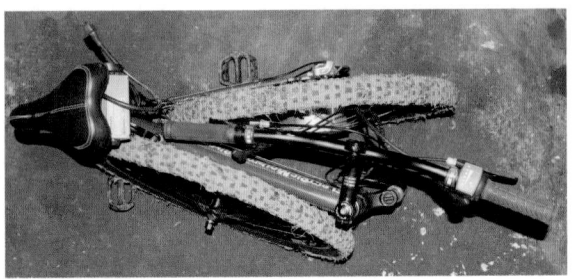

Heinzmann kits have been put to all sorts of heavy duty uses; here a high torque version is fitted to a folding mountain bike, the Montague Paratrooper. The battery (not shown) is usually rack-mounted but on this 'special', from Electric Mountain Bikes, is adapted to be carried in a small backpack.

Tongxin

This light, compact front wheel hub motor has become known in the UK as the 'Nano'. It certainly merits the name, because at 2.3kg it is one of the smallest, lightest motors available. Although fitted with a conventional pattern sun-and-planet gear system, the Tongxin is very unusual in employing friction rollers rather than gear cogs to transmit the drive.

Once the motor has been professionally spoked into a suitable rim you slot the front wheel into the forks, and fix the battery, controller and new brake levers onto the bike. Only a basic mechanical knowledge is required for fitting, but there are companies that offer a fitting service, and the exact set-up of control box and battery will depend on which company you buy from and what option you choose - controller and battery may be seatpost mounted for example, whilst on some earlier examples, the battery slotted into a special pannier rack.

The Nano is one of the few hubs that will fit into the narrow forks of the popular Brompton folding bike, as it comes in a narrow 80mm version. Again, mounting of the controller and battery vary according to which kit you choose (and both can be fitted by the kit supplier if you wish). Options include a handlebar-mounted controller and a large capacity battery in the front Brompton bag, or a small battery fitted into the front bag along with the controller.

Riders often comment on the surprising amount of power available from such a small hub. This may be an illusion caused by the near silence of the motor, the effect being rather like an invisible hand pushing you along. In fact, most hub motors are just as quiet, but conventional sun-and-planet gears can be quite noisy - not a problem with the Tongxin's friction-drive. According to the speed of hub motor chosen (it comes in 260, 210 and 190rpm versions), and the wheel size it is spoked into, the result will be either a high torque model for hill-climbing, or a motor providing gentle assistance at higher speeds - ideal for longer rides with fewer stops over moderately hilly country.

The future for the Tongxin looks very bright. At the time of writing Cytronex is promising a retrofit kit based around the Tongxin, that will suit a very wide range of bikes and be easy to fit compared to current kits, with full diagnostics so that any part of the system can be easily removed from the bike should it get damaged or become faulty. It would also be even lighter than current versions.

Most likely users

Whilst the Tongxin isn't the most powerful motor (though it is certainly no slouch) it scores very highly for light weight and silent running, making it one of the least conspicuous retrofit options. For an efficient, lightweight kit for all kinds of light and medium-duty use it has a lot going for it. The low weight makes it particularly suitable for folding bikes.

Kit weight Approx 5.2kg (with 370Wh Li-ion battery though see below on the various batteries available).

Battery type & capacity Several options are available, and these are liable to change in future. Consult retailers below for options.

Replacement battery cost & guarantee Varies depending on your supplier.

Bike Requirements One supplier and fitter claims the kit will fit 90% of bikes.

Price Approx £750

Contact www.tongxin.net.cn

UK availability www.electricwheel.co.uk   www.freedomebikes.com
                    www.cytronex.com

✛ Very lightweight and relatively easy to fit. Extremely quiet in operation.

▬ As with other hub motor kits, you will have to choose between high torque or high speed. There are more powerful hub motors, and the failure rate of two per cent or so is high by hub motor standards. There is some evidence that hard use can result in motor failure.

Whilst the Tongxin hub motor has retained pretty much the same appearance over the years, it has been sold with a large range of batteries and controllers.

This version uses a rack mounted battery, but current options include seatpost-mounted, 'water bottle' mounted, or for Brompton conversions, a choice of batteries housed in the front Brompton pannier.

Other kits

Some kits have come and gone while others, for one reason or another, remain on the fringes. But a number of these are worth keeping an eye on.

● One of the most promising, which now appears to be discontinued, is the **Sunstar** pedelec kit, highly unusual amongst kits in being a crank-drive. This is a rather elegant piece of engineering, the motor being clamped to the frame near the bottom bracket and driving a sprocket inboard of the main chainring.

As the Sunstar comes with its own bespoke bottom bracket and chainring, you are limited to a single chainring where a front derailleur would normally give a choice of three. But with today's multi-gear rear hubs this need not be a problem. The degree and timing of the power is controlled by three DIP switches inside the handlebar-mounted control unit, which can be set by the user to suit the wheel size and other parameters, including personal preference for power delivery. With the top of the control unit removed, it's possible to experiment with the switches until the power delivery suits you.

Possible quibbles are lack of raw power (the motor is rated at 180 watts), a very short motor-to-battery cable run (this really does limit where you can put the battery, which is clearly designed to be frame-clamped near the motor, 'amidships' on a conventional upright frame), a tiny 80Wh Li-ion battery and quite a lengthy fitting process. This involves removal of the bottom bracket and carefully fitting the Sunstar bottom bracket and pedal force sensor. The motor is fixed to the bottom bracket via an arm that allows it to slide in order to tension the drive chain.

Slightly tricky to fit, but there are many advantages – it's an extremely light set up (something over 4kg total kit weight, excluding charger) and with the controller integrated into the motor casing the Sunstar has a lovely clean appearance with the minimum of cable runs. Like other low powered crank-drives, the Sunstar is very economical, consuming just 9Wh/mile when tested on a recumbent. You may see Sunstar kits very occasionally crop up secondhand.

● **Stokemonkey** is an electric motor assist kit for Xtracycle cargo bikes - Xtracycle being a kit you can use to convert a conventional bicycle into a cargo carrying machine by, in effect, adding length to the rear part of the bike frame. The extra length and the power convert the ubiquitous 26-inch wheeled mountain bike into a load carrier. A throttle on the handlebars activates the frame-mounted motor, which drives the crank through a chain. The Stokemonkey claims exceptional torque allowing the rider to get heavy loads going quickly and climb steep gradients. The suppliers say they've managed to haul 220kg up a near 1:3 gradient. Because it's a crank-drive, the rider only needs to pedal at normal speed to keep the motor 'on the boil', and the kit can produce as much as 500 watts of assistance even at walking pace.. The kit weighs 9.5kg without batteries (36 volt, and not included in kit). From Clever Cycles of Portland, Oregon. Price $883 (£545). www.clevercycles.com

● **eZee** offer a conventional front wheel hub motor kit, worth considering if you want something that is disc-brake compatible in a variety of wheel sizes. Price £895.

The now hard to find Sunstar crank-drive pedelec kit was lightweight. Here it proves a valuable addition to a recumbent.

The Stokemonkey kit is unusual in that it's designed specifically to be used with the Xtracycle longtail kit. Some cyclists like the long, thin shape of this set up - good for getting through pinch-points and for storing the bike too.

Like the SunStar, the Stokemonkey motor drives the chainring, but in this case the motor is frame-mounted.

155

Moving loads the electric way

The easiest and most obvious way of moving heavy loads is to attach a trailer to an electric bike and this works well in the vast majority of situations. Children, pets, shopping, large loads....the list of what you can take on a good, solid flatbed trailer goes on and on. Most pedelecs make suitable towing machines, provided they have a good quality gearbox with some low ratios. If using an E-bike, look for a powerful machine with the accent on torque rather than speed (for regular load haulage a high torque Heinzmann motor would be an excellent choice). For general advice on towing with electric bikes see page 126.

At first glance, attaching power to the trailer itself looks quite a tempting idea. In theory, any conventional bicycle can be used to pull the trailer, then disconnected and ridden as a normal machine, but there are several difficulties. Without going into too much detail, it's a difficult and potentially expensive technical challenge to power the trailer smoothly and effectively in a manner that doesn't destabilise the bike it's attached to. A powered trailer strong enough to give the bicycle more than a token push must be treated with great caution, particularly with a heavy trailer, light rider and/or loose surfaces. In the final event, the complications, and possible dangers, weigh against the idea. None are currently in commercial production, although a number of hopefuls are selling plans on the internet for home-produced trailers. But when a good electric bike can tow a bigger payload (the trailer motor and battery add weight to the trailer, of course), there doesn't seem to be much point.

Although an electric bike and conventional trailer appears to be the ideal load carrying combination, some situations might demand the more radical solution of a specialist load carrier:

- **Extremely heavy or bulky loads** - for example business use, moving heavy machinery, bulk goods. There are several commercial electric trikes available, the Cargo Trike from Cycles Maximus in Bath being typical. Hauling the payload of 250kg is made relatively easy thanks to a choice of Heinzmann front hub motor, or a more sophisticated and powerful Lynch PowerDrive fitted under the floor and driving both rear wheels. Both options are claimed to give a range of up to 30 miles, and the more powerful Lynch is designed to haul 250kg up a 1:5 slope.

- **Non-cycling adult passengers** - As with load-carrying trikes, there are several pedicab trikes available. These can, of course, be ridden easily by one person in flat areas, but electric assist adds a great deal to their practicality for general passenger carrying. Most pedicabs are sold to commercial 'taxi' operators, but they have many uses on large work sites, or even as family transport, where the ability to carry up to three adults and/or heavy or awkwardly shaped freight, makes them extremely useful. Once again, power-assist tends to involve an under-floor Lynch motor or front Heinzmann hub.

One of the biggest successes, commercially and design-wise, has been the German pedal-assist semi-recumbent tricycle known as the Velotaxi. Designed to carry one driver and two passengers, the vehicle was originally made by Veloform in Berlin, but is now manufactured in the Czech Republic with some clones made in China. The machine is powered by a 500 watt front-wheel hub motor and two 12 volt batteries.

They are promoted as "advertising in motion" and are suitable for use at events such as trade shows as well as playing a useful role in urban transport systems. The Velotaxi company has run a fleet of taxis in Berlin since 1997, but elsewhere the taxis are generally operated by independent partner companies. A common arrangement is for the operator to take the advertising revenue, with the drivers taking fares as wages. A nice touch is that passengers receive a receipt showing how much CO_2 would have been generated for the same journey by car.

In the UK there's a successful operation running in Norwich, but the taxis don't seem to have caught on elsewhere, perhaps because their power and weight (about 145kg) take them beyond 'red tape-free' electric bicycle status. There was a short-lived operation in Cardiff, and there were plans in 2010 for a couple of taxis to operate in Sheringham, Norfolk.

Internationally, you'll find Velotaxis from Tallinn and Vilnius to Tokyo and Osaka. They are popular in Europe, especially Germany, and certainly seem to have hit the spot in Japan. There are few in service in America, although the country now has many pedicab services using different fleets.

Velotaxis can be found touting for business in many European city centres. This machine has just picked up a fare in Frankfurt's Romerplatz. Advertising is a key element in the success of the Velotaxi operation.

- **Keeping an eye on small tots** - Bakfiets are a design of bike or trike with a large carrying box placed in front of the rider - perfect for keeping an eye on a precious load, such as small children. There are now a number of electric-assist Bakfiets, such as the Babboe - a Dutch design now available in the UK - and Urban Arrow, an extremely practical-looking system.

The Urban Arrow is actually a Danish-style 'Long-John' bicycle, with a long narrow box placed within the wheelbase of a two-wheel bike. This arrangement means a degree of balancing skill is required at low speeds but is handy in urban environments for negotiating narrow alleys and pinch-points that may prove impractical to the three-wheel variants of bakfiets. Despite feeling unstable at low speed they are fine once underway, and thousands are in everyday use on mainland Europe. The Urban Arrow features the Daum crank motor which is able to provide plenty of power in the low gears for shifting heavy loads.

The Babboe (right) claims a carrying capacity of up to 100kg, is powered by a Protanium hub motor kit and has an RRP of £1899, although discounted on the internet (www.babboe.co.uk).

The Urban Arrow (above) is an altogether more sophisticated carrying solution, expected to be launched in the Netherlands during 2011 for €2750. Urban Arrow was also talking of a possible UK launch later in 2011. (www. urbanarrow.com).

158

- If your cycling environment isn't really suited to trailers because of pinch points, access controls and the like, you might want to consider a 'longtail'. This relies on the same principal as the Long-John, but with the load-carrying extension at the rear. (See also Stokemonkey page 154).

Longtails are handy for passenger and load carrying. Here a Velonom has been fitted with an eZee conversion kit. It's the brainchild of Claus Schroeder, whose company, Velvet Systems, has worked with Austrian electrical specialists elfKW to produce a new range of models for 2011. The street legal 250W model is priced from around €1800. A more powerful version requiring a 'leichtmofa' licence is under development.
www.velonom.com   elfKW www.elfkw.at
For a wide range of load carrying bikes in the UK see www.practicalcycles.com

Laid back power - electric recumbents

Recumbent bikes tend to be considered rather on the fringe of the cycling scene, especially in the UK and US, although in the more cycle-friendly northern European countries, where cycle paths several metres wide are the norm, recumbents are a much more frequent sight.

Electric-assist is well suited to some recumbents and can obviously help with hill-climbing in particular, an area where these bikes struggle against their more conventional upright cousins (or 'wedgies' as they are known to recumbent riders, for perhaps obvious reasons!). Thanks to their lower wind resistance, recumbents can keep up high speeds on the flat and downhill, so the addition of electric-assist for hill-climbing can make an ideal combination.

In the Netherlands and Germany in particular, several manufacturers have fitted electric-assist kits to recumbents. These are generally low-powered kits, often the same as those fitted to uprights. In the UK and US, where recumbents tend to be seen as sports machines rather than day-to-day transport, power-assistance is somewhat looked down on, and such machines are quite rare.

Surprisingly (although there have been many DIY experiments) commercially available high-powered, faired recumbents are rare, although in principal machines of this kind would make superb commuter bikes (or trikes). Such machines certainly exist; the Twike (as detailed in the *History* chapter) is in reality an electric car with human assist, costing between £21,000 and £30,000 according to battery options, with a claimed range of up to 150 miles. The Dutch Aerorider is a similar idea, but lighter and less expensive, the Sport model starting at €7,600.

Are fully-faired electric-assist recumbents the shape of the future? The Aerorider's vital statistics are 48 volt, 576Wh battery, top assisted speed of 45km/h and a weight of 55kg. Classed as a moped, such a vehicle can be used on many Dutch bike paths but would be restricted to the road in most other countries. www.aerorider.com

With recumbents being such 'individual' choices, and customers often ready to pay a premium for their dream machine, building motor-assist versions to customer order makes a great deal of sense. Australian firm Greenspeed does not produce a standard power-assisted recumbent, but quite a few machines are built to bespoke specifications.

Greenspeed must be one of very few companies in the world to have developed a solar-powered electric bike (albeit to special order, and in this case, a trike). The roof of the GTT is designed to carry a 60 watt folding solar array which charges the rear-mounted 544Wh Li-ion battery. Obviously range depends on sun, rider effort and road conditions, but without solar, range would be about 25 miles, more or less doubled to 50 miles on a bright sunny day.
www.greenspeed.com.au

The Cyclone motor sits just in front of the rear wheel, This compact little unit is available in five power ratings from 180 to 500 watts, the biggest motor being claimed to maintain 25mph on the flat without pedalling. All the motors are fitted with an internal 10:1 gear reduction and external freewheel, so the bike can be ridden more or less like any other when the motor is off. Greenspeed call this a Mid Drive, but the effect will be like a twistgrip-controlled crank-drive.

www.cyclone-tw.com

Whilst the tricycle recumbent design solves the problem of balancing whilst cycling in a straight line - something some cyclists find tricky on a recumbent, especially with the extra weight of electric assist - it makes the machine prone to tipping when cornering at speed. The idea of improving tricycle stability on bends with a 'tilting' function has been around for a while and there are even electric recumbents that feature it.

The Dutch Drymer - currently a prototype but intended for commercial production - has all three wheels tilting (some only have one) and is powered with a 250 watt brushless rear hub motor and a 48 volt lithium-ion battery. Maximum speed is restricted to 25 km/h, with range of around 70 kilometres. The cost is expected to be 6,000 euros with the body shell, 4,000 without.

The German Tripendo is a rather fine-looking recumbent tilting tricycle and can be supplied with power assistance as an extra in the form of a hub motor of either 250 watts or 1500 watts and two lithium-ion batteries. Examples of these machines seem to be few and far between.

Tilting tricycles with electric assist offer a whole new riding experience. The Drymer (below) seems to hold particular promise as it's designed to fall within European regulations for pedelecs, and would be classed as a normal tricycle.
The Tripendo (right) is similar. More details at www.drymer.nl and www.tripendo.com

A novel use of electric-assist; German recumbent manufacturers Hase hope this Kettwiesel trike with hub motor kit and full fairing will popularise laid back commuting. The fabric fairing is removeable and foldable for storage.

Electric Bikes from Around the World

World trends

From a position of almost total obscurity at the end of the last century electric bikes have started selling in quite startling numbers in several areas around the world. In China electric bike sales far outstrip car sales - over 20 million compared to around 12 million respectively for 2009.

Whilst China remains responsible for the vast bulk of electric bike sales globally, the principal driving force behind the sales boom there - a ban on petrol powered motorbikes in many large cities - has not been copied on a comparable scale in any other country. In effect electric bikes have replaced motorbikes and mopeds in numerous Chinese cities. By contrast India, another developing nation with a huge population, sells virtually no electric bikes. Clearly population size and wealth simply don't dictate the uptake of electric bikes - there is a complex mix of political, economic and social factors at work too.

Elsewhere the trends are still remarkable, even if they are on a scale dwarfed by the China phenomenon. The European growth in electric bike sales is truly incredible - from being on a par with Southeast Asia (not including China), an area of similar population, growth has accelerated unchecked by the global financial crisis of 2008-2009.

In 2007, Japan was second only to China in sales volume, but has since been overtaken by the EU and South-east Asia, and by 2010 the USA was snapping at its heels (although with a population twice the size). Just to put US sales in perspective, they were still only on a par with those of the Netherlands, whose population was only one-twentieth as large. The Netherlands, it is no surprise to learn, has enjoyed a bigger take up of electric bikes per head of population than any other country. British readers may be disappointed that the UK languishes way behind some other European countries, but though reliable sales figures are hard to come by, there was anecdotal evidence in 2010 that even here sales were starting to increase significantly.

These bare figures hide some interesting trends as well as revealing them. To take one example, most Dutch electric bikes are sold through smaller, independent bike shops, with buyers largely forsaking the 'stack 'em high and sell 'em cheap' merchants, possibly due to concerns about reliability and quality. By contrast, in the UK, budget brands such as Powabyke and Powacycle have been at the forefront of the market. This might change though, as 2010 saw the introduction by Raleigh of its high quality and higher priced range of bikes through a specially trained network of dealers, and the Raleigh launch has been followed by other top end brands, such as Daum, Gruber Assist and Storck.

Worldwide Electric Bikes Sales 2005 -2010

Note - these are estimates based on the best available information - gaps indicate a lack of data

Population Figures

China 1.3 bill India 1.2 bill SE Asia 593 mill **EU 501 million** USA 310 mill

Japan 127 mill Germany 82 mill   UK 62 mill Netherlands 16.5 mill

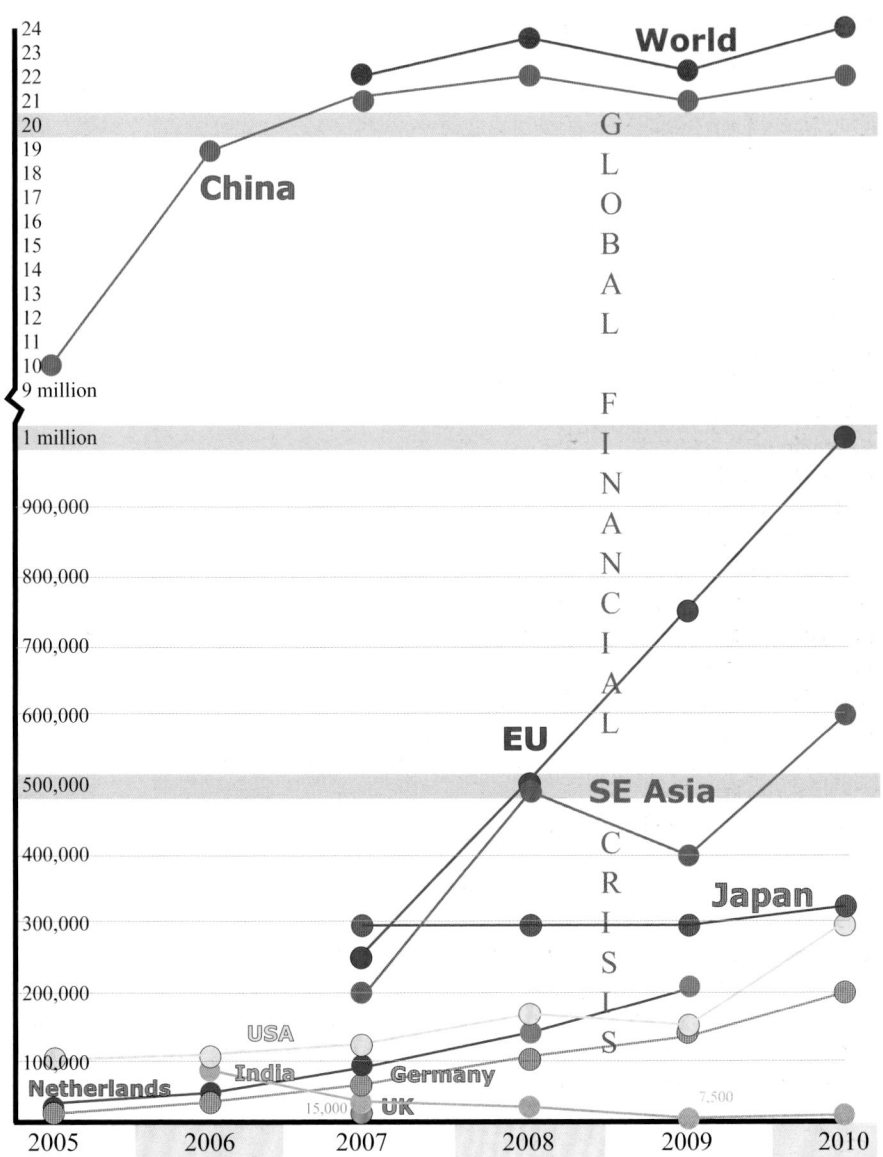

165

British individuals

Whilst electric bikes from other countries often conform to a pattern - sturdy Dutch town bikes, high-tech German and Japanese bikes and chunky Chinese machines built down to a price - the only remarkable thing about bikes designed in the UK is their variety.

In the early days the market was dominated by the reliable but rather tank-like Powabyke which arrived in the UK in the 1990s. More sophisticated competition arrived in the form of two imports - the redesigned newly-specified Giant Lafree, from Taiwan via the Netherlands, and the powerful hub-motored eZee bikes from Shanghai. Powacycle entered the market in 2006, aiming unashamedly at those on a budget, marrying a reasonable quality power-assist system with rather less high quality bike components.

Both Powabyke and Powacycle though, were companies with the means to provide a good level of backup to customers who had parted with their hard earned cash. This wasn't always the case with the many other importers of cheap and cheerful machines. In the early days electric bikes seemed to be struggling with an image problem and were perhaps also still suffering from the hangover effects of Clive Sinclair's failed C5 and the even more disastrous Zike and Zeta projects (see the *History* chapter for more detail).

What has really made the UK electric bike scene interesting have been the home grown products - most notably some of the lightest, most efficient bikes around, such as the Cytronex range, and the very innovative, demountable GoCycle, which makes regular high profile media appearances. With quality imports like Kalkhoff, Gazelle and Monark starting to make their presence felt in the UK, by 2008/9 there was a wide choice of quality bikes available, although the general profile of electric bikes, and therefore sales, remained tiny compared to the Netherlands and Germany.

Could this be about to change? 2010 saw major players enter the game. Raleigh introduced the high class and extremely capable Dover for £1799 (the same basic design as the £1595 Kalkhoff Agattu), and Halfords entered the market with the less sophisticated hub-motored Urban Mover range. Another traditional name, Claud Butler, launched the price-conscious Glide range, starting at £799.99. These widely known brands were complemented by smaller but rapidly expanding companies such as Alien and Freego. And, perhaps ominously for smaller retailers and even for large competitors, the US consumer electronics retail giant Best Buy opened its first store in the UK, promising to stock GoCycle, IZIP and Urban Mover. Five more store openings were promised in the same year along with '24 hour technology support', though what this actually consists of remains to be seen.

Powacycle (left) came on the scene after Powabyke, but rapidly established itself as one of the leading brands. Although very much built to a price, the company has certainly shown commitment to the idea of electric bikes, and has gone on to launch the Infineum, featuring stackable Li-ion batteries.

Cytronex - the world's lightest production electric bike

Electric bikes are often associated with the 'grey' market in the UK; that's to say older riders, and also those in need of a little help for fitness and health reasons. It didn't seem to have occurred to anyone that there was a latent demand for bikes that could be ridden like fast conventional bikes - speedy when not using power yet with an extra electric push when needed and also visually not out and out electric bikes. Enter Mark Searles' marrying of the Chinese Tongxin sensorless BLDC motor with a selection of carefully chosen bikes from a small number of makers. The operation is much more than a bolting together of third party bikes and equipment however - Cytronex designed its own battery (disguised as a water bottle!) and a clever system to control motor output. Unusually, the bikes are also put together at the company's Winchester base, and whilst demand is far greater than supply at the moment Searles says that production will expand soon with the introduction of the Cytronex kit. Outsourcing to China is apparently not on the agenda and the product will continue to be made within the European Union.

The Cytronex machines are designed to be ridden as 'normal' bikes for much of the time and, like the GoCycle, they utilise a push button system to engage or release power to the small but powerful front-wheel hub motor. Unlike GoCycle however, the system for multi-geared bikes offers two speed settings, the motor remaining engaged until you press the brake or the power button.

Although most Cytronex bikes are multi-speed, it's the single-speed Capo that seems to be the standout performer - an *A to B* magazine test showed it to be incredibly efficient in terms of power consumption, using just 7 Wh per mile, yet averaging 17.5mph over a hilly test course. That makes it probably the fastest road legal bike available in the UK.

Amazingly, it proved just as fast as a 24-speed model previously tested, but managed 24 miles on a single charge compared to the 18.5 miles of the 24-speed. Reasons? The Capo runs so freely, is so light and the riding position so aerodynamic that the efficiency gains outweigh the lack of gears. The single-speed system has only one button and bases the assistance on your speed of pedalling and therefore the speed of the bike. This results in fast acceleration from low speeds to get the rider up to the optimum cadence where both rider and system will be at their most efficient.

Early models could be powered from a standing start, but for safety and mechanical reasons the Cytronex bikes are now fitted with a pedal motion sensor, so a pedal stroke is required before the power kicks in. This is the only real downside to a superb system. However, the Cytronex kit promises to have ultra fast pickup, even higher efficiency, lower weight and longer range, plus compatibility with a wide range of bikes.

Most likely users
Speedsters who like sporty bikes but want a bit of help.

Weight 12.9kg-17.3kg
Range Approx 30km (18.5miles) to 39km (24.3 miles) (A to B tests Sept 08 & Aug 09) Range can, of course, be doubled by adding a second battery and some of the models have a second bottle mount, allowing two batteries to be mounted at once.
Motor type & power 250 watt Tongxin sensorless BLDC hub motor
Battery type NiMH ***Capacity*** 36v, 148Wh
Recharge time Maximum 1.5 hours
Replacement battery cost £195 ***Guarantee*** 1 year
Other features Superb integrated battery-powered lights (Busch & Muller Fly IQ and Cyo) and unique computer light. Current gear options include a single speed, 8-speed Shimano hub gear and a 27-speed derailleur model.
Price £1395 - £4450
Contact www.cytronex.com
UK availability Direct from the above website. Test rides available at the company's HQ in Winchester.

+ Power on demand at the touch of a button. One of the lightest and most efficient electric bikes around. A virtually silent motor. Fitted to light, efficient existing bikes and designed for minimal visual impact.
- Limited range and lack of battery capacity indicator. Standing starts not possible due to motion sensor.

Important note: At the time of writing Cytronex had been working on its retrofit kit for 18 months with the launch predicted for early 2011. The company says the new product will include new technology, will be lighter, have a longer range battery and will include a battery gauge.

The retrofit Cyctronex also offered the prospect of a power-assist tandem, for which a low-geared version of this light, compact system would be ideal. Tandems are fast downhill, free-running on the flat, but hard work up hills, so a low-geared Cytronex kit able to add power just on hills could be the ideal addition. There have been very few electric tandems, though in 2010 German manufacturer Bernds was offering one and Sparta of the Netherlands was planning to launch an e-tandem in 2011.

This 24-speed Cytronex Trek clearly shows the company's hallmarks: small but powerful hub motor and a water bottle battery mounted on a sporty bike. Typical of the meticulous detailing on these bikes is the speedometer light, visible on a stalk above the handlebars.

Powabyke X-byke

Powabyke was one of the first electric bike companies on the UK scene, arriving in 1999 with technology based around heavy lead-acid batteries housed in a long rectangular casing along the bike's top tube. Today these machines, approaching 40kg and using large brushed motors in the front hub, are widely dismissed as anachronistic. But the fact is they are still here, and still using lead-acid battery technology (albeit with the option of lithium-ion) which rather suggests that new is not always better.

So if you are looking for a cost-effective, reliable machine, and weight is not an issue, you should certainly try one of the 'Classic' lead-acid models (currently two 6-speeds, plus a tricycle).

If seeking something lighter, the new Mark 2 X-byke is lightweight and fast and now suitable for longer commutes as well as short hops around town. The X-byke is based around a conventional frame, with Raleigh having collaborated on many of the 'bike' aspects of the project, and Powabyke contributing the motor and a new lithium-ion battery weighing only 1.8kg but with a tiny 150Wh capacity. This very small battery, cleverly housed in a water bottle type receptacle, attracted some criticism, but in Mark 2 form it has doubled in capacity (but not size), promising a much greater range. The X-byke weighs around 24kg - pretty decent by electric bike standards.

In late 2010, the Mark 2 was only just arriving in the UK, but Powabyke says Mark 1 brake and gear issues will be sorted, with Shimano Alivio equipment on the 24-speed, and a reduction in weight to 21kg.

Most likely users
Those who want a light bike for a decent price.

Weight 21kg
Range Approx 40km (25miles), based on Mark 1 performance (A to B test Jan 09).
Range can of course be extended by buying additional batteries which are easily carried whilst riding.
Motor type & power 250 watt BLDC front-hub motor
Battery type Li-ion *Capacity* 200Wh (author tests)
Recharge time 2 hours 45 mins
Replacement battery cost £299 *Guarantee* 12 months
Other features Mudguards, pannier rack and kickstand. Men's and women's frames in two different size options. 6 or 24 speed derailleur options.
Price Lead-acid range £549 - £995 (latter price for tricycle option)
X-byke range £895 - £995
Contact www.powabyke.com
UK availability Widely available through Powabyke dealers.

+ Relatively cheap, quick and light.

- Battery mounting system has caused problems. Range will be improved, but still low by modern standards.

In Mark 2 form, Powabyke's X-Byke has been given improved gears, a powerful BLDC motor and a much bigger frame-mounted battery. The changes have reduced the weight slightly, and increased the rideability and power-assisted range.

GoCycle - Formula One inspired one-off

GoCycle is a UK electric bike designed from the ground up, and several years in the design and manufacture (designer Richard Thorpe founded Karbon Kinetics Ltd in 2002 to develop light electric vehicles, but it was 2009 before GoCycle hit the shops). This lengthy gestation is hardly surprising when you look at the technology packed into this groundbreaking demountable electric bike. It has a lightweight magnesium frame and wheels, tiny yet powerful hub motor and controller housed in the front fork, while the wheels slip easily off splined hubs. The GoCycle's sleek design has seen it compared to other icons of consumer design including Apple Mac computers and the iPhone.

Richard Thorpe came from the high-tech world of Formula One motor racing, so it's hardly surprising that a wide variety of new technologies were used to produce a radically different electric bike, although he chose (wisely as it turns out) to stick with relatvely heavy, but reliable NiMH batteries.

The magnesium frame and wheels are made using a process known as thixomoulding, often used to make notebook computer cases (like carbon fibre technology, it is lightweight but unlike carbon fibre it's not too expensive for the mass market). It can be used to make complex shapes that are of a consistently high quality.

According to Thorpe the company initially aimed to hand build about 100 'very cool, high-end bicycles' in the UK in carbon fibre that would sell for around £3,000 each. Changing tack, he decided to make the bikes mainstream, qualifying for a DTI development grant to research alternatives to carbon fibre and ended up with magnesium. The result was a lightweight product that could be made at a fraction of the cost of carbon-fibre.

As other designers of unique bikes have found, money and willing commercial partners can be very hard to come by and the process is time-consuming and gruelling. After many rejections, GoCycle finally secured some funding in January 2006, and though a manufacturing deal with Ideal Bikes of Taiwan collapsed, production did finally go ahead.

Early Go-Cycles suffered many teething problems, but continued development seems to have solved most of these issues. Rider reviews are consistently positive, praising the Go-cycle's speed and comfort, though noting a rather noisy motor. Free-rolling tyres and a 200% gear range mean you can easily nip up to around 15mph (the only real criticism being that you cannot fit an alternative hub gear or even change the gear sprocket on the rear wheel to get a greater top speed - it's fully enclosed and 'guaranteed for life'). Hit a hill or a headwind and you simply press the power button which easily powers you up to the legal assisted limit. This 'all or nothing' propulsion method seems a little crude against the high-tech nature of the rest of the bike, and there's no doubt a graduated power system would be a useful step forward (though GoCycle point out the bike is designed expressly for

The GoCycle is highly unusual in being a demountable electric bike. Whilst not packing down as quickly as a folding electric bike, and not really suitable for regular use on bus or train, it's still a handy characteristic.

the city environment, not touring style riding where sustained low level power is more important). Others have pointed out that - as with all new technology - time and repeated real-world use may well throw up other unforeseen issues.

The 'fold' is easy, though it takes a few minutes and involves removing wheels and folding the frame in half. You'll need a bag (GoCycle supply a bespoke one) to carry all the bits. A useful development would be to make the four separate parts clip or tie together, which would make a much more portable package.

Minor criticisms aside, the GoCycle remains a superb machine and a huge achievement in a world where the vast majority of electric bikes are made by bolting electrical systems onto conventional bike technology. It also seems to have captured the imagination of reviewers and retailers alike, making frequent high profile appearances on TV and in the broadsheets. The GoCycle has broken out of the specialist bike shop mould where so many good bike products seem to get trapped, making it onto the shelves of John Lewis department stores, as well as other non-bike shops.

Future GoCycle projects are said to include a 12.9kg version using Li-ion batteries, which compares well with the current model weight of 16.7kg.

Most likely users

Those with limited storage space, making stop/start urban rides. GoCycles PR targets commuters particularly strongly.

Weight 16.7kg

Range Approx 32km (20 miles) (A to B test Aug 09)

Motor type & power BLDC 250 watt

Battery type NiMH *Capacity* 216Wh, housed in the mainframe.

Recharge time 3 hours

Replacement battery cost £250 *Guarantee* 2 years.

Other Features 3-speed hub gear with 203% range. Free-running bespoke tyres produced for GoCycle by Vredestein. Disc brakes with protective shroud. The motor can be reprogrammed to a 'US spec' which will take it up to a maximum assisted speed of 18mph. The electronics are controlled by firmware (a mini computer programme) that can be updated via a USB port in the front fork. Stayless mudguards. Battery charger weighs around 1kg. Integral lock. Anti-theft bolt option and kickstand options.

Price £1495 - £1693 depending on accessories chosen

Contact www.gocycle.com

UK availability Direct from the above website or via one of GoCycle's authorised retailers (including a good number of independent bike shops as well as some non-bike shops). Details on the website. Good dealer network throughout many mainland European countries too.

+ Power on demand at the touch of a button. One of the lightest electric bikes around. Great innovation and design.

– Not suited for longer touring rides or quick folding to put on a train or bus. Gearing cannot be altered.

The GoCycle has a decent turn of speed.

Practical Dutch bikes mean soaring sales

Dutch electric bikes in many ways mirror their traditional non-electric cousins, the so-called 'omafiets' or 'granny bikes' that are a standard transport mode in cities like Amsterdam. Typical features include a step-thru frame (though 'men's' diamond frame models are available too), hub gears and brakes, mudguards and a 'sit up and beg' riding position. Similar, but with a sportier riding position, are roadster bikes, while the broader term 'city bike' encapsulates elements of both omafiets and roadsters. Whatever you call them, for convenience and comfort the typical Dutch bike is a design that's hard to beat.

In terms of sheer sales of electric bikes, the Netherlands has seen a remarkable increase in recent years, with many of the bikes modelled on this traditional, well-known and well-loved pattern that has stood the test of time. This buying frenzy has proved something of a boon to independent Dutch bike shops - in 2009 a third of all bicycle bucks spent in the country went on electric bikes, and the independents benefited.

The industry is dominated by the Accell group, which includes electric bike (and regular bike) Dutch-based manufacturers Batavus, Koga Miyata and Sparta plus German-based Hercules. Rather than outsourcing manufacture to the Far East, like many other companies, Accell retains manufacturing plants in the Netherlands and elsewhere in Continental Europe.

Dutch electric bikes tend to be of a very high quality, comfortable and extremely practical but often aren't great hill-climbers - for obvious terrain related reasons the Dutch tend towards bikes that will keep them going tirelessly at higher speeds on the flat! Ideal maybe, for UK buyers in East Anglia, but not really suited to hillier areas of the country.

The Netherlands also boasts many smaller independent electric bike companies offering a wide variety of bikes. Antec was one of the early pioneers of electric bikes in Europe in the early 90s, while Azor make bikes of absolutely classic Dutch design, with electric options. Johnny Loco has a much more upmarket image and uses the new Sunstar crank-drive system, available only on complete bikes. Babboe cargo bikes, made in the Netherlands, also have an electric option, available in the UK in 2010 for £1749.

The Koga Miyata above has classic Dutch bike features; low step-thru frame, hub braking, sturdy rack and powerful lights. It's hard to tell this is an electric bike, with the batteries well-hidden in the frame and the rear-wheel hub resembling a hub brake. Technology developed in classic Dutch bikes has recently migrated to racier machines like the Koga E-light (below), described overleaf.

Sparta Ion - traditional Dutch style meets high tech

Sparta fitted small petrol engines to bicycles in the 1980s and 1990s in the form of the popular Spartamet motor, perhaps prompting the Dutch public to associate bikes and power assist with Sparta, which no doubt helped to establish the popularity of its electric bikes.

Undoubtedly the biggest feather in Sparta's cap is that it claims to make the number one selling electric bike in Europe, its Ion model, 300,000 of which had been sold by 2010. It went down well with the industry too, winning the Bike of the Year award in 2004, the year after its launch.

The Ion range - up to eleven variants in 2011 - are undoubtedly city bikes par excellence. Features include a comfortable, upright riding position and substantial steel frame which neatly houses the NiMH batteries (and a Li-ion option from 2010) plus many traditional low maintenance features such as optional drum brakes and hub gears, while all models have mudguards, pannier rack and lights.

Electronics are integrated into the Ion's design, rather than being 'bolt-ons'. The nerve centre of the system is the handlebar-mounted computer that twists off and disables the bike. It stores a mass of data and contains a security code unique to the bike so that theft is rendered rather pointless (though all Ions come with a frame-mounted ring lock too). A diagnostics system tells the rider if something has gone wrong and the bike can then be plugged in to a registered dealer's computer system in order to sort the problem. Sparta has even established a network of recharging stations across the Netherlands.

Unusually, Ion models all feature a direct drive hub motor (see pg 92), a type that tends to lack torque for hill-climbing, but are ideally suited to making steady progress across the flat and often windy Dutch landscape. You can see why they are sold in Cambridge too. With batteries hidden in the frame and a virtually silent motor it's hard to tell that this is an electric bike at first glance.

As noted, Koga is part of the Accell group, and one of the standout bikes of Koga's 2011 range is the E-light, fully-equipped with all the usual Dutch features - sturdy rack, mudguards, lights, chainguard and kickstand plus a 36V, 370Wh Li-ion battery and packed to the gunnels with quality fittings designed for speed. These include Schwalbe Marathon Racer tyres, a lightweight racing fork, 21 derailleur gears (Shimano XT) and Koga's own quick-adjust handlebar stem letting you adopt any position from upright town rider to boy racer. A superb combination of speed and comfort.

Most likely users
Town riders and commuters

Weight 27-28kg
Range Approx 32km (20 miles) with 240Wh battery (*A to B* test Feb 07)
Motor type & power Accell direct drive hub motor with inbuilt sensor to determine pedalling pressure. 250 watt.
Battery type & capacity NiMH 264Wh Li-ion 370Wh
Recharge time 2-3 hours
Replacement battery cost £235   **Guarantee** 2 years, extendable to 5 years for an extra £150.
Other features Less expensive models use V-brakes whilst higher end machines have hub and roller brakes. Ion RX models have a detachable battery for those needing to take it away from the bike to recharge it. New for 2010 is the heart rate monitor that controls the level of power assistance by matching it to the riders heart rate. The same power assist system is available on several other Sparta models including a tandem and a cargobike.
Price £1540 - £2099
Contact www.sparta.nl (English language version available)
UK availability www.electricbikesales.co.uk

✚ Superb build quality and reliability with an excellent back-up program (in the Netherlands at least).

▬ Fairly heavy by current standards. Lack of torque makes it a poor hill-climber.

An early Sparta Ion. Sparta still use this easily recognisable step-thru frame, though it has been joined by a variety of other designs.

Gazelle

Whilst Gazelle started out with the excellent Panasonic crank-drive system it has now introduced its own hub motor design with a rack mounted battery. It has integrated high quality Dutch style weatherproof components into the design - for example hub gears with roller brakes (its own design of front-wheel hub motor has an integrated roller brake) on the more expensive models. Its lithium-ion batteries come in three size options (bronze, silver and gold) with a stated range of anything between 25 and 200km per charge, depending on battery size, power setting and the other usual variables. The UK spec bikes come with the smaller battery size with a tested range of around 30km. Weight is a very reasonable 25-27kg when you consider you are buying a fully equipped town bike.

Most likely users
Town riders and commuters

Weight 25-27kg
Range Claimed to be around 50 km / 30 miles in typical use (smaller battery size).
Motor type & power BLDC front hub motor, designed in collaboration with a Dutch engineering company. 250 watt.
Battery type Li-ion available in three sizes on mainland Europe
Capacity 252 Wh (bronze), 324 Wh (silver) and 396Wh (gold) - but the smaller version is most common in the UK.
Recharge time 3.5 hours (standard battery option).
Replacement battery cost £300 for standard battery option
Guarantee Battery guaranteed to hold an 80% charge for up to 3 years if fully charged less than 600 times.
Other features All models are fitted with Shimano hub gears (apart from the Medeo Innergy which has 24 derailleur gears) and roller brakes (except the bottom of the range Orange Pure Innergy).
Price £1540 - £2099
Contact www.sparta.nl (English language version available)
UK availability www.cycleheaven.co.uk

+ High quality electrical system and bike components. Smooth, quiet riding.
- Some tests have criticised a lack of power under load.

Gazelle's Innergy range are all built around the same front hub motor and lithium-ion battery. Frame and gearing options vary from model to model; the Orange Innergy (above) has eight hub gears whilst the Medeo (below) has 24 derailleur gears.

German technology - engineering their own path

The electric bike world of Germany, Austria and Switzerland is dominated by Panasonic and BionX drive systems - Diamant, Kalkhoff, Kettler, KTM, Maxcycles, Puch, Riese & Muller, Rixe, Swiss Flyer, Victoria and Vital all use one or other of these systems. Such is the scale of the German electric bike market that a specialist firm like Panterra, based at Löhne near Hannover, can purchase electrical components from such major companies as Sanyo and SAFT and mix and match them to suit bike manufacturers' needs.

However, quite a number of smaller, independent-minded companies in Germany, Switzerland and Austria have, rather refreshingly, gone their own way.

Daum - comfortable and high-tech bike for older riders

With a background in gym fitness machines that include electronics - ergometers, running machines and the like - Daum felt well-placed to develop its own German-made motor drive system in 2009 and enter the electric market. *A to B* magazine hailed the pedal torque sensor system as 'more sensitive and responsive' than the highly regarded Panasonic system - praise indeed. In practice this makes for a bike that accelerates quickly yet smoothly, with three power levels letting you choose just how quickly.

Visually the most striking feature is the electronic dashboard, which displays a whole host of information, including the remaining estimated range at your current power consumption (updated every few seconds) and a gauge showing how hard the motor is working - both highly unusual features for an electric bike, but hugely useful in helping you get the maximum range from your battery and preventing arrival at your destination without power.

Other features are arguably information overload, such as the ability to monitor your heart rate when attached to a chest belt (this isn't a racing bike after all) or to save route data onto an SD card. Dashboards on Premium models also incorporate an SMS text messaging function that will tell you if your bike has been stolen! The Premium variant also uses a 3D sensor to display hill gradients and has a GPS facility allowing routes to be imported via a GPS card.

Although it's at the higher end of the price scale the Daum still represents very good value for money when you consider the quality of the crank-drive system and the sophisticated electronics. These bikes will appeal to those who are always on the look out for the latest technology.

Older people might well like the large LCD information display and the 'pushing assistance' feature meaning you can push what is quite a heavy bike up steep gradients whilst dismounted.

A to B magazine's summary of the Daum seems a good one; 'these machines really do take the bicycle to a whole new level.'

Most likely users

Leisure riders who like plenty of comfort and close control over the amount of electric pedal assistance they get. Older riders might appreciate the large and very legible information on the backlit display panel. This has received some criticism for being too big and heavy but is certainly very easy to read.

Weight 26.9kg

Range 40-70 miles depending on power setting (A to B test Aug 2010)

Motor type & power BLDC crank-drive motor. 250 watt.

Battery type Lithium-ion **Capacity** 396Wh

Recharge time Approx 3 hours

Replacement battery cost £450 or £350 if bought as a spare with bike **Guarantee** 2 years.

Other features 700c size wheels. Suntour suspension forks, Shimano Nexus Inter 8 Premium hub gears, Busch & Muller lights powered from a hub dynamo (German law demands dynamo power - even though power from the battery would help reduce weight), Schwalbe Marathon / Marathon Cross tyres. The same system is fitted to two different frames - a Comfort step through frame (44cm & 52cm frames) and a Trekking hybrid type frame (women's / men's versions - 44 & 52cm / 48cm & 56cm frames respectively).

Price £1950 Premium version £2350

Contact www.daum-electronic.de (English language version available)

UK availability www.velospeed.co.uk

The Daum display is large and clear and displays a wealth of useful information (right). The crank motor (far right) is an equally impressive bit of engineering that will put considerable pressure on Panasonic.

The Daum's crank-drive system is actually less obtrusive than the rather downmarket unbranded Chinese battery.

+ Smooth, comfortable riding on a superbly efficient bike.

- Rather heavy by current electric bike standards. Not everyone is comfortable with the big display screen and large rack-mounted battery box. Several kilos could be lost with little or no extra cost to produce a lightweight version - for example, lighter tyres, smaller 'dashboard' and non-suspension forks.

The Daum's high quality crank-motor allied with hub gears makes for great hill-climbing, even when towing loads.

Storck Multiroad and Multitask - electric sports bikes

Storck made its name with high-end road bikes known for their very light, stiff frames. Its entry into the electric bike market may have surprised some racing purists, but it has applied the same uncompromising technological approach to the design and manufacture of a new motor, battery and control system branded as Raddar, working with German electronics specialist Marquardt.

Both Storck electric bikes, the Multiroad and Multitask, can be switched between pedelec and e-bike mode and use a gearless 'high torque' motor. Being gearless, the motor has a regenerative capacity, activated when you touch the brake levers, and the accent on performance means the motor will accept a Shimano cassette.

Most likely users

Long, fast rides on an extremely high quality bike. The Multiroad is an out and out road racing bike whilst the Multitask is more suited to touring and commuting.

Weight From around 20kg.
Range Approx 40-90km (25-56 miles) depending on battery choice.
Motor type & power BLDC gearless motor. 250 watt.
Battery type Lithium-ion **Capacity** 252 / 317 / 360 Wh options.
Recharge time Approx 3 hours
Replacement battery cost £449 **Guarantee** 2 years
Other features Optional GPS computer with cruising range info. Both models come with disc brakes.
Price From £2895
Contact www.storck-bicycle.de
UK availability Storck Raddar UK Ltd e-mail: ian@ian-hughes.com Website in the pipeline.

✚ High end technology seemingly applied in a sensible way.
▬ Pricey!

The Storck Multiroad (foreground) and the Multitask (background).

Dolphin / IZIP Express - the 500 watt fast class bikes

Dolphin is a very unusual electric bike company in that it makes machines specifically aimed at the 'fast-class' Swiss and German markets where a small amount of paperwork is required to make these more powerful bikes legal on the road. In the UK these bikes would have to be registered as mopeds.

The system is based on Dolphin's own patented hybrid drive that seamlessly combines pedal and motor power. Pedal power is transmitted to the rear hub in the normal way through a chain and derailleur gear system, while electrical power is transmitted from the frame-mounted motor via a toothed belt to the same rear hub. The clever bit is in the hub, where the human and electrical power are mixed. The working principles of the system are described on page 94. Previous incarnations of the design appeared as Swizzbee, a brand that seems to be no longer in existence. Its latest venture is in cooperation with US company IZIP and features the same hybrid rear drive, entirely re-engineered, says Dolphin, to give better performance and greater power. This Evo-Drive system, measures the pedal speed and provides electrical power to match. The result feels like a good crank-drive, but without the need for torque sensors. Six motor-assist levels let you find the right balance between range and speed.

The Izip Express has a stated 'cruising speed' of some 40km/h (around 25mph) and a claimed range of 50-70km (31-43 miles)! Whether these claims are accurate or not, the Express has an unusually large battery that should give quite good performance. Sadly, none of these machines are road-legal in the UK without a moped licence.

Most likely users
Those who feel the need for speed and don't mind a fairly heavy bike.

Weight 30kg
Range 50-70km (31-43 miles)
Motor type & power 'High-torque' differentially-geared motor (combining human and motor power). 500 watt.
Battery type Li-ion *Capacity* 666Wh
Recharge time Not known
Replacement battery cost & guarantee Not known
Other features Avid disc brakes front, V-brakes rear. The rear-wheel hub motor is compatible with Shimano and SRAM 9-speed cassettes and Dolphin models come fitted with 27 SRAM derailleur gears. The Dolphin Marathon has lower voltage and a lower capacity battery (486Wh).
Price Dolphin Marathon CHF3980 (around £2620) Dolphin Express 4680CHF (around £3080) Currie IZIP Express US$3499 (around £2220)
Contact www.velocity.ch / www.currietech.com
UK availability Not known

+ A high quality, well-engineered system with the feel of a top end pedelec without the same amount of chain and sprocket wear. Excellent speed and torque mix (i.e high speed on the flat combined with the ability to power more slowly up steep hills).

- Relatively heavy and expensive. The power and speed of these machines mean fuel economy isn't as good as less powerful models.

The IZIP Express (left) was launched in the US in 2010, and is based on the existing Swizzbee hybrid design. This US/Swiss co-operation seems unlikely, but legislation in both countries allows fast bikes of this kind

Cruising power - United States

For a country with a population of over 310 million - the third most populous country on the planet and one of the richest and most technologically advanced - the US buys relatively few electric bikes. Of course, in a country where the car is synonymous with modern life's convenience and comforts this may not be altogether a surprise.

US electric bikes take after their cars too, in that they tend to be more powerful and energy hungry than European and Japanese models. Why? Part of the reason might be embodied in the concept of America being a 'land of plenty', a belief that crops up throughout their history. There are more specific reasons too: US Federal law is relatively lenient, allowing motors up to 750 watts (three times the European maximum) and a top speed of 20mph. The country as a whole has little modern history of cycling as a mode of transport, and little in the way of cycling infrastructure outside of very localised pockets in cycle-friendly cities such as Portland, Oregon. This combination of circumstances has led to large and heavy E-bikes with throttle power - in other words ones you don't have to pedal if you don't want to. Prime examples of these monster electric bikes include the Tidalforce and the Pi bike, and of course the Izip Express...

As always, there are one or two exceptions to the rule. Schwinn (now little more than a badge owned by Pacific of Taiwan) has produced 'European' style bicycles. Its first venture with Protanium resulted in some reliability problems, but the company has recently teamed up with Toshiba to produce the Tailwind, a well equipped bike with a unique two-year/20,000-mile battery guarantee.

This is the Beast from US cycle manufacturer M55. Designed for 'off-road use' only, this powerful 1.3kW bike was due to be joined by the Daemon, a lighter machine, road legal in the US.
The Beast is a crank-drive - very unusual in America, where the twistgrip throttle is king. M55 says the Beast should be available in 2011.

Eplus bikes (also known as Tidalforce) are based on a concept originally developed in co-operation with the US military, and its flagship mountain bike (left) still undoubtedly bears a macho stamp. The company's website boasts the bike is 'approved for use by US Special Forces'. This limited edition model costs nearly $4500, but the mountain bike range starts at $2700.

Despite their military origins, Eplus bikes are now offered in several styles, including ladies, tricycles and 'comfort' bikes as shown below. Despite this attempt to widen the appeal of this innovative concept, the centre of the wheel is not an ideal place for a heavy battery. The increase in rotating unsprung weight will tend to put a strain on the wheel and other components and upset the ride and handling, especially off-road.

IZIP - continuing with lead-acid technology with the Aspen

European bikes like the Tailwind, with lights, racks and mudguards will always sell in a few areas in the United States, but the much brasher IZIP (the brand name for Currie Technologies) has emerged as the pre-eminent US electric bike company, and unusually one that has managed to make some inroads into the UK. The new Urbana (introduced as the Urban in the UK) is unusual for a US bike, being a lightweight folder with a small battery and shortish range. Aimed specifically at commuters, the Urbana weighs a reasonable 16.5kg.

The middle of IZIP's US range is dominated by cruiser-style bikes, often with the batteries in the frames, and decent quality components. Perhaps most notable though are the budget lead-acid options - IZIP is one of the few companies outside of the Chinese market to persevere with lead-acid batteries on bikes like the Aspen which is also equipped with the ever reliable Electro Drive motor, although unlike its kit equivalent it doesn't come with a throttle control - it's a pure pedelec.

Most likely users

Those wanting the reliability of lead-acid on a bike that won't weigh you down too much and is easy to pedal without power, the Aspen is one of the best options out there.

Weight 28.9kg
Range 15-25 miles depending on assist level.
Motor type & power Currie Electrodrive motor, chain drive via rear wheel (see chapter *Kits, Folders & Specials* for more details on the motor itself). 200 watt.
Battery type Sealed lead-acid battery *Capacity* 240Wh.
Recharge time 5-7 hours
Replacement battery cost £140 *Guarantee* 3 months
Other features An extra battery can be fitted on the rack, effectively doubling the range (though it adds an extra 7.2kg). An extra £200 will buy you a similar style bike, the Skyline, but with a lithium-ion battery mounted behind the seat tube.
Price Aspen £599.95 Skyline £799.95 Urban £1,199.95
Contact www.izipusa.com
UK availability www.moorelarge.co.uk

+ A good choice for low-tech enthusiasts and without a big weight penalty.
- The battery mounting high up at the back affects the handling of the bike and mid-frame style mounting is not available any longer. Range is quite limited.

The lead-acid budget model, the IZIP Aspen, comes in men's and women's versions.

Unusually for a US bike, the IZIP Urbana is small and light. The 20-inch wheel folder has a stated weight of 16.5kg, and the 120Wh Li-ion in-frame battery (removable for charging), is claimed to give a range of 12 miles. This is arguably more acceptable on a lightweight folder, where this kind of mileage would achieve most cross-town hops.

Japan

The Panasonic crank motor

The Panasonic crank-drive is probably the most popular system at the quality end of the European market, but originates in Japan. Panasonic-powered electric bikes began to appear in Western Europe in the early years of the century via Swiss firm Biketec (Swiss Flyer) and a few Japanese folders, such as the Porta Ranger and the Will, but the system was most notably popularised in the UK by the excellent Giant Lafree (see the entry under Classics and Flops in the *History* chapter) which brought it a reputation as a high quality, reliable system featuring a long-lived NiMH battery.

The crank motor subsequently re-emerged with a lithium-ion battery – very small at first, in classic Japanese style, but later big enough to give a much greater range. The new Li-ion crank-drive kept the wonderful torque sensor system that delivered seamless power and made Panasonic bikes so like a conventional bike to ride.

The Monark Eco is the cheapest of the crank-drives at £1250
www.monarkexercise.co.uk

The power settings were now more subtle too, with three levels of support (adding 50%, 100% or 130% of rider pedal effort) instead of the two on the old system. As with the original NiMH powered crank-drive, the speed range over which power is available is easily modified by changing the gearing on the rear wheel.

It's simply a delight to ride - responsive to pedal without power and when used on a bike with a good gear range it makes light work of hills and adds speed on the flat. In 2009 *A to B* magazine labelled it simply 'the best system in the world', and although other crank-drives have come along since, such as Daum and the latest Sunstar it is certainly still a prime contender for top spot. Today it's employed on a huge range of bikes from a wide variety of manufacturers. The main UK brands are described left and opposite, but it's also available in Western Europe on the French brand Gitane and Swiss Flyer (as the name suggests, from Switzerland).

The Panasonic-powered Raleigh Dover led the iconic British brand back into the UK electric bike market in 2010 and initial levels of interest seem to mark out a bright future. www.raleighebike.co.uk

Like many other bicycles, the Spanish E-motion uses the Panasonic crank-drive, but unusually, it runs the power through a normal derailleur gear system, apparently without technical issues. The range has expanded rapidly in recent years to include the City, Avant, Express and Sport. Pictured is E-motion's folder. It has a stated weight of 20kg, a 6-speed derailleur and battery powered lights.
£1600-£2400.   www.bh-emotion.com
UK sales: www.onbike.co.uk

Kalkhoff, like Raleigh has long been a division of the US Derby Cycles group, although it is now independent. Imported by 50 Cycles of Loughborough, it was one of the first high quality electric bike brands to make real inroads into the UK market. The sporty Pro Connect model is pictured. This bike is also sometimes sold in 'derestricted' form, in effect, a moped. £1495 - £2295.
www.kalkhoff-bikes.com
UK sales: www.50cycles.com

China & Taiwan

China has taken electric bikes more seriously than any other country. As early as the 1960s the Mao government was experimenting with their potential, but wisely decided battery and motor technology were not yet advanced enough for widespread adoption. However, by 1991 China's National Science Board named electric bikes as one of ten key scientific development priority projects in the 9th Five Year Plan. The truly massive uptake of electric bikes in China over the last two decades has not been without its problems. Seen on the one hand as a low cost solution to the transport needs of millions of low income citizens (especially in the wake of local bans on certain forms of petrol-powered transport), electric bikes have also been subject to bans by city authorities and the target of an aborted crackdown by central government. By some estimates there are 120 million e-bikes on China's roads. There were only 50,000 or so a decade ago. At first they were viewed as a quieter and cleaner alternative to gasoline-powered scooters, with Tianjin

banning hydrocarbon powered two-wheelers in 1994 and Shanghai suspending new licences in 1996; 1998 saw similar bans in several more cities.

But it wasn't long before a backlash against their electric counterparts began. It quickly became obvious that the national bike standards that came into force in 1999, imposing a 12mph limit, were being almost universally flouted. The typical Chinese machine was more akin to an electric moped that just happened to have pedals than to a bicycle, and many were capable of illegal moped-type speeds. After a new law in 2,000 allowed electric bikes to use bike lanes, the conflict with non-electric cyclists and pedestrians grew.

Chinese electric bikes more often resemble mopeds with pedals stuck on, rather than bicycles. They are pressed into use to carry all manner of things - frequently both shopping and passengers.

The city of Fuzhou banned electric bikes, but by this time electric bike users and manufacturers represented a powerful vested interest and the ban was subsequently overturned in the courts. Two years later, in 2002, Beijing stopped registering new electric bikes, but social trends pushed illegal electric bike use ever higher, with a big surge in sales accompanying the 2003 SARS virus, which seems to have driven bus users towards less crowded forms of transport. A new law in 2004 allowing electric bikes to stay in bike lanes but at a maximum speed of 9mph (15km/h), proved wholly ineffective.

In short, the laws aimed at restricting electric bikes simply weren't in tune with reality, and such was the pressure that in 2006 Beijing rescinded its previous ban. More city bans culminated in late 2009 with proposed new national restrictions on electric bikes, but they were 'postponed' almost immediately amidst public outcry while rampant illegal use continued unabated. In one crackdown, Changsha city traffic police handed out 60,000 tickets in five days for electric bikes that violated weight and speed restrictions or didn't have proper registration. Wenzhou police confiscated 5,000 illegal bikes at one point.

Other problems have emerged too. Around 95% of China's e-bikes use lead-acid batteries, and some studies have suggested that these batteries emit more lead into the atmosphere than many other forms of transportation.

But all this doesn't mean bikes exported *from* China are overweight, lead-acid powered monsters (though they may be relatively heavy compared to European designs). In fact, the world's biggest maker of quality bikes, Giant, recently opened a dedicated electric bike factory in China, whilst the company itself remains based in Taiwan, another major centre of electric bike manufacture. There is certainly something of a paradox with the electric bikes coming out of China - bikes at the cheaper end of the market are of a noticeably lower quality and often much heavier than European bikes and more prone to electrical failure. But when the R&D is good, and there are no corners cut in production, the Chinese can design and/ or manufacture some great machines. The Tongxin sensorless BLDC hub motor is an example of a high quality product. Another well regarded motor was the 8Fun, produced by Suzou Bafang. This was fitted to many eZee bikes, eZee being another Chinese-based company that has turned out well-regarded machines, in this case since 2001.

Giant - getting themselves in a Twist?

The *History* chapter details the glories of the original Giant Lafree (2001-2006) - a true classic, but now only available secondhand and becoming quite rare.

The Lafree was replaced by the much cheaper hub-motored Suede. This was a bit of a technical and commercial failure – the motor had no freewheel, the pedal sensing system was crude and tended to knock the chain off, and overall efficiency was poor.

Still attempting to take a share of the growing Dutch E-bike market, Giant then tried to go upmarket with a revamped Sanyo-motored bike, once again called the Twist. This was better thought through, with big batteries and quite a reasonable range, but it was expensive, it still lacked a freewheel and it somehow lacked class too.

It didn't last for long. In 2008, Giant replaced the Twist with the Express/Freedom range (now called Express/Esprit) and this has evolved into a much better machine, faster and lighter than its predecessors. Like the 2007 Twist, it's based around a Sanyo hub motor, but this is now fitted with a freewheel. Sanyo has developed the system with regenerative technology (see Sanyo Eneloop's entry under Japan), but this isn't currently available on Giant bikes. Lack of regenerative capacity means this particular hub motor set-up, though quite a competitively-priced electric bike, looks rather inferior technically and performance-wise against the most keenly-priced Panasonic crank-drive machines (currently the Monark Eco at £1250). In particular the Giant hub motor system is weak on hills whereas the Panasonic crank system has the benefit of applying power throughout the gear range and hence over a greater speed range. It's also worth noting that 'fuel consumption' is actually greater than the classic Giant Lafree (12.8Wh per mile compared to 10.8Wh per mile, as tested by *A to B* magazine).

The Twist comes in two basic variants: the Express (derailleur gears and a single battery) and the Esprit (hub gears and dual batteries - previously known as the Freedom), with range in excess of 40 miles. Despite the unfavourable comparison with the Panasonic crank-drive - whose predecessor Giant had ditched after using it on the Lafree - the latest Twist models use quite an effective pedal sensing technology. Unusually, a pedal sensor is mounted in the rear axle dropout on the chain side. The forward pressure of the axle in the sensor when pedalling sends a signal to the control box which translates the pedal force to a proportionate amount of power in the front-wheel hub motor. The system gives a very bike-like ride, so it should be ideal for newcomers to electric bikes who have only ever ridden non-electrics. However, some riders have reported drag in the hub when riding unpowered, despite the freewheel.

Most likely users
Longer rides in moderately hilly country.

Weight 22.9kg plus
Range Approx 32km (20 miles) with one 234Wh battery *(A to B test March 09)*
Motor type & power Sanyo BLDC front hub motor. 250 watt.
Battery type Li-ion **Capacity** 234Wh (or 468Wh on the Twist Esprit models).
Recharge time Around 5 hours
Replacement battery cost £300 per battery **Guarantee** 2 years
Other features Sporty, hybrid style aluminium frame. Unique pannier mounted
battery system, allowing the mounting of an extra battery and a doubling of range.
Three power levels selectable on handlebar-mounted control panel. 700c wheels
make for a comfortable ride with assured handling. Adjustable handlebar stems and
a choice of frame sizes mean most shapes and sizes can find a bike to fit.
Price range £995-£1895
Contact & UK availability www.giant-bicycles.com

✚ Reasonably light weight and good build quality. Good dealer network from the
world's largest maker of quality bikes should ensure good back-up.
▬ Lack of torque makes it a poor hill climber. Some riders report drag from the hub
motor, despite the freewheel.

*The 2011 Giant Twist Esprit. This top of the range model has two batteries - one in
each pannier - giving a nominal capacity of around 500Wh - that would give a range of
around 40 miles, based on the A to B magazine test of the similar Express (March 2009)*

eZee Sprint Eco - one of the fastest bikes around for the money

By contrast to the giant that is Giant, eZee electric bikes are largely the creation of one man, Wai Won Ching, the bikes being made in a dedicated factory in Shanghai. Mr Ching's approach to electric bike design is based unashamedly on what he thinks will be future trends. He sees Chinese-style hub motor machines as eventually overtaking both European designs such as Heinzmann and also the Japanese technology - both crank-drive and hub motor - and coming to dominate just about all markets. The European law, he says, was 'drafted to keep the Chinese competition away', but will only have a small effect in 'holding back the Chinese tide'.

eZee made its name with the Torq, best known for its powerful and quiet hub motor, capable of assisting to well over 20mph when derestricted for 'off-road use', something quite astounding when it was introduced in 2005. It went on to win the Tour de Presteigne electric bike race three times. Unfortunately, later Torq models became heavier and less efficient.

All eZee bikes are well made, well-specced and well-equipped, but with the more expensive models now costing as much as European-made Panasonic crank-drives, the budget end eZee bikes, such as the Sprint Eco, now look better value. In its early days the Torq was plagued by problems with Phylion branded lithium batteries, but the quality appears to be improving and recently eZee has started sourcing batteries from Samsung Korea. In keeping with the Chinese trend for larger and larger battery capacities, eZee recently introduced the option of an extra rack-mounted battery wired in series with the normal battery to increase the range. In 2010 eZee was still finalising its top of the range offering - the Torq T1, with full titanium frame and many other titanium parts. Final price and weight are unknown, but the prototype was claimed to weigh around 20kg.

The Sprint Eco stands up very well in the quality it offers against similar priced Chinese machines, offering better value performance and equipment (this was also the case with the even more reasonably priced Liv, though this is no longer imported into the UK). As you'd expect from eZee, the bike is based around a powerful hub motor that quickly gets you up to 15mph and beyond and powers you quickly over moderately hilly country (up to 1:6 gradients) with the aid of seven hub gears. Despite the extra power consumed by higher speed, the big battery gives a decent range too and the bike is easy to ride should you run out of juice.

On the standard version assistance only kicks in when the pedals are rotating forward at a road speed of more than 6mph.

There are currently two eZee batteries with capacities of 370Wh and 518Wh, the cheaper models coming with the smaller battery. Either battery can be teamed up with the 370Wh range-extending battery on the rack, giving a maximum capacity of 888Wh, enough to give range of about 50 miles. This should give both batteries an easier life as peak current drawn (which puts a strain on them) will be shared

The eZee Sprint Eco in action (above) is a good value bike at the budget end of the eZee range.

between them and deep discharges and recharges will be less common, another factor that can reduce battery life.

Being sold throughout the world, eZee bikes are fitted with motors that can run at different speeds. The slowest 200rpm motor will give a road speed of 15-16mph with a 26- or 27-inch wheel, and is legal anywhere. The faster 250rpm motor will usually be held back to 15mph by a simple controller adjustment if sold in Europe. It can be easily derestricted to give a top speed of 19-20mph. eZee also produces a 300rpm motor for the US market, with a top speed of up to 24mph. The faster bikes are a lot more fun, but they are of course, also illegal in many markets, and have a shorter range and reduced battery life.

Most likely users
Speedy commuting and touring.

Weight 26.5kg
Range Approx 50km (30miles) *(MMM magazine test Oct 2010)*
Motor type & power BLDC hub motor. Throttle activated with pedal motion sensor. 250 watt.
Battery type Li-ion **Capacity** 370Wh or 518Wh
Recharge time 4-5 hours
Replacement battery cost £400 (370Wh) or £500 (518Wh) **Guarantee** 1 year
Other features Shimano Nexus 7-speed hub gears. V-brakes front, roller brakes rear. LED lights front and rear powered by the main battery. Pannier rack, mudguards and kickstand. Whilst pricier models offer broadly similar performance and weight they have better gears, brakes and other components.
Price Sprint Eco £999 Other models range up to £1800 (extra battery option costs extra)
Contact www.ezeebike.com
UK availability www.onbike.co.uk

+ Good speed from an efficient hub motor.
− Not particularly light in electric bike terms, though comparable with similar specced bikes at the same price.

Author Richard Peace took an eZee Forza nearly 2,000km around France in 2007 - including through the Pyrenees.

Other Chinese machines

In recent years, many other Chinese brands have arrived in the UK. These tend to have large unbranded Li-ion batteries and BLDC motors, whose general design weaknessses are described elsewhere.

Having said that some firms have clearly made efforts to improve the quality of manufacture in China and to offer a decent level of service and backup to UK customers. Wisper is one such long-established company which has recently extended its range upmarket, introducing Alfine hub gears on Alpino models. Wisper offers a two-year battery guarantee if the battery capacity drops below 70% of the claimed figure. Other firms making progress in the same area include Freego, Byocycles and Juicy Bikes.

Chinese machines such as this Byocycle have had a measure of success at the budget end of the market. £600-£700 buys a large lithium-ion battery offering good range, but it will be unbranded, and generally sold with a rudimentary guarantee. Savings will also have been made in the components, such as bottom-bracket bearings, gears, brakes and suspension forks.

The Future

We've already talked a lot about the history of electric bikes and their current state, but what about the future? Is there a technical fix to the limitations of range and battery life? And is a world full of battery-powered vehicles really possible, or sustainable?

Technological trends

The battery hurdle

It is always difficult to predict in which direction technology will go, particularly with products like electric bicycles, which are changing very fast, but we can draw a few lessons from the current state of play. In the early years of this century, with the widespread adoption of light, cheap, and apparently reliable lithium-ion batteries, it looked as though the electric bike was about to come of age. That this has not been the case so far is down to the battery technology - although these batteries have been around for nearly a decade now, the original promise of lithium-ion has yet to be fulfilled. The batteries are certainly light, and their storage capacity in relation to their size and weight continues to improve, but they remain expensive, with a disappointingly short life.

In the world of electric cars, petrol or diesel/electric hybrids are now well established, but so-called 'plug-in' machines - able to go a reasonable distance on battery power alone - look as remote as ever, for the reasons mentioned above. A lithium-ion battery can have a considerable life when used as a 'buffer', providing short-term power storage. This is why they work well in hybrids, where the battery is primarily used to absorb braking energy and releasing it to give increased acceleration, but they still have limited range and charge cycle life under more arduous charging and discharging conditions.

So the future of electric vehicles depends on the development of the lithium-ion battery; if performance, reliability and price improve, the future will be about batteries. If not, the search will continue for a better alternative.

An interesting recent development in tram and heavy road vehicle applications is a combination of supercapacitors and lithium-ion batteries, and this may point the way forward for bicycles too. Unlike batteries, supercapacitors can recharge very fast and are more or less indestructible, but their storage capacity is limited, so they are still not practical on their own.

Combining the two technologies to get the best from both would involve some complex technology, but as Li-ion batteries already require a Battery Management System, not necessarily that much *more* complex. This sort of power pack would recharge in a matter of minutes and offer a reasonable riding range from a smaller (and hopefully cheaper) lithium-ion battery.

Fuel cells, whether hydrogen or methanol, certainly appear to be struggling in their current form for all sorts of practical reasons, although that might change very quickly with the right breakthrough. A small petrol/diesel or methanol internal combustion (IC) motor might make more sense in the short-term. As with the supercapacitors, this could operate in tandem with a smaller lithium-ion battery to produce an IC/battery hybrid of the kind now familiar in the motor industry. There are many complications in applying this technology to a bicycle, principally legislation - this would have to change in many parts of the world - not to mention the barriers posed by size, noise and weight. But it looks as though hybrid motorcycles will be the first development, with their near-future introduction likely to be driven by tighter pollution legislation rather than any perceived consumer need.

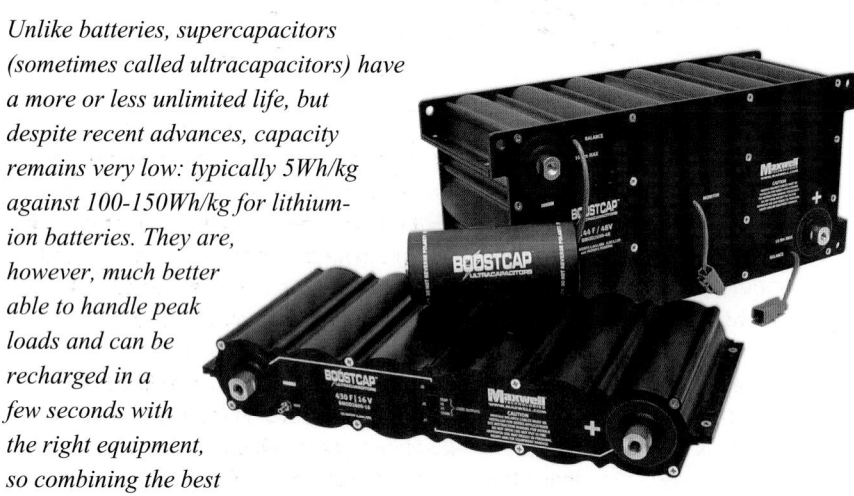

Unlike batteries, supercapacitors (sometimes called ultracapacitors) have a more or less unlimited life, but despite recent advances, capacity remains very low: typically 5Wh/kg against 100-150Wh/kg for lithium-ion batteries. They are, however, much better able to handle peak loads and can be recharged in a few seconds with the right equipment, so combining the best of both technologies in a supercapacitor/battery hybrid might make sense.

Motor and gear developments

Electric bike motors and drive systems are a fascinating area, and like the battery world, it's changing month by month. In theory a crank-drive is by far the best option, but developments have been slow, partly because for many years the market was dominated by a single company, Panasonic. With the return of Yamaha, a third generation system from Sunstar and entirely new crank-drives from Daum and Bosch, there are now five systems available, and it looks likely that cheaper, lighter and more innovative crank-drives will arrive as the market expands.

The advantage of crank-drives – that the power passes through the bicycle gearing – is also its Achilles heel, making these machines tricky to drive smoothly, and they are tough on gear systems too. These problems could be solved with a continuously variable gearbox (CVT), and Kalkhoff and Raleigh are about to release the first such production machine, combining a Panasonic crank motor with a NuVinci CVT.

The NuVinci continuously variable rear hub may herald the arrival of a fully automatic electric bike.

Riding such a machine is a great deal easier than a conventional electric bike, because you simply pedal and adjust the gear control to get the most comfortable pedal speed. As this can easily be sensed automatically, a fully automatic bicycle cannot be too far away. It would start off in the lowest gear and thereafter maintain a comfortable motor/pedal speed by adjusting the gear setting to suit road speed, gradient and power input. Despite the relative inefficiency of CVTs, this sort of system might even improve battery range because of the improved pedal and electrical efficiency of keeping at or near the ideal crank/motor speed.

A simpler way to keep the motor running close to its ideal speed is to fit a hub motor with its own internal gear system. Multiple gears are unlikely, but a two-speed system could be derived from the sun-and-planet gears, which are fitted to most hub motors anyway. A two-speed hub would pull away faster from road junctions and climb hills better in the low gear, yet cruise more comfortably at higher speeds in the high gear. Operation between the two gears would have to be automatic, but this technology has been used on mopeds for many years.

Overall efficiency and rideability would be much improved, but the two-speed hub is in some ways a less elegant solution than a crank-drive and CVT because it continues to utilise seperate gear systems for muscle and electrical power, involving unnecessary weight and complication, both of which are unwelcome on a bicycle.

The simplest system of all is the direct drive hub motor, which holds the promise of great things: near silent operation, low maintenance and easy regenerative braking. The only weaknesses are weight (these motors need to be large), low torque (making them weak on steep hills) and poor cooling under tough conditions. But the motors are improving all the time, and already up to the standards of less powerful geared hubs. With just another technological push, the direct drive motor may finally become an everyday fitment.

Another possibility is an entirely electrical system – a so-called 'series hybrid' – which seems to offer many theoretical advantages, but as yet, no practical ones! Power from the rider would be converted to electrical power in a small generator, combined with power from the battery and supplied to a normal (or of course two-speed) hub motor. This is a compelling idea, doing away with the gears and chain altogether, but at the moment the small loss of efficiency at each stage adds up to a serious loss of performance when compared to the remarkably adaptable, cheap and efficient Reynolds chain, which still dominates the bicycle transmission market after more than a century.

Driving down weight

Whatever the technology, the lessons of history suggest that bikes, motors and batteries will continue to get lighter. Ten years ago, hub motors weighing 4 or 5kg were not unusual, but the latest prototype hubs weigh as little as 1.6kg, and with improved materials and a continuing downward spiral in size, this is bound to reduce further. Ten years ago, batteries weighing 14kg were the norm, but the best batteries in 2010 weigh around 3kg, with output of 150 Wh/kg, so a 2kg battery with substantial range is certainly achievable very soon.

Perhaps most astonishing is the reduction in the size and weight of control units and peripherals. Something that might have weighed half a kilogram in the late 1990s, had been cut to 300g five years later, and the same speed control can now be achieved with a unit weighing less than 30 grams, small enough to fit inside the motor itself. Bulky, complex cables and connectors can, and are, being replaced by digital control, either wireless, or using the power wires as a databus. The real push for miniaturisation has come from the radio-controlled aircraft world, where the saving of a few grams on the battery, controller or motor can make a real difference to performance. Bit by bit these size and weight reductions are moving up into electric bikes.

In late 2010 a conventional (i.e. hub motor) power kit with output of 250 watts and range of 35 miles could weigh as little as 4kg, although no-one has yet put all the necessary elements together. The gross weight depends on the weight of the host bike, of course, but 8kg is not particularly high tech these days, giving an on-the-road weight of 12kg. So an electric bicycle no longer needs to weigh more than a typical bike, and they will no doubt get lighter still. A weight of 10kg is perfectly achievable. Less rugged products are already on sale weighing a lot less. The Pedalix friction drive comprises a 200 or 270Wh Li-ion battery and a radio-control type BLDC motor with a claimed continuous rating in excess of 250 watts. The claimed weight for this odd mixture of high tech and low tech (the drive is transmitted by a toothed belt to an aluminium roller rubbing on the tyre) is just 2.6kg. The manufacturers claim a range of up to 31 miles, which sounds achievable, but subject, of course, to the usual friction-drive caveats – poor starting and hill-climbing, and complete failure in the wet.

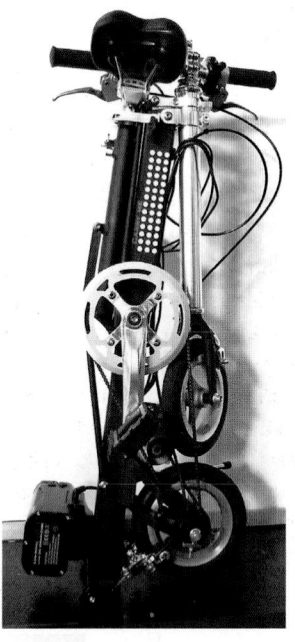

The Pedalix friction drive motor, battery and control circuitry adds just 2.6kg to the weight of a bike.

This micro-folder from Pacific Cycles of Taiwan uses a motor borrowed from the world of radio-controlled modelling to drive the rear wheel via a chain.
Total weight is said to be around 12kg, though miniaturisation looks set to take electric bikes even lighter.

Boom or bust?

Writing in late 2010, a Western European electric bike boom is underway, and the Dutch, as the Western World's foremost cycling nation, are being keenly watched. Electric bikes now account for around 10% of new bikes sold in the Netherlands and their relatively high prices have been a boon to independent bike shops, which make up nearly 90% of Dutch cycle outlets.

But could this - as suggested by some industry commentators - be a sales bubble that is about to burst? The argument goes that with big stack 'em high and sell 'em cheap' retailers arriving in the Netherlands, prices will crash and the market will collapse, the ripples spreading out to damage other markets too. Large retail chains, such as Walmart and Tescos, are already taking an interest in electric bikes in the UK and the USA, and there are signs that the drive to reduce prices is already damaging quality. The UK supermarkets are often vilified in the cycle press for the poor quality of their non-electric bicycles, and complete lack of maintenance back-up and technical know-how.

If the opposite happens, and sales continue ever-upwards, could electric bikes eventually replace traditional bikes in the Western world on a mass scale, as they have in China? Unless governments take to banning or at least restricting petrol-powered transport, as they have in many Chinese cities, this seems unlikely. However, a 2008 Dutch report conjectured on what might happen if electric bikes replaced traditional bikes in Dutch society and concluded '......promoting the use of electric bicycles may positively affect mobility, health and the environment. The Dutch will cycle more often and longer. This will probably not lead to less congestion, but will result in better accessibility. More Dutch will gain weight at a lower pace. And finally a net positive effect can be expected on climate change, due to reduction of CO_2 emissions.' In effect, the report predicted, more electric bikes would mean longer cycle trips, a meaningful percentage of which would replace car journeys.

From local networks to global resources

The birth of local charging networks

What if your electric bike could be topped up with electricity, just like pulling into a garage to refuel with petrol? Installation plans are already underway for the Netherlands' first city-wide recharging system, in what looks to be a race between the Dutch cities of Amsterdam and Rotterdam.

In 2009 Amsterdam opened the first electric recharging station, with technology provided by Californian-based company Coulomb Technologies. The city's aim, it says, is to be the first European city to welcome electric vehicles. In Rotterdam electric bikes and scooters may be charged by means of the OV-chipkaart, the Dutch public transport pass that had its first charging station in the guarded bicycle parking facility on the Rotterdam Meent (one of the main thoroughfares). And moves are afoot nationwide too; energy company Eneco and electric bike manufacturer Sparta have plans to open over 800 NRGSPOTS recharging stations. The new charging station includes a dedicated connection for Sparta ION e-bikes, besides a general connection suitable for all small vehicles, allowing chargers to be left at home.

An even more ambitious pilot scheme for pedelec rental was also just getting underway in Berlin in late 2010. When the scheme goes live in spring 2011, the 50 pedelecs will be available for hire from dedicated rental/charging stations. This is part of a wider concept which aims to integrate the largely electrified rail system with electric bike and car sharing to cover long and short journeys. Bosch, whose brand new crank-drive system is detailed in this chapter, was a partner in the scheme. Whilst good news for electric bikes in one sense - effectively expanding their range - these emerging public charging networks appear to be aimed just as much, if not more so, at electric cars. As noted in the first chapter, a widespread move to electric vehicles would place a huge strain on the electricity generating infrastructure.

But other recharging systems are already emerging as potential competitors. The E-bike Mobility solar charger, as its name suggests, is aimed purely at electric bikes. Examples

are already in use, designed specifically to suit the ubiquitous Li-ion Panasonic battery, popular on many crank-drive machines. The E-bike Mobility system has the advantage that it's essentially a sun-powered battery exchange scheme, using green electricity to charge a battery that is ready and waiting for you. But there are many potential pitfalls. The Panasonic battery may be ubiquitous, but it's by no means universal, and batteries continue to come in all shapes, sizes and voltages, some fitted with one of many charger plugs, while others (like the Panasonic) slot into a brand-specific docking station. Standardisation seems as far away as ever. And while battery life remains so limited, an exchange scheme means users will never quite be sure what they're getting!

The E-bike Mobility system, in this example using solar power to recharge Panasonic batteries, is already on the market and seeking customers.

Lithium - the new oil?

With the age of oil now drawing to a close it seems electricity is set to replace hydrocarbon combustion in vehicles - or at least it seems that way if you give any import to the recent activities of the world's major car companies. For example Toyota has publicly stated that it will mass-produce electric cars for the Chinese market from 2012 - a statement of serious intent if ever there was one. If the mass production of Li-ion battery electric vehicles really is just round the corner, can we be sure we are not just replacing the problems associated with oil supply - ranging from wars to economic instability - with similar problems based around a massive international market for, and dependence on, lithium?

What is clear is that the attitude of the car industry is now a million miles away from that of 1998 - the year it fought Californian legislation mandating 2% of vehicles sold in that year to be electric. Their opposition was based, in the words of a contemporary news article, 'on the grounds that electric vehicles are incapable of replacing internal combustion-engined cars. The automakers claim that battery storage is inadequate for the demands of commuters, charging technology is insufficiently advanced to maintain reliability, and the cost of producing electric cars will be uneconomic.'

Clearly we are getting beyond the scope of a book on electric bicycles, but it seems, if current trends continue, that demand from the car industry for lithium could well drive up the price of batteries for electric bikes. A few facts also suggest at least a note of caution as we appear to be welcoming in the lithium age:

- The bulk of easily accessible lithium deposits are in South America and China, so a lithium-based transport system would simply introduce two new areas of energy security concern for the US and Western Europe.

- Accessing the lithium reserves of South America on a greater scale would mean industrial exploitation of the world's largest salt flats - where it is estimated 50 to 70% of currently mined lithium reserves can be found. A particularly large and largely untapped resource is located in a vast Bolivian salt flat, the Salar de Uyuni. At present it is mined by local cooperatives who oppose mining by multi-nationals. The Bolivian government wants to develop its own lithium extraction plant to extract lithium in modest quantities.

- Global demand for lithium is expected to triple in the next fifteen years.

The big boys move in

Late 2010 saw a flurry of multi-national companies enter the electric bike arena. Details of real-world performance, accurate pricing and availability are somewhat sketchy in November 2010, but here is an outline of products that should arrive in the shops in 2011.

Shimano STePS

Shimano says its new electric-assist system will appear both as original equipment on electric bikes and as a retrofit kit. At first glance the system appears conventional enough - a front hub motor is fed by a rack-mounted battery. Unusually though, the system boasts regenerative power and a tiny 96Wh battery

that claims a charge time of less than an hour and a useful life of eight years in normal conditions! Shimano says the system will appear in the UK in 2011 and complete bikes should be in the range of €2,000-€3,000 (or the £ equivalent) **www.shimano.com**

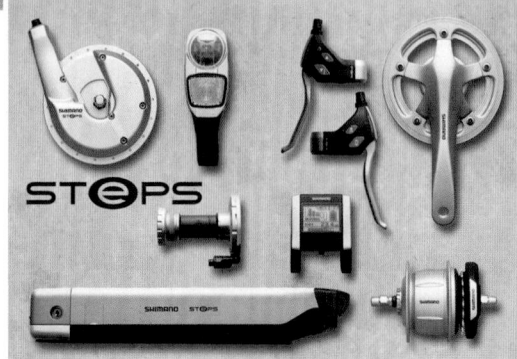

The STePS kit in use (above) at Eurobike 2010. Despite appearances, it's not just the usual hub motor set-up; it includes integral light, control unit, bottom bracket with sensor, brake levers and a hub gear option featuring electronic shifting.

Bosch

When a German based multi-national engineering company with no bicycle history enters the electric bike market it's a fair assumption it sees mass market popularity ahead for electric bikes. And backed by a multi-billion Euro research and development budget and a background in power tools and automotive electronics, expectation of success is inevitably high.

The Bosch system uses a common crank-drive motor but with a number of battery options: rack-mounted (below), frame-mounted (left) and Cannondale's own development, a battery doubling as a seatpost.

Launched at Eurobike 2010, the first electric bikes from Bosch's partnership with US bike giant Cannondale were aiming for a 2011 launch in Continental Europe with bikes at around the €2,800 mark. Cannondale couldn't confirm an exact UK launch date or price range. It looks as though competition will be fierce for Cannondale, with Bosch announcing it has also licensed the system for use by many other bike manufacturers, including one of Cannondale's main US rivals, Scott.

The paper spec certainly looks good - a conventional sounding pedelec built around a crank-drive motor designed and built by Bosch, featuring torque, speed and cadence settings and offering a range of support levels from 30% to 250%. The Li-ion battery is a smallish 288 Wh and claims a recharge time of two and a half hours.
www.bosch-ebike.de

Suntour HESC
Another announcement at Eurobike 2010, the Suntour HESC system (Human Electro Synergy Components) is a rather more conventional looking hub motor system. Exact launch details have been hard to come by.
www.srsuntour-cycling.com

Another giant of the cycle industry goes electric - Suntour's HESC system.

213

This Raleigh Velo-City prototype may look like just another electric bike, but it could break the mould of electric bikes in the UK when introduced in 2011. Along with the Velo-Trail, the Velo-City has quite an enviable spec list, including a high quality hub motor used on some top-end Dutch bikes, an effective pedal torque sensor making for smooth power transmission and a 370Wh battery with a two year guarantee. At just under four figures, the bike seems to have the value-for-money potential to knock similarly-priced UK competition flat and bring electric bikes to a truly mass market. Of course, the technology must pass muster in real world conditions, but 2011 certainly should be a fascinating year for UK electric bikes, one way or another.

Legal Matters

Legal matters - theory and practice in brief

The legal tangle untangled

In most countries where electric bikes are recognised in law, they are treated as 'normal' bikes - usually meaning no requirement for tax or insurance (and often no necessity to wear a helmet), but with a restriction on motor power and a speed limit at which power assistance must cut out. This lack of 'red tape' puts electric bikes in a very privileged position, but in practice the legislation has proved to be confusing, especially in the UK and US. Here's why.

The UK passed laws in 1983, stipulating two main criteria necessary for an electric bike to escape classification as a motor vehicle and thus avoiding road tax, insurance etc. These were:

- 15 mph maximum assisted speed, although you may exceed this limit if the motor is not giving assistance (a fairly easy matter on the flat).
- The bicycle's motor must provide no more than 200 watts continuous power (250 watts for tricycles and tandems).

Other criteria imposed by the 1983 Act include a minimum legal riding age of 14 and a weight limit of 40kg for electric bicycles (60kg for electric tricycles). Construction and Use Regulations from 1983 also specify requirements for this new breed of Electrically-Assisted Pedal Cycles (EAPCs). These include a requirement to display the manufacturer, the nominal voltage of the battery, and the continuous rated output of the motor.

This law is now apparently contradicted by a European Directive passed in 2002, which takes legal precedence in the case of a conflict. Speed and power caps dictated by the 2002 directive are:

- 25km/h (15.6mph) maximum assisted speed – again, you can exceed this limit if the motor is not assisting you.
- The bicycle's motor must provide no more than 250 watts of continuous rated power, and crucially, the 2002 Directive also states that the motor alone cannot be used to propel the bicycle i.e. it must be augmented by pedal power.

The UK's Department for Transport still quotes the 1983 / 200 watt law as definitive in its most recent consumer advice sheet, merely acknowledging the existence of the European law with a website link. However, the European government has pressed for the UK to clarify its own laws so as to bring them into line with Europe. Ultimately only action by the UK government, the European Commission (which has ultimate power to enforce the UK to comply with directives) or the European Court of Justice can resolve the situation.

The US's legal confusion results from the fact that federal law passed in Washington – putting a 750 watt cap on the motor rating and a maximum speed of

20mph – is consumer law only. State, county and city traffic laws may all put local interpretations on the types of vehicle that are allowed on their roads and what the technical requirements are.

Buying tips

Where does all this leave electric bike users and potential buyers in the UK and the US? In practice, you are unlikely to be stopped for riding an electric bike unless it is clearly travelling way above the legal limit under power. Electric bikes styled as mopeds however, are more likely to be stopped by the police, even when ridden at legal speed, usually because the 'moped' rider may not be wearing a helmet. One lady in the UK was stopped 17 times in one month for this reason! But despite their idiosyncrasies, the electric bike laws are there for your own safety. Should you be involved in any accident the law could well come into play.

So what steps can you take to ensure you are buying a legal electric bike?

• If you are buying a throttle-controlled machine - i.e an E-bike - ask exactly how this operates. This is the main practical point of conflict between UK and European law. Current and planned European Directives effectively class 'open' throttles as mopeds, but machines whose motor cuts out when you stop pedaling and also reduce power up to the cut out at 25km/h are likely to be regarded as electric bikes (in this respect at least). Much more debatable are 'off-road' switches that allow the rider to 'flip' between road-legal and 'moped' modes and these should be avoided by those worried about potentially falling foul of the law. Note that the European Directive of 2002 was phased in and was not retrospective, so pre-1999 throttle-only bikes will be classed as electric bikes in this respect and a few are still available secondhand. With machines manufactured and / or imported into the UK from 2000 to 2003 the law is particularly complicated. From 2004 to the present the machine should certainly not be throttle only (i.e.pedalling should be required to get power).

• Ask your retailer (or seller if buying second hand) if the bike falls within the law and preferably get that in writing.

• If they sound hazy or uncertain you could ask what the rated power of the motor is, and also the maximum assisted top speed. Check this falls within the limits listed in the table on pages 228 to 231. Note that very few will have independently tested the maximum speed of the bikes they sell, and figures supplied by the manufacturers are unlikely to be accurate.

• In any event check to see if the bike has any stickers or stamps on it indicating the continuous rating in watts (W) of the motor and/or the assisted speed limit, battery voltage and manufacturer. Also check for the CE mark (see following section).

• If you are buying a retrofit kit remember this will fall outside the scope of European law but will still be subject to the UK power and speed caps of 200 watt / 15mph.

- In the US you may want to check with the relevant state transportation department (for more detail on US state law see www.electricbicyclesbook.com). One strange anomaly of the UK's legal system is that Crown Dependencies, such as the Isle of Man, Jersey and Guernsey, have their own legal systems, effectively being outside the EU's legal obligations. Buyers and users of electric bikes there are advised to contact the local road transport departments.

UK and Europe head towards tighter standards

A 2004 Directive on electromagnetic compatibility, and a 2006 Directive laying down health and safety requirements for the design and construction of machinery, impose further requirements on electric bikes. It was confirmed in 2010 that road-legal electric bikes within European Union member states are subject to these Directives. Only if a bike conforms with both the Machinery and the EMC Directive can it to be sold in EU countries. In future compliance with a European technical standard, EN15194, will become compulsory for electric bikes and will amount to the same thing as complying with both directives. If you see EN14764 on an electric bike this actually refers to standards laid down for the manufacture of the cycle parts of the product and this can be found on many conventional bicycles too. What does it all mean in practice? The buyer of a new electric bike should check to see that the CE mark is displayed on the bicycle somewhere. This tells you that the bike has passed the tests as set down in the Directives (the same CE mark can be found on most household electrical items too). It also gives a powerful hint that the manufacturer or importer intends to be around to honour the warranty and deal with other issues – they will have spent large sums of money sending bikes for testing to gain official approval, or investing in equipment to 'self-certify' the machines.

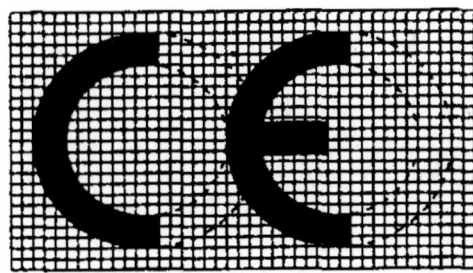

The CE mark should be present on any new electric bike you buy and tells you that it has been through a lengthy safety testing procedure.

Beyond 25km/h – fast electric bicycles and the law

Generally speaking, electric bikes exceeding the power or speed limits set down by Europe (or having an open throttle) will be classed as road vehicles (usually mopeds), and legal requirements for riding them on public roads will then depend on the laws of the EU state they are sold and/or used in. Under European law something called 'Type Approval' applies to all electric bicycles with power assistance above 25 km/h and/or continuous rated power exceeding 250 watts, as well as to all electric bicycles that can be propelled by the motor itself. In effect they become road vehicles subject to road traffic law.

Companies actually making and marketing such electric bicycles 'above board' (some are illegal US spec machines imported and sold as 'legal' bicycles) are becoming increasingly common in certain European countries.

In the UK an electric bike exceeding power and/or speed caps needs to jump through the legal hoops that apply to a moped i.e. a road tax disc (though as an electric vehicle it would actually be exempt from payment, insurance, helmet and - once the vehicle reaches a certain age - an MOT test certificate.

However, in some European countries there is a legal category lying between true electric bicycles and a full moped classification. Some requirements attach to this category of electric bikes, but they are less onerous than those attached to mopeds.

• In Germany, if the bike is capable of being electrically assisted up to 45km/h by a motor rated up to 500 watts it becomes a 'leichtmofa', or light moped class vehicle, requiring a licence and insurance, but not a helmet. Leichtmofas are not allowed to use urban bike paths in Germany. Hence manufacturers such as Riese & Müller have brought out 500 watt models capable of speeds of around 30mph, allowing them to mix with faster traffic on the highway.

• Similarly in Switzerland, bikes capable of assisted speed between 25km/h and 45km/h require a licence plate, but riders may also go helmetless. Bikes made specifically for this 'Swiss fast class' include some models from Velocity and Swiss Flyer.

How will future law develop?

Greater clarity on the more powerful classes of electric bike (i.e. those exceeding the current regulations) looks to be in the pipeline. After much wrangling between various trade associations - a conservative 'don't change anything' stance being taken by the representatives of some manufacturers of traditional bicycles and a liberal, deregulatory approach (including E-bikes) by others - it seems the future is looking a little clearer, with European legislation due in 2011 or 2012. The most recent draft directive suggests the creation of new classes of 'L' category vehicles (the term used in European law for certain 2- , 3- and 4-wheeled electric and combustion-engined vehicles). The proposed directive would replace the previous 'patchwork' of directives.

Electric bicycles would be categorised as follows:

- Category L1e "light two-wheel powered vehicle" with two subcategories.
  - L1Ae – Powered Cycle. Maximum assisted speed limited to 25 km/h as now, but the motor's continuous power rating would be raised to 1kW. Tricycles that met certain criteria would also fall within this category.
  - L1Be – Two wheel moped. Maximum speed 25km/h. Continuous motor output limited to 4 kW.

Looking further ahead, another proposal is for compulsory onboard diagnostic systems, to be phased in from 2017. Legal obligations on manufacturers to provide access to vehicle repair and maintenance information have also been proposed.

It seems electric bikes travelling up to 45km/h (like the Riese & Müller Delite on the right here), won't have their own European category; in 2010 the European authorities turned down such a suggestion in their proposed revision of European law on electric bikes. .

Battery rules

Yet another European Directive, known as the Battery Directive, applies to all batteries, including those commonly used in electric bicycles. These are classified as "industrial batteries" and the directive lays down regulations intended to ensure their safe disposal and/or recycling. Battery producers must cover the cost of collection, treatment and recycling of waste batteries.

The producer is defined as the person in an EU member country who supplies or makes available to a third party, batteries (including those incorporated into vehicles) for the first time in that country.

Particular regulations apply to industrial batteries. Producers (or their agents) must take back waste industrial batteries. All collected industrial batteries must be recycled, so they may not be disposed of in landfills or by incineration. By 26 September 2011, battery recycling processes must meet minimum recycling efficiencies of 65% for lead-acid batteries, 75% for nickel-cadmium batteries and 50% for other batteries.

Industrial batteries must be readily removable from electric bicycles. If the battery is integrated in the bicycle, it has to be accompanied by instructions showing how the batteries can be safely removed and who is the best person to do this. Batteries must be labelled with a crossed out wheeled bin and chemical symbols indicating the heavy metal content. Producers must be registered in the national register of all European member states countries where they place batteries on the market for the first time.

Old electric bike batteries should be taken to the nearest battery disposal point – most large council recycling centres have this facility. Please make sure you do this – rechargeable batteries contain some very unpleasant chemicals and heavy metals that will remain in the soil for a considerable time.

Lithium-ion battery carriage

Due to the unpredictable and occasionally explosive nature of lithium, there are strict regulations on the quantity that can be carried by air. Lithium-ion rechargeable batteries are considered safer than lithium primary cells, but the danger is still present. Regulations do not affect very small batteries, such as those fitted to laptops and cellphones, but they are certainly applicable to larger electric bike batteries.

The restrictions used to apply to batteries containing more than a set quantity of metallic lithium, the weight of lithium in grams being calculated from the formula: cell capacity in Ah x 0.3 x the number of cells. Thus a typical 10Ah, 37 volt electric bike battery would contain 3 grams of lithium per cell and with ten cells, 30 grams in a battery. Another useful formula assumes that the battery contains around 8 grams of lithium per 100 Wh of capacity. So by this route, the same typical battery would have a 370Wh capacity, giving a total lithium content of 29.6 grams.

In 2008, batteries containing more than 25 grams of lithium were banned from aircraft hand luggage, and in 2009 the restriction was tightened to two batteries of 160Wh (12.8 grams of lithium per battery), so carriage of most electric bike batteries is now banned. Lithium batteries should never be transported as checked-in baggage.

The American Department of Transportation reckons that lithium batteries may have been responsible for up to 40 incidents aboard planes since 1991, and the batteries have been implicated in connection with several hitherto unexplained crashes. It seems certain that legislation will continue to tighten.

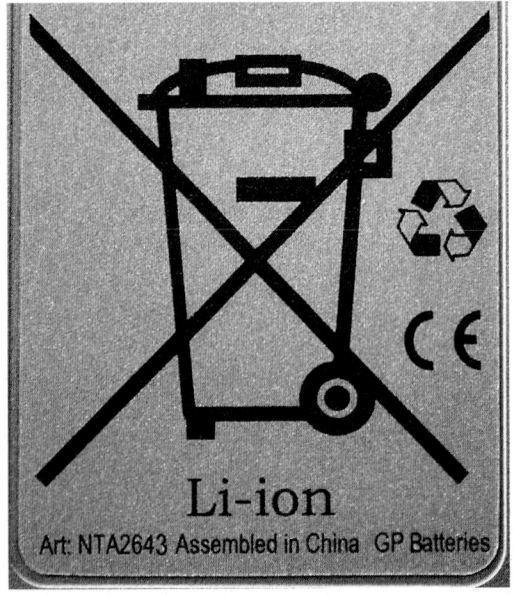

These markings on a lithium-ion battery sold in the UK in 2010 are typical.
The crossed out wheelie bin, advises you not to throw the battery in the bin, and the three little arrows indicate that the battery is made from recyclable material. The CE mark is explained on page 217.
Although the battery has been put together in China, because it is sold inside the EU it needs to conform to these legal standards.

The US and Canada - national and local laws

United States

As in the UK, electric bikes have barely hit the radar of lawmakers, with similar inconsistency as a result. US federal law says that electric bicycles are 'any bicycle or tricycle with a low-powered electric motor weighing under 100 pounds, with a top motor-powered speed not in excess of 20 miles per hour.' Federal law also lays down a maximum motor power rating of 750 watts.

However, this federal law only defines electric bicycles. This same law specifies that whether and how electric bikes can actually be used depends on state and local regulations. Unfortunately state law varies widely in this respect. Continuing this hierarchy, county law and city law can lay down further strictures. As an example, New York state does not - in theory - allow electric bikes on state and city roads, but in practice they are and without any practical problems or much attention from the police. A move was afoot to amend state law in line with the reality of electric bike use, but the senator proposing the amendment died and the impetus was lost. Boulder City, Colorado bans E-bikes of over 400W from bike lanes. In practice, if they are actually concerned about the legal situation most riders of electric bikes will look to state law - this regulates where electric bikes are allowed (public highways, bike paths etc) and requirements for riding such as age limits, helmet wearing, insurance etc.

The good news is that prosecutions for riding electric bikes illegally appear to be almost unheard of - as in the UK, if an electric bike is more bike-like than moped-like in appearance it will probably not attract the attention of the long arm of the law. The reason for the apparently confused legal state of affairs is that in many states electric bikes appear to be caught unwittingly by legislation aimed at either cycles fitted with small petrol engines or small mopeds.

What shape is future legislation likely to take? Eric Sundin, of Seattle's Electric Bikes Northwest, is in no doubt; 'It can safely be assumed that US statutes shall become ever more lenient as far as still allowing throttle control only and more power and speed'. This is in stark contrast to some Canadian states like Ontario, whose recent laws seem aimed at excluding powerful moped style machines from the electric bike category of vehicles.

www.electricvehiclesnw.com

Canada

Canada's Motor Vehicle Safety Regulations (MVSR) define Power Assisted Bicycles (PABs) as two- or three-wheeled bicycles with a 500 watt motor limit and 32 km/h speed limit. Both pedelecs and e-bikes are allowed, but the latter must have a power cut-off when the brakes are applied and the former when pedalling is stopped.

As in the US, local Canadian jurisdictions can pass supplementary laws - and nine have passed laws explicitly allowing electric bikes for public road use and are treating these vehicles as conventional bicycles and not as motor vehicles. These are Alberta, British Columbia, Manitoba, Nova Scotia, Newfoundland and Labrador, Ontario, Quebec, Saskatchewan and the Yukon Territory. Five of these jurisdictions have a minimum age requirement - 12 years in Alberta, 14 in Manitoba and 16 in British Columbia, Ontario and Quebec.

Ontario in particular paid quite some attention to its law, conducting a three-year pilot study, resulting in detailed legislation in 2009. Unusually, Ontario's law stated that, to fall outside motor vehicle legislation, electric bikes must have wheels with a minimum diameter and width of 350mm and 35mm respectively - presumably a move aimed at outlawing scooter type machines, but a requirement that may also unintentionally catch some of the smaller-wheeled electric folders. Machines must also have two independent braking systems for front and rear wheels that are capable of bringing the bike to a full stop within 9 metres from 30km/h. Users will also need to wear a helmet. Despite these strictures this law represents a considerable degree of liberalisation in Alberta and has effectively legalised many machines previously considered mopeds, bringing down the price as a consequence.

Justin Lemire-Elmore of Grin Technologies, a firm specialising in electric kit sales, notes that once the kits are fitted to bikes and put on the public road they have to fall in line with the above regulations. Yet, despite the plethora of regulations, Justin confirms that very few riders - however compliant (or not) their bike - are getting into trouble with the law.

www.ebikes.ca

UK consumer law and electric bikes

An outline

In the UK consumer law (mainly in the form of the Sale of Goods Act 1979 and the Sale and Supply of Goods Act 1994) affords a lot of protection and is much underused.

Not only should the product conform to any description given of it by the retailer or manufacturer (e.g. a description on a label or tag or in a catalogue) but it should be of 'satisfactory quality'.

What is satisfactory, of course, will always be open to debate in any particular case - but this law is still a powerful tool for those who feel they have been sold a genuinely sub-standard electric bike. 'Satisfactory quality' is judged by a number of criteria, based on what a 'reasonable person' would find acceptable with regard to:

- Price paid
- Fitness for purpose specified
- Appearance, finish and freedom from minor blemishes
- Safety and durability

If it becomes apparent that an item is not of the quality you were led to expect, that you were not aware of this when you bought it, and you bought from a seller acting 'in the course of a business' (i.e. from someone who is a trader, rather than a private individual), you are quite within your rights to go back to the retailer, even after some months of use. If a product develops a fault within the first six months, the assumption will be that this defect was present at the time of purchase and you will not have to prove anything. If you are returning an item after this six-month time period, this automatic assumption does not apply, and it will be up to you to prove the fault did not occur through misuse.

Occasionally buyers might have an incident or accident because a bike is simply dangerous to ride. For example, one test bike tried by one of the authors decided to accelerate away on its own at full power, even without the throttle twistgrip being touched - had this happened at a different time it could have lead to a very nasty accident. And some cheap and cheerful pedal sensing mechanisms leave a delay of several seconds before the motor kicks in - hardly an ideal situation for controlled and relaxed riding.

Unsafe goods are generally covered by the Consumer Protection Act which says, critically, that some damage such as personal injury or damage to private property (other than the bike itself – damage to this is not covered under this Act) must have occurred (if not there may still be scope for action under the Sales of Goods Act). Obvious caveats apply - the fault must have caused the damage and you shouldn't have used the bike inappropriately or ignored safety instructions.

This law complements and can be used alongside any warranty given with the bike - it doesn't replace it. All credible electric bikes should come with a year's warranty *at the very least* (a two-year warranty is obviously preferable, and may soon be the norm). As lithium-ion battery failure has been all too common with some makes of bike, some manufacturers have applied a shorter guarantee period just to the battery - for example a six-month guarantee for the battery and 12 months for the rest of the bike. Beware of this tactic! (see the chapters *The Battery* and *Choosing, Using & Maintaining* for more detail on lithium-ion batteries).

There are a couple of other legal points worth knowing:

● If buying by credit card remember the card issuer is jointly liable with the retailer if something goes wrong. This gives you the choice of claiming your money back from the retailer or the credit card company. You still have to prove your case of course - or have it accepted by the retailer or credit card company. This could be a useful piece of knowledge though, should the retailer happen to become untraceable or go bust.

● When you buy online or from a catalogue, you can cancel your order at any time up to seven working days from the day after you receive the goods. Consumers must be given clear information including details of the electric bike offered, delivery arrangements and payment, the supplier's details and the consumer's cancellation right before they buy.

Faulty goods - practical steps

You should always attempt to solve the problem via the seller before taking any further steps. Giving the retailer several attempts to remedy the problem may well do the trick and, in any event, if action is taken a court will always look to see if both parties have made every effort to resolve the dispute. If you haven't it may well count against you, especially with regard to the costs of the case.

If all reasonable approaches to the retailer have failed, the next question will be whether to consult a solicitor or use what is known as the 'small claims court' (this is the special procedure for handling smaller value claims in the County Court). The latter is generally done in person by the disgruntled buyer. Whilst this procedure may seem daunting to those with no legal background, it's actually pretty user-friendly for a layman. The main features of the small claims procedure are:

● The claims limit is £5,000 and so should cover the vast majority of electric bike purchases.

● Several court and claims fees may be payable, but may be reclaimable from the other side if you win the case (you may be exempt from these if receiving one of the qualifying state benefits).

● Option of one month's 'breathing space' to allow both parties to try and settle the claim.

● Free mediation service where an independent court official will talk to both parties and try and settle the dispute.

● A hearing may not be necessary - the judge may decide to use written evidence only.

- If the case does come to court you can choose another person to speak for you. It may well be worth having an initial consultation with a solicitor in any event and especially if your case appears complex - they could advise you on your chances of success and suggest tips, even if you end up going down the small claims route by yourself. For claims of more than £5,000 consulting a lawyer is highly advised.

A real-life example

The buyer's electric bike developed a battery problem within the first few months after purchase. Several mechanical problems also emerged but battery reliability was the main ongoing defect. The battery range had declined rapidly after fewer than 100 partial recharges whereas the seller's website indicated they should be good for 500 recharges (quite a popular claim). A replacement battery was organised but this began to decline in range after just 30 recharges.

The seller took the second battery back for testing, but said the test results did not reveal a problem. The situation then reached an impasse with the seller claiming it had never advertised the battery as being capable of 500 recharges and also that the buyer could have discharged it below a 'safe' discharge voltage. This would have been virtually impossible to achieve in practice, because all Li-ion batteries are protected by an internal Battery Management System. And if the BMS had failed, it would imply a fault with the battery rather than any maltreatment by the buyer.

The small claims procedure was invoked and the buyer won, the judge finding that the seller had indeed claimed at the time of the sale that the battery would survive 500 recharges before deteriorating to 80% of its new capacity, despite the sellers protestations to the contrary. The bike was picked up by the seller with the buyer paying around £100 for the benefits he had received for use of the bike (technically known as 'betterment'), which was deducted off a full refund.

Clearly there are several lessons to be learned from one of the few court cases involving electric bikes:

- At several stages in the negotiations the buyer agreed to the seller's attempts to remedy faults but always stated he was 'reserving his position' - in other words reserving his right to ask for a full refund should the problems persist.
- Written notes were made by the buyer of all conversations with the seller.
- The buyer got advice from the legal helpline that came with his household insurance policy, so check your policy to see if it covers any aspect of a potential claim.
- Keep a copy of any claims made by the seller at the time of purchase e.g. pages from their website which may later be removed.
- One final important point is that there are strict time limits for various claims, so it is important to act quickly and, preferably, take some sort of advice at the outset.

www.communitylegaladvice.org.uk

www.adviceguide.org.uk

Bikeline (Alyson France & Co. Solicitors) www.bikeline.co.uk

Spares and repairs

Unfortunately there is no obligation in the UK for manufacturers to supply spares or after-sales service for electric bikes - even if they are still in production. Traditionally, bike shops have been reluctant to get involved with electric bikes for the very reason they may be asked for after-sales service in an area where they have little experience - or where they do not trust the manufacturer or distributor to provide advice and spares.

If a spare is not available you may be able to fall back on the Sale of Goods Act or the guarantee if it seems to be a case of malfunction rather than 'wear and tear' over a lengthy period. Guarantees are normally offered by the manufacturer but may also be offered by retailers and are in addition to your statutory rights under the Sales of Goods Act. It can also be worth asking household insurers whether electric bike repair is covered under their policy and if not what the extra cost might be.

There is a move in the UK industry to provide a higher and more uniform standard of after-sales backup. The British Electric Bike Association (BEBA) are currently working on accredited training for cycle mechanics and electric bike technicians via Cytech (the bike maintenance qualification arm of the Association of Cycle Traders). An electric bike module should be available as part of a Cytech bike maintenance qualification or as a course in itself, to members, cycle shop employees and members of the public. Hopefully such voluntary moves will drive up standards over time, as will a willingness by disgruntled buyers to take legal action if really necessary.

www.thecyclingexperts.co.uk
www.beba-online.co.uk

COUNTRY / AREA	RELEVANT LAW	MOTOR POWER LIMIT
UK	The Electrically Assisted Pedal Cycles Regulations 1983 (however note it is extremely likely that Directive 2002/24/EC also applies in full to electric bikes currently sold in the UK, though this has not been tested in a court of law). EAPCs also need to comply with Directive 73/23/EEC (commonly known as the Low Voltage Directive) and the Electromagnetic Compatibility Directive 89/336/EEC. Confirmation should be sought via the Department of Trade and Industry.	Bicycle 200w Tandem / tricycle 250w continuous rated power
EUROPEAN UNION COUNTRIES	Directive 2002/24/EC (though note a new replacement Directive is due in 2011 or 2012) European standard EN 15194 adopted by all EU countries, aimed at consumer safety and product reliability. EN15194 lays down details of tests required to which will enable complying electric bikes to be marked with the CE sticker. EN 15194, in effect, implements two Directives: 2006/42/EC (the 'Machine Directive') 2004/108/EC (the 'Electromagnetic Compatability Directive').	250W
SWITZERLAND	Although Switzerland is not in the EU is has similar domestic laws on electric bikes - see Directive 2002/24/EC above.	250W

MAX ASSISTED SPEED	PEDELECS OR E-BIKES ALLOWED?	MIN AGE BIKE WEIGHT	BIKES EXCEEDING LEGAL LIMITS
15mph / 24km/h Models fitted with 'off-road' switches allowing greater speeds are probably not within the law	Both	14 40kg (60kg for trikes)	Considered to be a motor vehicle requiring a tax disc, insurance and registration. Helmet also required.
25km/h	Pedelecs only (i.e. throttle-only models classed as mopeds)		Considered to be 'low performance mopeds' if the motor does not exceed 1kW and the maximum speed of 25km/h. Low-performance moped classification will bring with it some restrictions, depending on the the country; for example compulsory wearing of a helmet, an age limit, obtaining a number plate and having a driving licence. Low performance mopeds may be excluded from some legal requirements for standard mopeds.
25km/h	Pedelecs only (i.e. throttle-only models classed as mopeds)		There is a so-called 'Swiss fast class'. There is a power limit but no speed limit on qualifying electric bikes. However, such models must get 'type-approval' which in practice effectively limits speed to around 35-45km/h, depending on the individual rider's fitness.

COUNTRY / AREA	RELEVANT LAW	MOTOR POWER LIMIT
US	Public Law 107-319 passed by Congress 2001 classes electric bikes within certain criteria as bicycles. They are then subject to the Consumer Product Safety Act and also to State law on bicycles. This means there may be *extra* legal requirements passed by individual states.	750W
CANADA	Motor Vehicle Safety Regs 2001 These define Power Assisted Bicycles (PABS) Power-assisted bicycles must also comply with the requirements of provincial and territorial regulations. Each province or territory may adopt the federal definition as is, or add further restrictions to meet their own specific needs. Consumers interested in determining whether power-assisted bicycles can be used in their province or territory should contact their provincial or territorial Ministry of Transportation	500W

MAX ASSISTED SPEED	PEDELECS OR E-BIKES ALLOWED?	MIN AGE	BIKES EXCEEDING LEGAL LIMITS
Max speed less than 20mph	Must have functional pedals	A matter for state, county or city law	A matter for state, county or city law
20mph / 32km/h		A matter for local jurisdiction	A matter for local jurisdiction

Technical Glossary & Listings

Glossary of technical terms

AC - Alternating current. The direction of current periodically reverses. Tends to be used for higher voltages and long distance power transmission for reasons of safety and efficiency. Mains current in the home is AC, and will generally be reduced in voltage using a transformer and 'rectified' into DC (Direct Current) for charging an electric bike

Amps (A) - Short for Amperes. A measurement of the 'volume' or 'quantity' of electricity in a circuit. The flow of amps in an electric bike varies from about 10 amps to 60 amps - the latter requiring thick wiring and substantial switchgear.

Amp Hours (Ah) - This is the measure of current flow against time. It is used by battery manufacturers to indicate the capacity of battery cells, and has also been used by bike manufacturers to show the capacity of a whole battery, but it doesn't do this! To find the capacity of a battery, Ah must be multiplied by the voltage of the battery to get watt-hours (Wh) - a much handier measure, enabling direct and meaningful comparisons to be made.

Battery Management System (BMS) - Now, almost universal in lithium-ion batteries, BMSs control many aspects of battery operation, including the maximum current output (to neutralise an accidental short circuit), restricting charging when the battery is full, and constantly monitoring the battery cells' condition. In lithium-ion batteries the BMS acts as a failsafe mechanism to prevent permanent damage and even fire.

Belt Drive Toothed rubber belt used to transmit drive to the wheels. The smooth reverse side of the belt may be used to transmit power direct to the tyre as in the Sinclair Zeta, but more usually the toothed belt transmits motor output to the rear hub.

Brushes / Brushless Motors - In a DC electric motor brushes are used to transfer the current from stationary wires to the moving parts of the motor (they are also used in some alternators and generators to take a small current to the rotating field coils). Brushed motors have been around since the 19th century. Brushless motors were developed to overcome the main disadvantage of brushed motors - their reliance on the physical contact of the brushes which results in friction and wear. Brushless (BLDC) motors use 'Hall Effect' sensors within the motor to determine which winding in the motor requires power. Sensorless BLDC motors sense position by monitoring small voltages in the windings, thus doing away with the sensors.

Cells (Battery Cells) - The units of which batteries are made, consisting of positive and negative plates which allow it to store electrical energy. Cells are often called batteries, but a battery is technically a group of cells in series.

Controller - Also known as the power controller. In electric bike terms the controller controls the timing, direction and strength of the current to the motor to give precise and efficient control.

Crank Motor - A motor that delivers power to a bike through the pedal crank area. Makes of crank motor include Bosch, Daum, Panasonic and Sunstar.

Current (or Electrical Current) - A flow of electrons in a circuit.

DC - Direct current i.e. electric current running in one direction only. Electric bike batteries supply direct current, and some motors use it, but in most the direct current is broken up into pulses by the control unit. See also AC.

Depth of Discharge / Discharge - The amount of energy removed from the battery, expressed as a percentage. 70% depth of discharge means a battery still has 30% of its energy remaining. 'Deep discharge' is the discharging of all energy in the battery to the point where it will not deliver any more power. Most electric bike batteries do not like constant deep discharges and prefer to be kept topped up. NiMH batteries, however, benefit from periodic deep discharges. This 'refresh' function may be achieved with a suitable charger (the Giant Lafree charger has such a feature).

EAPCs - Electrically-assisted pedal cycles - also known as pedelecs. Electric bikes that deliver power when you push on the pedals. You may also see references to EPACs (electric pedal-assisted cycles) which are the same as EAPCs!

E-bike - Also known as EPVs (electrically-powered vehicles). Put simply, they are electric bikes controlled by a throttle twist grip rather than through pedal assist. Also see EAPCs and Pedelecs.

EPVs - Electrically powered vehicles. See E-bikes.

Friction Drive - Direct transmission of power to the wheel, using a roller or belt applied to the tyre. Sometimes used in the early days of electric bikes, the ZAP being one of the most popular examples.

Fuel Cell - A device that converts a fuel (examples include compressed hydrogen gas and liquid methanol) into electric current. They have been used to power 'concept' electric bikes but have yet to find practical use in bicycles and tricycles.

Hall Effect Sensors - Used in brushless DC motors, these tiny components measure the position of the motor's rotation very accurately, feeding the information back to the controller and allowing the correct amount of current to be delivered to the correct winding. See also Sensorless BLDC motor.

Hub Motor - The commonest design of electric bicycle motor. It can be housed in either the front or rear wheel hub of the bike (though front-wheel drives are more usual). See also Belt Drive, Crank Motor and Friction Drive for other types of drive system.

Lead-Acid (LA) - The commonest type of rechargeable battery technology in the world, but becoming rare on electric bikes due to its high weight to energy ratio. Now found only on some of the least expensive models.

Lithium Ion (Li-ion) - Becoming the dominant electric bike battery technology due to its superior energy density compared to other types. Early doubts over safety are being overcome, but a question mark remains over the Li-ion's ultimate life and reliability.

Memory Effect - A partially discharged battery losing some of its ability to charge fully. NiCd batteries are prone to this.

Nickel Cadmium (NiCd) - A mid-1990s battery technology, now almost unheard of. Overtaken by Nickel Metal Hydride which offered better performance and didn't feature dangerous cadmium that was difficult to recycle. NiCd batteries also suffered from the Memory Effect.

Nickel Metal Hydride (NiMH) - Still seen on a small number of electric bikes today, NiMH batteries succeeded NiCd technology due to their better energy to weight ratio and easier recycleability.

Ohms - Unit of measurement for electrical resistance against the flow of current.

Open Circuit Voltage - The voltage of a battery or other electricity generating device (e.g. solar panel) that is not connected to a circuit. It is higher than the voltage under load (i.e. when the generating device is connected to a circuit and doing useful work).

Parallel Connection - Batteries connected together so that the voltage remains the same but the current (and therefore the Ah capacity) is multiplied. Two 12 volt, 7 amp hour batteries in parallel would give a 12 volt, 14 amp hour power source.

Pedelec - Electric bike with power provided only when pedalling. Also known as electrically-assisted pedal cycles (EAPCs) or electric pedal-assisted cycles (EPAC).

Photo Voltaics - Cells that convert solar radiation (primarily sunlight) into direct current electricity - solar panels to me and you.

Resistance (or Electrical Resistance) - The degree to which a given material opposes the flow of electrical current - a good analogy in the mechanical world is friction. Some early electric bicycles used resistors to control the amount of power reaching the motor. Electrical resistance is measured in Ohms (Ω).

Reverse Polarity - If a DC circuit is wired backwards, so that the positive wire is given a negative charge and vice versa, it is said to have reverse polarity. This is not normally possible on an electric bike, but if it is done happen, the delicate electronics in the controller and/or motor may be destroyed. Reverse polarity can also occur within a battery if one of the cells drops to zero volts and the machine continues to be used. Power will then effectively be forced backwards through the weak cell which can be very damaging, particularly with Li-ion, where the Battery Management System (BMS) should stop reverse polarity from occurring.

Sealed Lead-Acid (SLA) - One sub-type of lead-acid battery that is classed as maintenance-free, in that it cannot be topped up with water. The electrolyte is in the form of a gel, but there will always be a safety valve to prevent explosion if the battery is misused. SLA batteries can even be used upside down..

Sensorless BLDC Motor - One of the most recent advances in motors, these designs are a derivative of the brushless DC (BLDC motor that is able to sense the motor position without the complex and troublesome sensors used on previous brushless motors.. See also Hall Effect Sensors.

Series Connection - Battery cells connected together in a string,positive to negative, so that voltages are cumulative (e.g. ten 1.2 volt cells make a 12 volt battery), with an amp hour capacity the same as only one of the cells. See also Parallel Connection.

Switchgear - General term for the switches used to control the electrical current in a circuit.

Torque (*T*) - A measurement of force, typically the turning force on a shaft, generally measured in newton metres (Nm). Torque multiplied by the speed of the shaft gives the power output, usually measured in watts. If an electric bike with a given wattage of power output is geared to provide high torque and low speed, it will be good hill climbers. If it is geared to produce low torque and high speed, the bike will perform badly on hills but go better on the flat. A bike with greater power output will be stronger in one or both areas.

Valve-Regulated Lead-Acid Battery (VRLA) - In the Valve-Regulated Lead-Acid battery vented hydrogen and oxygen are recombined and returned to the electrolyte, so that the cell can be partially sealed. Safety valves are still fitted to allow any excess gas to escape.

Volts / Voltage (V) - A measurement of the 'strength' or 'pressure' of electric power. Electric bikes tend to use batteries of 24 volts and above.

Watts (W) - A measurement of power output and the most important figure when looking at an electric bike system. The electrical input power to a motor can be found by multiplying the voltage of the battery by the current drawn. Roughly speaking, electric bike systems have peak power inputs in the 250 watt to 1,000 watt range. The mechanical power output from a motor can be found by multiplying speed by torque. Stored power in a battery or similar device is measured in watt-hours (Wh). So, for example, X Wh in a battery might can be converted into a turning force of Y newton metres at Z speed for M minutes, resulting in forward motion!

Put the glossary into practice! The two most useful tools for measuring electricity in relation to an electric bike are a plug-in meter and a multimeter (below, left and right).

The plug-in meter lets you measure the watt-hour capacity of a battery, vital to monitor its condition. A good quality multi-meter lets you measure battery voltage levels as well as current and resistance levels in wiring.

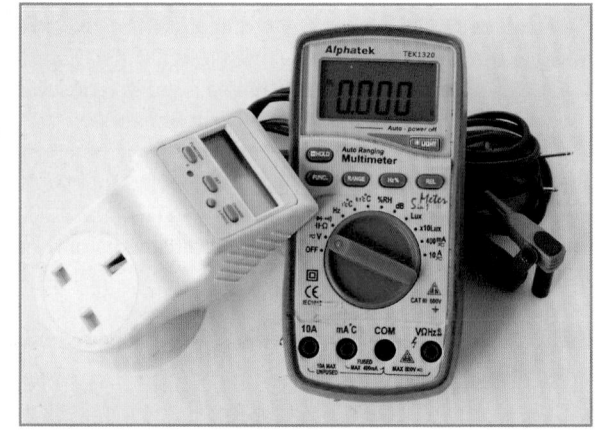

Where are electric bikes made and does it matter?

As a British publisher, it's nice to be able to point out products with a significant British input. This isn't just blind patriotism (well, maybe a bit...), it has an environmental aspect too, because the more locally components are made, the lower their carbon footprint in getting to the consumer. It's an argument for Europeans to buy European-made bikes, the Chinese to 'buy Chinese' and so on. Even if the components are imported, local assembly will still keep a slice of the bike's value in the local economy.

As well as nationality, another big issue is the type of manufacturer. Specialist manufacturers such as Cytronex (electric sports bikes), Cycles Maximus (load-carrying trikes) and Nano-Brompton (electric folders) produce machines designed by cyclists who have invested a lot of their own knowledge, time and money in perfecting the design. For an excellent all-round pedelec, you can't beat the big resources of Raleigh, E-motion or Kalkhoff, but the smaller concerns can offer in-depth knowledge for niche products which may be just what you are seeking.

In this book, we have often warned about the dangers of low-quality Chinese E-bikes. But the Chinese industry is quite capable of producing decent quality equipment, such as the efficient, quiet and relatively powerful Tongxin motor. The difficulty lies in sorting the good from the bad and the indifferent; something this book will hopefully help you do.

For a huge interactive database of more than 160 manufacturers worldwide see

www.atob.org.uk

Electric Bike Manufacturers

Name	Description	Manufacture	Design	
Akkurad	Manufacturer of electric-assist velo mobiles and add-on kits.	-	-	-
Antec	Hub-motor pedelecs.	China	Netherlands	
Anthrotech	Recumbent tricycle manufacturer with electric-assist option.	-	-	-
AS Bikes	Budget folders.	China	China	
Ave	German-made city-styled pedelecs.	Taiwan	Germany	
Babboe	Dutch cargo bikes in the 'bakfiets' style.	-	-	
Batavus	Dutch style city bikes - part of the Accell group, so extremely similar in style to Sparta.	Netherlands	Netherlands	
Batribikes	Range of hub motor bikes.	China	China	
Bauer	Hub-motor pedelecs.	Multiple	Germany	

Where Can I Try Out Electric Bikes?

There a number of specialist retailers in the UK who are happy for you to try out electric bikes at their premises:

50 Cycles www.50cycles.com 0800 0288116
Test ride centres at Richmond Park and Loughborough.

Atmosphere Electric Bikes www.electricbikes.org.uk 0117 9087153
Demo areas at Bristol and Coventry.

Cycle Heaven www.cycle-heaven.co.uk 01904 636578 / 651870
Stock several brands of quality electric bike in York.

Cyclesense www.cyclesense.co.uk 01937 844068
Range of demonstration models available to try out in very quiet conditions (subject to weather!) at Cyclesense's Thorp Arch site in Yorkshire.

E-Bikes Direct www.e-bikesdirect.co.uk 01580 830959 and 0207 7207973
Test facilities at Bodiam, East Sussex and Battersea, London.

Electric Cycle Company www.electriccyclecompany.co.uk 0131 552 0999
Demonstrator models and electric bike hire at Granton, Edinburgh.

Electric Mountain Bikes www.electricmountainbikes.com 01751 432936
Experienced electric mountain-biker Steve Punchard offers a range of kits and bikes at Kirkbymoorside in the North Yorks Moors. Try-outs by prior arrangement.

Electric Transport Shop www.electricbikesales.co.uk sales@TETS.biz
0117 955 2271   01223 247410   0207 4822892   01865 243937
A chain of shops with outlets in Bristol, Cambridge, London and Oxford.

Kinetics www.kinetics.org.uk 0141 0141 942 2552
Long-established shop run by very knowledgable owner Ben Cooper in Bearsden, Glasgow.

OnBike www.onbike.co.uk 07944 636080 / 01299 251514
A wide range of makes on offer at shops in Presteigne and Kidderminster.

Raleigh's dealer network Full list of dealers at www.raleighebike.co.uk
Visit the website to book a free test ride at one of 57 local dealers.

Velospeed www.velospeed.co.uk 01635 579304
Daum, E-motion, GoCycle and Velospeed electric bikes at Aldworth in Berkshire.

US and Canadian readers might like to try:

Electric Wheels Northwest www.electricvehiclesnw.com 206 5474621
Store in Seattle, Oregon.

Nyce Wheels www.nycewheels.com (800) 6923943
New York city store.

Grin Technologies www.ebikes.ca 604 5690902
Specialists in kits located in Vancouver, Canada. .

Events & Shows

Cycle Show www.cycleshow.co.uk
Premier UK showcase for all things cycling. 2011 show at NEC Birmingham 29 September – 2 October (first day trade only, otherwise open to all). Huge number of stands. Try out facilities. Favourite launch pad for new products. Presentations from industry experts and cycling celebs.

Eurobike www.eurobike-show.de
A trade show with a huge range of exhibitors from around the world. The electric bike area has grown year by year and the test track is incredibly popular. Usually held in early October each year.

SPEZI www.specialbikesshow.com
Annual show of all kinds of 'special' bikes, including electric ones. Held each spring in Gemersheim, Germany.

Tour de Presteigne www.tourdepresteigne.co.uk
The self-styled 'world's premier electric bike race' seems to have become an annual fixture in this small town on the Welsh border. Hill-climbs, races, exhibitors and try-outs and lots more.

John Hymas looks to be combining business and pleasure on a Giant Suede at Presteigne in 2008. (Photo courtesy of Phil Key, OnBike).

Consumer websites

A to B www.atob.org.uk 01305 259998
Hugely comprehensive site on car-free travel and carbon-neutral living. Features electric bike reviews, buyers' guide and manufacturers listing. Also covers folding bikes and taking bikes on trains.

www.bikeradar.com
Huge website cover many types of cycling but concentrating on road bikes and racing. It covers electric bike developments too.

www.electricbikemag.co.uk
Plenty of reviews and features. There's a free paper magazine out bi-monthly as well as the digital edition.

www.recyclenow.com
Type in your postcode and see your local recycling facilities. Includes a filter that lets you see battery recycling points (though note electric bike batteries are only likely to be accepted at the larger council depots - many of the battery recycling points listed here will only take smaller batteries).

Experts & forums

http://users.tinyworld.co.uk/flecc/
Lafree guru Tony Flecchia's site on how to keep the Giant Lafree Twist series on the road. Information and repair pages for the Panasonic motor units produced from 2001 onwards.

www.pedelecs.co.uk
Lively electric bike forum with lots of interesting facts and snippets posted. Some good reviews and articles elsewhere on the site, though some are a bit dated. Good small ads.

Trade & professional bodies

BEBA www.beba-online.co.uk
Founded to promote electric cycles and develop the market. Members are electric bicycle manufacturers and distributors.

ETRA www.etra-eu.com
The European Twowheel Retailers Association is a Europe-wide lobbying and promotional association especially involved with promoting cycling, including electric bicycles, at government level.

Ecobatterien www.ecobatterien.lu/en
Site for producers and importers of batteries, givng advice on the European battery directive

PRESTO www.presto-cycling.eu
A superb central collection and dissemination point for the best policy in European cycling. They promote electric bikes too and do an excellent policy guide on them.

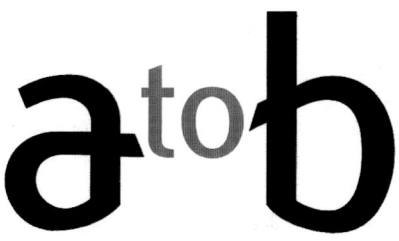

www.atob.org.uk

A to B magazine specialises in car-free sustainable alternatives of all kinds including: folding bikes, electric bikes, trailers, trikes, public transport, solar-power, children's bikes and much more

- Bi-monthly magazine, with starter pack offers, paper and / or digital subscription. Two million word back catalogue!

- Wide-ranging website including bike buyers' & price guides to electric and folding bikes, world list of electric bike manufacturers, electric motorbikes, bike rail travel, sustainable living and the exclusive chance to buy signed copies of the author's books, *Brompton Bicycle* and *Electric Bicycles*

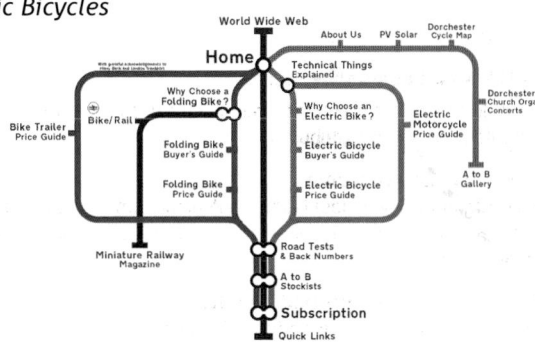

- Expert e-mail and telephone advice lines

(01305) 259998   atob@atob.org.uk
A to B, 40 Manor Road, Dorchester   DT1 2AX UK

Index

www.electricbicyclesbook.com

The updating site for Electric Bicycles~The Complete Guide

Updated performance graphs - More facts and figures

The latest law - New technology - Events -

New try out facilities - And much more....

www.electricbicyclesbook.com